RTI Team Building

The Guilford Practical Intervention in the Schools Series

Kenneth W. Merrell, Founding Editor
T. Chris Riley-Tillman, Series Editor

www.guilford.com/practical

This series presents the most reader-friendly resources available in key areas of evidence-based practice in school settings. Practitioners will find trustworthy guides on effective behavioral, mental health, and academic interventions, and assessment and measurement approaches. Covering all aspects of planning, implementing, and evaluating high-quality services for students, books in the series are carefully crafted for everyday utility. Features include ready-to-use reproducibles, lay-flat binding to facilitate photocopying, appealing visual elements, and an oversized format. Recent titles have companion Web pages where purchasers can download and print the reproducible materials.

RECENT VOLUMES

Child and Adolescent Suicidal Behavior:
School-Based Prevention, Assessment, and Intervention
David N. Miller

Cognitive Therapy for Adolescents in School Settings
Torrey A. Creed, Jarrod Reisweber, and Aaron T. Beck

Motivational Interviewing for Effective Classroom Management: The Classroom Check-Up
Wendy M. Reinke, Keith C. Herman, and Randy Sprick

Positive Behavior Support in Secondary Schools: A Practical Guide
Ellie L. Young, Paul Caldarella, Michael J. Richardson, and K. Richard Young

Academic and Behavior Supports for At-Risk Students: Tier 2 Interventions
Melissa Stormont, Wendy M. Reinke, Keith C. Herman, and Erica S. Lembke

RTI Applications, Volume 1: Academic and Behavioral Interventions
Matthew K. Burns, T. Chris Riley-Tillman, and Amanda M. VanDerHeyden

Coaching Students with Executive Skills Deficits
Peg Dawson and Richard Guare

Enhancing Instructional Problem Solving:
An Efficient System for Assisting Struggling Learners
John C. Begeny, Ann C. Schulte, and Kent Johnson

Clinical Interviews for Children and Adolescents, Second Edition: Assessment to Intervention
Stephanie H. McConaughy

RTI Team Building: Effective Collaboration and Data-Based Decision Making
Kelly Broxterman and Angela J. Whalen

RTI Applications, Volume 2: Assessment, Analysis, and Decision Making
T. Chris Riley-Tillman, Matthew K. Burns, and Kimberly Gibbons

Daily Behavior Report Cards: An Evidence-Based System of Assessment and Intervention
Robert J. Volpe and Gregory A. Fabiano

RTI Team Building

*Effective Collaboration
and Data-Based Decision Making*

**KELLY BROXTERMAN
ANGELA J. WHALEN**

THE GUILFORD PRESS
New York   London

© 2013 The Guilford Press
A Division of Guilford Publications, Inc.
72 Spring Street, New York, NY 10012
www.guilford.com

Printed in the United States of America

This book is printed on acid-free paper.

Last digit is print number: 9   8   7   6   5   4   3   2   1

Library of Congress Cataloging-in-Publication Data is available from the publisher.

ISBN: 978-1-4625-0850-1

*In memory of Kenneth W. Merrell,
a mentor in every sense of the word*

And to Eric, for his love and support

—KB

*In memory of Kenneth W. Merrell,
for encouraging me to write this book*

And to Brian, Jackson, and Nora, for your support

—AJW

About the Authors

Kelly Broxterman, PhD, is Associate Professor in the School Psychology Department at The Chicago School of Professional Psychology, where she teaches courses in response to intervention, assessment, intervention, systems change, and best practices in school psychology. She is the coordinator of the service learning program in the School Psychology Department and has been nominated for excellence in teaching and service learning on multiple occasions. Dr. Broxterman currently consults with schools implementing response to intervention in Illinois. Prior to becoming Associate Professor, Dr. Broxterman worked as a school psychologist and professional learning and leadership consultant for the Heartland Area Education Agency in Iowa. Her professional interests include data-based decision making, response to intervention, and instructional coaching. She is coauthor, with Rachel Brown-Chidsey and Louise Bronaugh, of *RTI in the Classroom: Guidelines and Recipes for Success*. Dr. Broxterman has presented nationally on academic assessment and intervention and is a nationally certified school psychologist.

Angela J. Whalen, PhD, is Assistant Dean for Academic Programs and Student Services at the University of Oregon College of Education. Dr. Whalen served for 9 years as a faculty member and Co-Director of the School Psychology Program at the University of Oregon, where she taught courses in response to intervention, assessment, consultation, practicum, clinical supervision, and school psychology principles and practices. Before joining the faculty at the University of Oregon, Dr. Whalen worked as a school psychologist, data/literacy facilitator, and staff development specialist for the Heartland Area Education Agency in Iowa and Vancouver Public Schools in Washington. Dr. Whalen's primary professional interests include academic assessment and intervention, school improvement efforts that promote student achievement, training, and supervision issues in school psychology. She was Project Coordinator for a personnel preparation grant, funded by the U.S. Department of Education Office of Special Education Programs, to train school psychologists with expertise in response to intervention, and has presented and consulted with schools nationally on topics related to response to intervention and data-based decision making.

Acknowledgments

This book would not have been possible without the encouragement and advice of the late Kenneth W. Merrell, a colleague, mentor, and friend, whose keen insight and constant support helped make this book come into being. We would also like to thank the people who helped us in the process of writing *RTI Team Building: Effective Collaboration and Data-Based Decision Making*, including all of the professionals at The Guilford Press with whom we worked. Thanks to Natalie Graham, Mary Beth Wood, and Anna Nelson for their efforts. We especially appreciate the suggestions and feedback from Chris Riley-Tillman. Finally, thanks to our families for their encouragement and support.

Contents

List of Figures, Tables, and Forms

FIGURES

TABLES

FORMS

CHAPTER 1

Introduction

Data-Based Decision-Making Teams and Their Role in Schoolwide Response-to-Intervention Models

This book is about the school teams that exist at the heart of response-to-intervention (RTI) implementation: teams that provide leadership, analyze student performance data, and use data to make decisions impacting individual students, classrooms, and schools. We believe that these teams, particularly grade-level data teams, play a critical role in improving student outcomes. Yet, many schools struggle to establish effective team-based collaboration and data-based decision-making practices within RTI models. These practices are new to many educators and require an investment of resources, such as time and professional development, to develop and fully implement.

You may work for a school district in the early stages of RTI adoption and implementation, in which data-based decision-making teams have not yet been established or fully implemented. If so, this book will provide a roadmap for how to establish and structure your teams for success. Alternately, you may serve as a member of an RTI team in a school district that has been implementing RTI for several years. You may be looking for ways to improve specific aspects of team functioning, such as collaboration or productivity of team meetings. If that is the case, this book will help you examine what is working well for your current team, and explore strategies for improving team functioning.

We believe that an investment in team development during the early stages of RTI implementation can promote buy-in among educators to the broader RTI model and practices and set the stage for productive team meetings for years to come. However, it is never too late to make the investment in the development of team functioning. It is common for RTI teams that have been working together for years to experience challenges that disrupt the process of team-based decision making. For example, teams may experience drift from the original purpose and goals, or face barriers to maintaining a regular meeting schedule. Over time, team members may transition on and off the team, resulting in disruption to the collaborative relationships or col-

1

lective expertise among team members. In these situations, revisiting some the basics of team development, planning, and collaboration can be a worthwhile investment.

With this book, we aim to provide RTI team members and facilitators with practical strategies to promote effective team-based collaboration and data-based decision making. We offer ideas, resources, and tools for you to use before, during, and after team meetings to improve team functioning. We also provide suggestions and strategies for building consensus and strengthening buy-in among team members for RTI practices, as well as identifying and responding to roadblocks experienced by the team during RTI implementation. Because RTI teams become a permanent addition to a school system, and because teams experience turnover among their membership over time, we also provide ideas and resources to help teams plan for sustainable team collaboration and data-based decision-making practices once they are established.

WHAT IS RTI?

The main focus of this book is on practices for effective team-based decision making within an RTI framework. But before jumping right into a discussion of team-based decision making, we would like to begin with a brief discussion of what we mean when we say "within an RTI framework," because we've observed that educators' use of the term *RTI* varies substantially. The term *RTI* has been used to describe systems-level practices involving prevention of academic difficulties, as well as practices involved in the identification of individual students with specific learning disabilities. As we discuss team-based decision making throughout this book, we are working from a conceptualization of RTI rooted in the following broad definitions.

Shortly after the Individuals with Disabilities Education Improvement Act (IDEIA) of 2004 was passed, the National Association of State Directors of Special Education (NASDSE) published a book outlining RTI policy and implementation considerations. This document provided the following definition of RTI to guide the work of states and school districts:

> Response to Intervention (RtI) is the practice of providing high-quality instruction and intervention matched to student need, monitoring progress frequently to make decisions about change in instruction or goals and applying child response data to important educational decisions. RtI should be applied to decisions in general, remedial and special education, creating a well-integrated system of instruction/intervention guided by child outcome data. (NASDSE, 2005, p. 3)

More recently, the National Center on Response to Intervention (NCRTI) released the following definition of RTI based on an analysis of existing research and evidence-based practice:

> Response to intervention integrates assessment and intervention within a multi-level prevention system to maximize student achievement and to reduce behavioral problems. With RTI, schools use data to identify students at risk for poor learning outcomes, monitor student progress, provide evidence-based interventions and adjust the intensity and nature of those interventions depending on a student's responsiveness, and identify students with learning disabilities or other disabilities. (NCRTI, 2012, p. 2)

Working from these definitions, we conceptualize RTI as a multicomponent framework for the systematic use of data to promote student achievement throughout an entire school. The RTI framework, or model, consists of a schoolwide, multi-tiered system of academic supports in which high-quality core instruction and universal screening are provided to all students. At-risk and struggling students are identified and provided with interventions matched to their instructional needs. Student progress is monitored, and the effectiveness of interventions is evaluated at the individual student and systems levels. Based on students' RTI, the intensity of instructional supports are increased or decreased as

> **We conceptualize RTI as a multicomponent framework for the systematic use of data to promote student achievement throughout an entire school.**

indicated. Throughout the multi-tiered system, including general and special education, data are used to drive decision making and efficiently allocate resources to promote student outcomes. This framework is illustrated by the depiction of the RTI model in Figure 1.1. Data obtained through a school's RTI practices may be used as part of a process to identify students with specific learning disabilities in accordance with IDEIA (2004) and state regulations, and may prove useful in identifying appropriate goals and services for individualized education programs (IEPs); however, the identification of students with specific learning disabilities is not viewed as the primary goal or driving force behind a school's adoption and use of an RTI framework.

RTI will not look the same in all schools because contextual factors will vary significantly from district to district, and school to school. The details of a school district's RTI model will depend on contextual factors such as district size and organizational structure, leadership and local expertise, available resources, and demographic characteristics. For example, one district may have a newly purchased evidence-based core reading program in place and a moderate annual budget for purchase of reading intervention curricula. A neighboring district may require teachers to choose between using an outdated basal program and teacher-made materials for instruction until the district budget crisis allows for adoption of a new core reading program. Similarly, schools may serve student populations with differing instructional needs due to differences in cultural or linguistic factors, early literacy and numeracy skills, prekindergarten educational or social experiences, or other factors.

Based on unique contextual factors, school districts should develop an RTI model that demonstrates strong contextual fit, in order to promote buy-in among stakeholders and high fidelity of implementation. The specific policies and procedures included in the district RTI

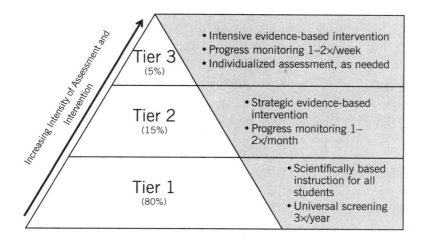

FIGURE 1.1. RTI model.

model should reflect the mission and priorities of the school district, and there should be a reasonable likelihood that the RTI model will meet the needs of the population of students served. The RTI model should take advantage of the district's strengths and available resources, while also reflecting a realistic picture of what is feasible to implement in the current context.

Although the details of RTI models and practices will differ across school districts, there are several critical components essential to any district's RTI model (e.g., NASDSE, 2005; Brown-Chidsey & Steege, 2010; Glover & Diperna, 2007; NCRTI, 2012). These critical components include:

- *Multi-tiered system of supports.* A multi-tiered prevention system is established to provide a continuum of instructional supports of increasing intensity, with an emphasis on fidelity of implementation. Tier 1, primary prevention, involves provision of scientifically based core instruction to all students. Tier 2, secondary prevention, involves provision of targeted interventions of increased intensity to at-risk or struggling students. Tier 3, tertiary prevention, involves provision of intensive, sometimes individualized, interventions of increased intensity to struggling students who do not respond to Tier 2 interventions.
- *Ongoing student assessment*
  - *Universal screening.* At least three times per year, all students within a grade level are assessed using a brief screening measure. Results are used to identify at-risk and struggling students who may need additional supports to achieve expected learning outcomes.
  - *Progress monitoring.* On a frequent basis, the academic performance of at-risk and struggling students is assessed using repeated measures designed for monitoring progress. Progress is monitored with increasing frequency for students receiving interventions at Tier 2 (e.g., once every 2 to 4 weeks) and Tier 3 (e.g., once every 1 to 2 weeks), to provide educators with timely feedback on the effectiveness of intervention delivered.
- *Collaboration.* Administrators, educators, specialists, and parents work together to implement RTI and promote positive student outcomes. Teams of educators meet regularly to analyze data and improve practices at the district, school, classroom, and individual student levels. Parents are active partners in problem solving when individual students are not responding to instruction and supports provided.
- *Data-based decision making.* At all levels of the multi-tiered system of support, decisions are made based on an analysis of student performance data. Major types of data-based decisions made by RTI teams include screening, instructional planning (e.g., grouping, selecting, and implementing intervention), evaluating student progress in response to intervention and identifying the need for intervention modifications, and evaluating the effectiveness of instruction at the systems level.

> **At all levels of the multi-tiered system of support, decisions are made based on an analysis of student performance data.**

- *Development and sustainability of systems-level capacity.* RTI leaders build capacity throughout the system for initial implementation and institutionalization of new RTI practices. Leaders identify and address variables required for sustainable systems change, such as development of an organizational framework, leadership, readiness, resources, policy development, and professional development.

- National Center on Response to Intervention
  www.rti4success.org
- RTI Action Network
  www.rtinetwork.org
- National Center on Student Progress Monitoring
  www.studentprogress.org
- Center for Response to Intervention in Early Childhood
  www.crtiec.org
- Technical Assistance Center on Positive Behavioral Interventions and Supports
  www.pbis.org

FIGURE 1.2. RTI-related Internet resources.

A comprehensive discussion of broad RTI models and the specific core components of RTI is beyond the scope of this book, which is intended to focus on effective team practices within RTI; however, many recent books, professional journals, technical reports, and policy guides have been published with extensive coverage of the evidence supporting RTI models and core components. We refer readers looking for up-to-date information about RTI models, practices, and implementation considerations to recent books by Brown-Chidsey and Steege (2010), Burns and Gibbons (2012), and Burns, Riley-Tillman, and VanDerHeyden (2012). Figure 1.2 also provides a list of RTI-related websites that provide information and resources related to RTI models, practices, and implementation.

CURRENT TRENDS IN RTI ADOPTION

It is clear that RTI adoption and implementation levels are on the rise nationwide, resulting in large shifts in school practices related to instruction and intervention, assessment, and decision making. Since 2007, an annual national survey of school administrators has been conducted by Spectrum K12 School Solutions, in collaboration with the American Association of School Administrators (AASA), the Council of Administrators of Special Education (CASE), the NASDSE, and the RTI Action Network/National Center on Learning Disabilities (NCLD), to collect data on RTI adoption and implementation. Although not a scientific survey, the results of the Spectrum K12 survey efforts arguably represent the best available estimates of current trends in RTI adoption because there is no national reporting system, database, or published scientific study on the topic to date. At the time of this publication, the most recent survey was completed in the spring of 2011, and included responses from 1,390 school districts across the nation (Spectrum K12 School Solutions, 2011). Some of the major findings illustrating 2011 levels and trends in RTI adoption and implementation include the following:

- Of the school districts that responded, 94% indicated some level of RTI implementation: 24% reported full implementation, 59% reported some level of districtwide implementation or limited piloting, 16% reported investigating or planning for implementation, and 1% reported not considering implementation.
- Trends indicate steady increases in the percentage of responding school districts indi-

cating their district was either fully implementing RTI districtwide, in the process of implementing RTI districtwide, or piloting RTI, from 44% in 2007 to 71% in 2009 to 83% in 2011.

- RTI is more likely to be implemented at the elementary level than secondary levels.
- RTI is most likely to be implemented in the area of reading, followed by math and social behavior.
- Approximately two out of three districts have school-based leadership teams responsible for RTI implementation at the school level, in place at the majority of buildings in the district; 27% of districts report having school-based teams in place at *all* buildings in the district (Spectrum K12 School Solutions, 2011).

In the context of this book about RTI teams, it is interesting to note that RTI leadership teams are one component of RTI models not yet consistently implemented. Only 27% of districts reported having established RTI leadership teams in *all* school buildings. Similarly, a minority of districts reported full implementation of regularly held collaborative meetings focused on analysis of grade-level group data to guide overall core instruction (26% of districts) or problem solving for individual students (26% of districts). In contrast, 72% of districts reported full implementation of a core reading program, and 47% reported full implementation of universal screening three times per year (Spectrum K12 School Solutions, 2011). Based on these data, there is a need for continued focus on establishing school teams that provide leadership and promote data-based decision making at the systems and individual student levels.

ROLES AND FUNCTIONS OF TEAMS WITHIN RTI

RTI requires both shifts in thinking and practice related to the level of collaboration involved in teaching. Historically, teachers have been assigned a class of students for whom they were responsible. Teachers were expected to teach this assigned class of students in a fairly isolated manner ("each classroom an island unto itself"), with acknowledgment that each general education class would consist of students with widely ranging skills and instructional needs. In this context, teachers were accountable for covering the annual grade-level curriculum. Little emphasis was placed on providing differentiated instruction matched to student needs, or on accountability for student outcomes. In recent years, teachers have faced increasing accountability for student outcomes, along with increasing diversity among students and their instructional needs. When a school district adopts RTI, teachers are no longer expected to meet the diverse needs of students alone, but rather to do so in collaboration with teams of educators. School resources are pooled and multi-tiered systems of support are established to promote collaboration across classrooms, general and special education systems, supplemental and remedial programs, and so on. Multi-tiered support systems provide a continuum of instructional supports of varying levels of intensity, to address the diverse instructional needs of students within a school.

This is not business as usual. With RTI, educators must actually *work together* to meet the diverse needs of students. The enormity of this shift in thinking and practice should not be underestimated. When making the shift to RTI, educators are expected to commit to core beliefs such as "All educators must work together to meet the diverse needs of students served in schools today" and "We should make decisions based on what is best for our students rather than what is most convenient/enjoyable/and so on for us as adults." These changes mean that general education teachers, specialists, related service personnel, administrators, and support staff will need to share expertise and resources (e.g., instructional assistant time, budgets, materials, access to pull-out intervention programs), and support each other to improve student outcomes. Collaboration is not an optional RTI activity, or a practice reserved for the specialists who work with struggling learners. Instead, RTI fundamentally changes the way *all educators* serve students, so that collaboration becomes an integral part of teaching for all general and special education teachers, specialists, related service providers, administrators, and staff. Although specific collaboration practices may "look" different from school to school, what remains critical to successful RTI implementation is that schools create team structures in which *all* teachers participate in team-based decision making, and allocate time during which collaboration is expected to occur.

> **When a school district adopts RTI, teachers are no longer expected to meet the diverse needs of students alone, but rather to do so in collaboration with teams of educators.**

Without teams, or without full participation of *all* educators on RTI teams, it is unlikely that collaboration and data-based decision making will be fully implemented throughout the school system. In our work, we often encounter schools that have invested heavily in collecting assessment data for the purposes of RTI decision making and have purchased a variety of evidence-based intervention materials, but struggle to get teachers to *use* the data to drive decisions about instruction. In these schools, it is often the case that a district/school leadership team makes decisions in a top-down fashion, telling teachers and interventionists what to do and when to do it. Most educators don't have the chance to engage in using data collaboratively to make decisions about screening, instructional planning, or evaluating outcomes. Other times, grade-level teams are left to their own devices to determine when to meet and how to make decisions, without sufficient knowledge or skills in problem solving and data-based decision making. In these circumstances, meetings may occur inconsistently, or may end up with decisions made largely based on professional judgment. Data-based decision making never becomes a part of the day-to-day teaching practices of the school. It remains an "additional" task to be completed as part of yet another educational initiative. For RTI implementation to be sustainable over time, it is essential that teams are housed within school systems that institutionalize team collaboration and data-based decision making as a standard part of everyday practice.

Once established, RTI teams should become a permanent structure of the district and school systems. These teams are not short-term committees convened to accomplish a specific task (e.g., select intervention materials for purchase, write a school improvement plan). Instead, they exist to provide a mechanism for *ongoing* decision making focused on providing high-quality instruction and intervention to ensure that each and every student is successful. The work of RTI teams is not finished after 1, 3, or even 5 years of successful RTI implementation. The process of ensuring educational success for each and every student never ends; it repeats year after year as new groups of students enter our schools with changing educational needs. Teams play a crucial role in routinizing collaboration and data-based decision making, and establishing sustainable evidence-based RTI practices within the educational system.

Types of RTI Teams

As school districts adopt and implement RTI, new teams will be created and some preexisting teams may need to be restructured or reorganized to promote efficiency in teaming across the district and avoid duplication of purpose across teams. There are generally four types of teams integral to successful RTI implementation in any district: (1) district RTI leadership teams, (2) school RTI leadership teams, (3) RTI data teams (a.k.a. "grade-level teams"), and (4) problem-solving teams (e.g., Brown-Chidsey & Steege, 2010; Burns & Gibbons, 2012). Each type of team plays an important role in the success of a district's overall RTI model. Some teams will provide leadership, resources, and oversight. Other teams will implement RTI assessment and intervention practices, and make decisions about the needs of individual students. All teams will use data to drive decision making within the RTI model. Table 1.1 provides a list of the roles and the focus of decision making for each type of team.

RTI adoption and implementation begins with establishing leadership teams. A district-level RTI leadership team consists of key administrative leaders and stakeholders who are given the charge of setting the vision and assuming responsibility for the change process across the district (Sugai & Horner, 2006). District-level leadership team members identify and implement a clear organizational framework to set district improvement goals, assess needs, coordinate implementation, and evaluate the effectiveness of the RTI model over time. Leadership teams apply data-based decision making to a variety of activities at a district level, such as securing and allocating resources, developing policies and procedures, planning and providing professional development, and addressing roadblocks. District-level teams build and provide guidance to school-level leadership teams, which requires team members to make a substantial and long-term commitment of time and resources for several years as leadership capacity and sustainable practices are developed throughout the district.

In addition to a district-level leadership team, each school needs a leadership team because the details of RTI implementation are unique to each school. The school-level RTI leadership team should include members representing administration, the various grade levels of the school, and related service providers within the school. School-level RTI leadership teams play a key role in building consensus among school faculty and staff, securing and allocating resources, providing support to ensure the RTI model is implemented with fidelity, and evaluating outcomes at the school level. Similar to district-level leadership teams, the school-level leadership teams must make a substantial and long-term commitment of time and resources to the development of leadership and sustainable practices within the school building.

Although necessary, leadership teams alone are not sufficient for successful RTI implementation. Each school also needs teams more directly linked to day-to-day classroom operations, and to the learning outcomes of each and every student in the school. RTI data teams, sometimes called grade-level RTI teams, are made up of teachers, specialists, and other service providers responsible for providing instruction and intervention to students within the multi-tiered system of support. These teams are integral to the actual implementation of RTI practices (e.g., assessment, intervention, collaboration) and decision making, such as identifying at-risk and struggling students, making decisions about grouping and instructional supports, examining individual student progress data, and evaluating the effectiveness of interventions at the grade and classroom levels. Schools typically set up multiple RTI data teams within a building, so that teams can focus their attention on a logical subgroup (e.g., grade level, primary/intermediate) of

TABLE 1.1. Summary of School District Teams Involved in RTI Decision Making

Type of team	Roles of the team	Decision-making focus
District RTI leadership team	• Develop a vision and blueprint for RTI implementation throughout the district. • Build consensus among district administration and leadership, develop capacity for RTI leadership at the school building level. • Assess district needs, allocate resources, develop policies and procedures that promote sustainable RTI practices, and provide professional development. • Identify and address barriers to RTI implementation and ongoing systems change efforts. • Use data to evaluate effectiveness of the RTI model at the district and school levels. • Use data to identify the need to provide support to struggling schools.	District level; school level
School RTI leadership team	• Translate the district vision into a vision at the school level, and support implementation of RTI at the school level. • Build consensus among key stakeholders at the building level, develop capacity for RTI leadership at the grade level. • Assess school needs, allocate resources, support implementation of policies and procedures that promote sustainable RTI practices, and provide or arrange professional development for school staff. • Identify and address barriers to RTI implementation. • Use data to evaluate the effectiveness of the RTI model at the school and grade levels. • Use data to identify the need to provide support to struggling teachers/classrooms within the school.	School level; grade level
RTI data team (a.k.a. grade-level team)	• Develop a vision for RTI implementation, including collaboration and tem-based decision making, at the grade level. • Implement RTI practices established by the district and/or school leadership teams. • Meet regularly to collaborate and provide support to each other regarding implementation of RTI. • Identify and address barriers to RTI implementation. • Use data to evaluate the effectiveness of the RTI model at the grade level and classroom level, and modify supports when needed to improve student outcomes. • Use data to conduct universal screening and identify students needing intervention within the grade level.	Grade level; classroom level; individual student level

(continued)

TABLE 1.1. *(continued)*

Type of team	Roles of the team	Decision-making focus
RTI data team *(continued)*	• Use data to conduct instructional planning (e.g., group students with similar needs for intervention, select and modify instruction/intervention provided across tiers). • Use data to evaluate student progress in response to intervention, and modify interventions as needed to improve student outcomes at the grade level.	
Problem-solving team	• Provides assistance to teachers throughout the school regarding individual students who are not responding to interventions across Tiers 1 and/or 2. • Provide assistance regarding individual students when more time or expertise is needed for problem solving than what can be provided on the grade-level RTI data team. • Use a problem-solving model to conduct individualized assessment to identify student needs, plan and support intervention implementation, and evaluate student progress. • Work with other school teams to determine when special education should be considered for struggling students.	Individual student level

the school population. This allows educators to share responsibility for student outcomes among a group of students with whom they are familiar, and for whom they are involved in intervention delivery.

Finally, schools implementing RTI will need one schoolwide problem-solving team that provides assistance to teachers of students who are not responding to interventions at Tier 1 or Tier 2 (Brown-Chidsey & Steege, 2010). Even in the most effective of RTI prevention models, we can expect that a small percentage of students will need individualized assessment and intervention using a problem-solving approach to identify and meet their educational needs. This type of individualized problem solving requires expertise in use of a problem-solving model, and can be time intensive. As a result, this type of individualized problem solving is often beyond the scope of what can be reasonably addressed during grade-level RTI data-team meetings. The schoolwide problem-solving team supplements the efforts of grade-level data teams to address the needs of struggling students, especially at Tier 3, and can assist in making recommendations regarding if or when a comprehensive evaluation to determine the need and eligibility for special education is warranted for struggling students. Problem-solving team membership should include representatives of teachers from multiple grade levels and specialists with expertise in use of a problem-solving model. The teachers and parents of struggling students should be included in the team problem-solving process for individual students.

Organization of RTI Teams

Although most districts implementing RTI should develop the four types of teams described above, the exact configuration of RTI teams and the relationships among teams within a school district will vary depending on contextual factors unique to each district. When creating a team structure, factors to consider include the size of the district and schools, the number of teachers within each school and grade level, the number of at-risk and struggling students within schools and grade levels, and other existing teams (e.g., positive behavioral interventions and supports, administrative, school improvement, student study team). For example, most small to midsized school districts only need one district-level RTI leadership team, but some larger districts may decide to create two RTI leadership teams and divide responsibilities (e.g., elementary and secondary, academics and social behavior, geographical regions). Alternately, some very small districts may need only one combined district and school RTI leadership team, such as rural districts with only one K–12 school building.

Because the details of RTI practices and implementation will vary from school to school within a school district, it is necessary that each school building identify RTI teams to serve both leadership (school RTI leadership-team) and operational (grade-level RTI data-team) functions. In most schools, a logical team structure involves one school-level leadership team, along with one data team at each grade level, as illustrated in Figure 1.3. Some smaller schools, such as schools with only one teacher per grade level, may find that grade-level teams are not a logical structure that works for their context. Instead, it might make more sense in small schools to form teams based on combined grade levels, such as one team of primary grade (K–2) teachers and one team of upper elementary grade (3–5) teachers.

Figure 1.4 illustrates one possible configuration of RTI teams within a school district with elementary schools of varying sizes. Note that each of the three schools within this district have organized RTI data teams in a unique manner, based on the size and resources of each school. School A created six data teams, with one at each grade level. School B created only two data teams, consisting of teachers grouped by primary and intermediate grade levels. School C created four data teams by grouping teachers at some, but not all, grade levels. These groupings made the most sense to the faculty of School C, because the school used a "blended-grades"

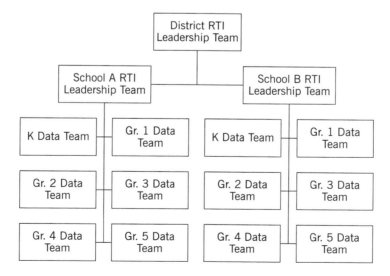

FIGURE 1.3. School district organizational chart for RTI leadership and data-based decision-making teams: Two schools.

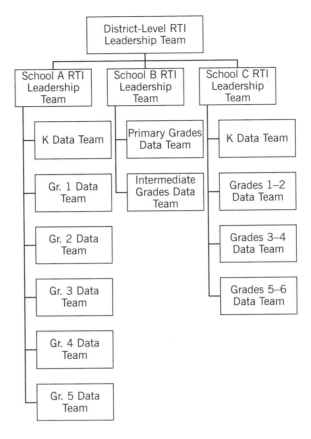

FIGURE 1.4. School district organizational chart for RTI leadership and data-based decision-making teams: Three schools.

model and frequently provided instruction in cross-grade group settings. Other alternatives are possible; the idea is to find a team structure that can be sustained in your district or school over time, and capitalizes on the resources and strengths of your school and local context.

SUMMARY

This chapter has provided a broad overview of RTI, current trends in RTI adoption, types of data-based decision-making teams, and their role in RTI models. Throughout the remainder of this book, our discussion of RTI teams and their role in data-based decision making is based on the following assumptions. First, we assume that the primary purpose for implementing RTI, and therefore RTI teams, is to prevent achievement problems and promote positive academic outcomes for all students. We assume RTI teams will be created in school districts that have adopted and are striving for full RTI implementation, and that those school districts provide professional development to RTI team members (and all staff) to develop a basic understanding of RTI and key components such as evidence-based intervention, assessment for universal screening and progress monitoring, data-based decision making, and collaboration. Finally, we recognize that RTI teams exist within the complex systems of schools and school districts, and as a result, will take a variety of forms. Despite these unique differences due to contextual factors, we assume that collaboration and data-based decision making are desirable activities for all RTI teams.

We now shift our focus to the main purpose of this book: promoting effective data-based team decision making within RTI leadership and data teams. For the purposes of this book, we've elected to focus our discussion primarily on grade-level RTI data teams at the elementary level, and on the application of RTI to promote academic achievement. We acknowledge the potential of RTI for promoting positive outcomes in secondary settings and in the area of social behavior, although there are unique considerations for teaming with each of these applications of RTI beyond those discussed in this book. Despite our focus on RTI teams for the promotion of academic outcomes, we believe many of the practices for effective team-based collaboration and data-based decision making described in this book are applicable to other school-based teams that differ in focus or setting.

The remainder of this book is divided into three parts, addressing activities that promote effective teaming before, during, and after RTI team meetings. Part I examines premeeting activities that set the stage for productive meetings, including setting up teams, establishing routines, and premeeting planning. Part II takes a closer look at what happens during team meetings, such as facilitating productive meetings, preventing and confronting common roadblocks, and making decisions for screening, intervention planning, progress monitoring, and outcomes evaluation. Part III focuses on activities occurring after team meetings, including creating contingencies that promote fidelity of implementation of teaming and other RTI practices, addressing logistical challenges of RTI collaboration, and building capacity and sustainable team practices that will endure over time.

PART I

BEFORE THE TEAM MEETING

CHAPTER 2

Getting Started
Establishing Your Team

Teams play a key role in RTI implementation, providing a structure in which collaboration and data-based decision making occur with regularity and predictability. The quality of team functioning and data-based decision making can make or break the success of a school's RTI efforts. Yet, a majority of school districts struggle to fully implement RTI leadership teams in each school building, and to regularly hold collaborative data-team meetings focused on the review of grade-level and/or individual student progress data (Spectrum K12 School Solutions, 2011). We believe addressing the barriers to full implementation of data-based decision-making teams begins with an investment in the initial stages of RTI team development. In this chapter, we examine how to work collaboratively as a team to establish your team, by defining the team's purpose and its relation to other RTI teams in the district, ensuring team membership is sufficient for accomplishing the team's purpose, developing a mission statement, and identifying team member roles and responsibilities.

DEFINING YOUR TEAM
AND GETTING THE RIGHT PEOPLE AT THE TABLE

Defining Your RTI Team as a Leadership Team or a Data Team

The first task facing your team is to identify the purpose of the team and how it relates to other RTI teams in the district and/or school. Without a clear understanding of the purpose of your team and its relation to other RTI teams in the district, you may waste time duplicating the work done by other teams or experience frustration among team members as a result of differing expectations about the priorities for team decision making. At a basic level, you must first identify whether you're part of an RTI leadership team or RTI data team. Working with your team members and school or district leadership, consider which of the following (leadership team or data team) best describes the purpose and expected functions of your team.

RTI Leadership Teams

RTI leadership teams are housed at the district level and at the school level. Although the scope of work may vary, the primary purpose of all RTI leadership teams is the same: to provide *leadership* as new practices are adopted and implemented. Leadership teams focus on the "big-picture" issues that must be addressed to promote change at the district or school level, such as:

- What is RTI?
- Why is it important and valuable (i.e., why should we care about it)?
- What will RTI look like in our district/school?
- How will the necessary resources be obtained to actually implement RTI in our schools/classrooms?
- How will we overcome local barriers to implementation?
- Over time, are we meeting our goals for improving student outcomes throughout the district/school?

Major tasks typically expected of leadership teams include:

- Setting the vision for the adoption of an RTI model and practices.
- Building consensus among school and community stakeholders.
- Identifying specific practices for districtwide implementation (e.g., assessment, intervention, teaming, data-based decision making).
- Providing professional development, coaching, and support to all faculty and staff.
- Monitoring fidelity of RTI implementation.
- Data-based decision making, including:
  - Evaluating the effectiveness of instructional supports at the grade and classroom levels.
  - Allocating district/school resources to attain goals.

RTI Data Teams

In addition to having a school-level RTI leadership team, each school building will house multiple RTI data teams (a.k.a. "grade-level teams"). The primary purpose of RTI data teams is to bring together educators involved in RTI intervention and assessment activities for collaboration and data-based decision making, focused on ensuring positive student outcomes. RTI data teams deal with the day-to-day operations at the grade, classroom, and individual student levels. These teams address questions such as:

> **The primary purpose of RTI data teams is to bring together educators involved in RTI intervention and assessment activities for collaboration and data-based decision making, focused on ensuring positive student outcomes.**

- Based on universal screening results, what percentage of students at our grade level are successfully meeting benchmark goals for academics and/or social behavior?
- How many and which students are at risk, and in need of supplemental academic and/or behavioral supports?

- What do instruction and intervention supports look like across tiers at our grade level?
- How should we group students and provide the needed intervention supports?
- Based on student progress data, which students are responding to intervention and which students may need modifications to the interventions they receive?
- At the systems level, how effective are our interventions?

Major tasks typically expected of RTI data teams include:

- Implementation of the RTI model and practices adopted by the district/school.
  - Multi-tiered system of instructional and intervention supports.
  - Ongoing assessment for universal screening and progress monitoring.
  - Team-based collaboration.
- Data-based decision making, including:
  - Identifying students in need of intervention.
  - Grouping students for intervention.
  - Selecting goals and interventions for at-risk and struggling students.
  - Formatively evaluating student progress and intervention effectiveness.
  - Evaluating the effectiveness of instructional supports at the grade and classroom levels.
- Identifying and addressing barriers to implementation.

Understanding Your Team's Relation to Other District and School RTI Teams

Once your team has clarified its status as either an RTI leadership or data team, the next step is to examine how your team fits into the organizational structure of RTI teams across the district and/or within your school. As discussed in Chapter 1, the configuration of RTI teams and the connections between teams will depend on contextual factors specific to each district. Most districts committed to RTI implementation will begin by identifying a district-level leadership team, which coordinates the selection and development of the school-level leadership teams, and drives systems change efforts during the initial 5 to 7 years of implementation. In some very large districts there may be more than one district-level leadership team; for example, two leadership teams may split up tasks related to the coordination of RTI implementation at the elementary and secondary settings, or across multiple domains (e.g., academics and social behavior). Individual schools will typically have one school-level RTI leadership team, along with several grade-level (or similarly configured) RTI data teams.

At this stage of the game, establishing your team involves making sure that all team members understand how your team fits into the larger organizational structure of RTI teams across the district and within the school. Understanding which teams exist, and for what purpose, will help keep your team focused on its primary objectives, without duplicating work done elsewhere by other RTI teams. Form 2.1 at the end of this chapter provides a tool for your team to use to build understanding of the structure and purpose of RTI teams existing within your district and school.

Team Membership: Making Sure the Right People Are at the Table

Once you've established the type of team you're on (leadership or data team), its major purpose, and its relation to other teams in the district and school, it is worth spending some time in team discussion about whether the "right" people are included on the team. It may be helpful to identify a temporary team facilitator at this point, who will facilitate these early conversations and coordinate initial team planning and organization activities. Natural leaders will likely emerge over time or through formal assignment of roles and responsibilities; meanwhile, the team may function more efficiently if one person is tasked with leading the team through the initial planning activities described subsequently in Chapter 3.

Although there is no formula for identifying the perfect team, your team should discuss whether it possesses the collective expertise needed to accomplish the major tasks expected of the team. Considerations related to the knowledge, skills, and experience needed to accomplish the major tasks of RTI leadership and RTI data teams are provided below. Working with your team members and/or school or district leadership, discuss the relevant considerations below for your type of team (leadership team or data team), and whether you've got people at the table with the qualities needed to accomplish the purpose and expected functions of your team.

Considerations for RTI Leadership Teams

Leadership teams require a group of individuals with the collective knowledge, skills, and access to resources necessary to set a vision for RTI implementation, develop and carry out a plan to fulfill that vision, and provide the necessary professional development and other support to staff at either the district or school level. Consider whether your team membership includes individuals who can contribute substantive knowledge, skills, and experience in one or more of the following areas:

- RTI models and implementation.
- Evidence-based instruction and intervention for academics and/or social behavior.
- Assessment for universal screening, progress monitoring, and/or program evaluation.
- Data-based decision making.
- Interpreting data at the systems level (district/school).
- Team-based collaboration.
- Instructional leadership.
- Effective communication skills.
- Authority to allocate resources (e.g., money, personnel, materials, space) for RTI implementation.

> **Leadership teams require a group of individuals with the collective knowledge, skills, and access to resources necessary to set a vision and develop a comprehensive plan for RTI implementation.**

Additionally, consider whether your leadership team includes individuals who represent critical groups of stakeholders in the district (e.g., administrators, general and special education leaders, curriculum and assessment leaders, classroom teachers, parents) or school (e.g., principal, primary and intermediate grade teachers, special education teachers, interventionists, school psychologists, coaches). Stakeholder representation is important to ensure careful and thorough consideration of the implications of proposed decisions for groups impacted by the team's decisions, and may have a positive impact on educators' buy-in to adopted RTI practices.

Considerations for RTI Data-Team Membership

RTI data teams require a group of individuals with the collective knowledge and skills needed for data-based decision making focused on providing effective instructional supports to each and every student within a subgroup of the school (e.g., grade level, primary or intermediate level). When identifying data-team membership, it is important that *all* individuals involved in instruction and intervention for students at the focus grade level(s) are part of the team. Each of the teachers, specialists, interventionists, coaches, and so on, who provide supports have information relevant to decision making. It is important that each of these individuals shares ownership in the success of each student within the grade level(s), in order to promote collaboration and sharing of resources among team members. Consider whether your team membership includes individuals who can contribute substantive knowledge, skills, and experience in one or more of the following areas:

- RTI models and implementation.
- Evidence-based instruction and intervention for students at the focus grade level(s).
- Administration, scoring, and interpretation of assessments for universal screening and progress monitoring at the focus grade level(s).
- Interpretation of data at the grade, classroom, and individual student levels.
- Team-based collaboration.
- Demonstrated skill in meeting facilitation.
- Effective communication skills.

Recruiting Team Members with Complementary Expertise

Based on the results of your team discussion, consideration should be given to the need to recruit others to serve on the team as permanent or consulting members, to make sure adequate knowledge, skills, and experience for decision making are present among the team's collective membership. For example, school psychologists may be recruited to join or consult with data teams to support data interpretation or individual problem solving. Reading specialists may be recruited to support intervention planning or resource allocation. When coaches are available, they may be sought out to provide coaching of team functioning and data-based decision making during the initial phases of RTI implementation, and to provide targeted ongoing professional development within grade-level data teams over time.

As you read this book, it may be the case that your team membership has already been established by someone else (e.g., district/school administrator) and you may not have the authority to select or recruit new team members on your own. Further, asking individuals to attend additional team meetings to provide consultation may raise contractual issues in some districts. Despite these challenges, we believe it is worth the effort for your team to work with the appropriate administrators to advocate and get the right people on the team to promote early team success, which is crucial to establishing buy-in among team members and building the capacity of teams to sustain teaming practices with increasing independence over time.

DEVELOPING A SHARED TEAM MISSION AND GOALS

RTI implementation can be particularly challenging because *all* staff will be involved in the RTI process in some capacity. Although some educators will be interested and supportive of RTI approaches, others will be skeptical or outright resistant to RTI approaches. As districts move forward with RTI implementation efforts and begin to mandate specific practices (e.g., use of evidence-based core reading program, use of curriculum-based measurement [CBM] to monitor student progress, teacher participation on grade-level RTI data teams), many educators will be faced with a need to learn and implement new assessment, instruction/intervention, and/or data-based decision-making practices. The change process is difficult, can be anxiety provoking, and people often just don't like being told what to do. Complicating things further, teachers, specialists, and administrators may have different values and priorities related to RTI goals and practices. Without a common vision or goal, it can be difficult to establish staff buy-in and motivation to implement new practices.

Once an RTI team has been established through the steps described above, the process of developing a team mission statement can help to bring team members together through the development of a shared purpose and set of common goals. A collaborative approach to developing the team's mission also allows each RTI team to build a vision that fits the unique context in which the team functions. Each team member should have the opportunity to provide input that shapes the focus and priorities of the team's future work. When all team members support a mission statement, that mission statement can be revisited over time and updated as needed to reenergize and refocus team members' commitment to working toward a common goal.

A collaborative approach to articulating a team's mission can also prevent later problems with team member resistance to change during RTI implementation, because it allows team members to identify and address any differences in underlying beliefs or values in the early stages of teaming. If left unaddressed, these differences in beliefs or values may hinder the team's ability to accomplish its goals during ongoing RTI decision-making meetings.

What Is a Mission Statement?

A mission statement is a clear, concise statement that describes the purpose of a team, the team's goals, and reflects the values of team members. It may be a short phrase or a paragraph in length, but it should convey the team's shared vision clearly. A powerful mission statement will connect emotionally with team members, motivating individuals to actively work toward team goals. A well-written mission statement provides guidance for future actions and decisions of the team.

> A powerful mission statement will connect emotionally with team members, motivating individuals to actively work toward team goals.

Each RTI team will have a unique purpose and set of goals, based on the unique school system in which it exists, the values of its members, and the tasks that need to be accomplished.

TABLE 2.1. Sample RTI-Team Mission Statements

Type of RTI team	Mission statement
District-level RTI leadership team	The RTI leadership team strives to provide a vision, leadership, resources, and support to our district's educators as they implement the ABC district RTI framework. We believe that through implementation of evidence-based practices and data-based decision making, we can have a positive impact on children's lives, and help all K–12 students achieve academic success.
Kindergarten RTI data team	The K team is committed to working together to establish the early literacy skills of all kindergarten students, preparing them for future reading success. By providing high-quality instruction and an enriching environment, we can provide a strong foundation for future learning and personal success for our students.

For example, the purpose and goals of district-level RTI leadership teams will likely be quite different from those of a kindergarten RTI data team, just as the priorities and focus of a kindergarten data team will likely be quite different from those of a sixth-grade data team. Because of the differences in purpose, values, goals, and context across RTI teams, it is important that each team take the time to develop its own mission statement and obtain the commitment of each team member to their team's shared vision. Sample mission statements for RTI leadership and data teams are provided in Table 2.1.

Develop Your Team Mission Statement

Your RTI team exists for a purpose. Your first task as a team is to define that purpose and develop a mission statement that will guide your work over the long term and communicate your team mission to others. In a clear and concise manner, your mission statement should accomplish at least three things:

1. Reflect the values/beliefs of the team.
2. Describe the purpose of the team.
3. State the goal(s) of the team.

Because the mission statement can be a powerful tool in promoting team members' buy-in and commitment to the change process required when implementing RTI, it is worth taking the time needed to build consensus among all team members when developing your team's mission statement. Although it may be easier for a team leader to simply write a mission statement defining the purpose and goals of the team, taking this approach results in a missed opportunity to bring team members together in a manner that sets the stage for future collaborative teamwork. We recommend that teams begin by discussing team members' opinions and perceptions about the team values, purpose, and goals before actually beginning the process of writing a mission statement. This may be a quick or lengthy process, linear or circular in nature, depending on the culture of the workplace or individuals' preferences. Form 2.2 at the end of this chapter provides a resource for your team to use during development of your team mission statement.

Identify Team Values/Beliefs

A critical component of successful RTI implementation at the district or school level is whether sufficient buy-in is established among teachers and other stakeholders. RTI requires a paradigm shift; a new manner of thinking about student learning and our role as educators in promoting the success of all students. Brown-Chidsey and Steege (2010) identify the following principles as necessary for all key staff members to commit to:

- All children can learn.
- All children have a right to an efficacious education.
- Not all children have disabilities, but they all might need extra help at various times as they make their way from kindergarten through grade 12.
- Differentiating instruction for individual students is an important part of general education.
- Education outcome data are effective tools for determining what types of extra support a student needs.
- Multi-tier standard protocols and problem-solving methods are effective ways of addressing the learning needs of all students. (pp. 139–140)

Professional development provided by a school district as part of the RTI adoption and planning process must include foci on the rationale for RTI adoption and the shifts in beliefs and assumptions about student learning that are needed for successful RTI implementation. As part of this process, it is important to address what these changes in beliefs and practices mean for the various stakeholder groups. Misconceptions and fears will need to be identified and addressed to promote buy-in and prevent resistance to change.

Similarly, a critical determinant of whether your RTI team will be successful is whether sufficient buy-in is established among team members. If team members do not understand the rationale for implementing new practices within RTI, such as team-based collaboration or data-based decision making, there will be little motivation for change. When team members do not see how their participation on the RTI team will benefit them as an individual, low buy-in and ineffective teams will likely result.

Before jumping in to identifying specific team priorities and goals, RTI teams can promote initial buy-in from members through targeted discussion about team member values and beliefs. Some questions that may help to stimulate discussion about team values and beliefs include:

- Over the last few years, what has been working well and what have been the challenges of our current service delivery system?
- How do we feel about the district/school's decision to adopt and implement RTI? What are perceived benefits and drawbacks?
- What have we heard about RTI from colleagues in other districts, or from the professional literature?
- How do the proposed/adopted RTI practices align with personal beliefs about the role of teachers and the educational system?
- How important is this team to the overall success of our district/school/grade level/students?

- How do we view our individual roles and responsibilities in ensuring all students meet expected performance standards?
- What role should assessment data play in our decision making about the instruction and intervention provided in our district/school/grade level? What other sources of information should be considered in these decisions?
- To what extent should evidence-based practices be emphasized in day-to-day instruction and intervention?
- Do we believe standards for accountability (e.g., all students proficient readers by third grade; school improvement goals) in our state/district are reasonable and attainable?
- With regard to RTI and our participation on this RTI leadership or data team, what is in it for us?

Identify Team Purpose

Identifying your team purpose involves answering the question "Why does this team exist?" There is no right or wrong answer to this question, just as there is no one way to implement RTI. Although your team has likely already identified its general purpose, refining and building consensus among team members regarding expected team outcomes can assist with the process of finding the team's shared mission. Some questions that may help to stimulate discussion about the team purpose include:

- What have we been told about the reason this team was created?
- How does this team fit into the overall district and school structure of RTI teams?
- What are the district or school expectations for this team?
- Who is this team designed to serve/support (students, teachers, principals, school-level RTI leadership teams, etc.)?
- What is currently working well in relation to RTI implementation in our district/school/ grade level?
- Which aspects of RTI implementation need to be improved in our district/school/grade level?
- What are our priorities in relation to RTI implementation this year? Over the next 3 to 5 years?
- What decision-making authority does this team have? What are the limits to our decision-making authority?

Delehant (2007) suggests that "While teams are defining a purpose, some also find it useful to define the *nonpurpose*. . . . Knowing what the group is *not* going to address can greatly increase the group's effectiveness" (pp. 6–7). Teams may find it useful to identify topics that are outside of the team's authority, or issues that the team cannot control, in order to refine the purpose and mission of the current team. For example, a school-level RTI leadership team whose purpose includes "supporting teachers at ABC Elementary to implement the district RTI framework" may identify a nonpurpose of "We will not discuss our disagreements about the new literacy assessments required in the district RTI framework." Development of nonpurpose statements can be useful as part of team consensus building, although they are not typically written into the final team mission statement.

Identify Team Goals

A mission statement is strengthened by the inclusion of one or more clear goals for what the team hopes to accomplish. One to two overarching "big-picture" goals with measurable criteria for success may be more useful to the team than several more specific or vaguely written goals. For example, a school-level RTI leadership team mission statement including a goal to "provide the necessary coaching and support to school staff to achieve implementation scores of 90% or better on each domain of the district RTI Implementation Integrity Checklist at each grade level, K–5" provides clear direction about what the team hopes to accomplish, and success can be measured. In contrast, although a similar mission statement including a goal to "support school staff to improve RTI implementation" provides a general sense of what the team hopes to accomplish, team members may not hold a shared vision for the criteria that would indicate successful improvement in RTI implementation. Without a shared vision and agreed-upon criteria to indicate successful goal accomplishment, commitment to working toward team goals may wane over time.

It is possible that your team may wish to define multiple short-term and long-term goals, or a set of more detailed goals or objectives. Although this type of goal setting may be outside the scope of what is needed for development of a team mission statement, do not discourage this discussion. Rather, suggest that the team first prioritize writing a broader mission statement, and then follow up at a later date to set more specific goals.

In relation to development of the team mission statement, discussion of one to two broad goals should focus on defining (1) what the team hopes to accomplish, and (2) how the goal(s) will be measured. Some questions that may help to stimulate discussion about team goals include:

- What does our team hope to accomplish? For example, are we primarily interested in:
  - Improving student outcomes?
  - Closing the achievement gap among subgroups of students in our school or district?
  - Increasing implementation integrity of the RTI model or specific RTI-related practices?
  - Reducing the number/percentage of students eligible for special education?
  - Reducing the disproportionate representation of minority students in special education and other intervention programs?
- What are the district or school expectations for this team?
- What do we know about the instructional needs of the students we serve?
  - What are the historical trends in academic achievement data for the school or district (e.g., performance on state assessments or district CBM benchmark assessments)?
  - What else is known about the academic, social, linguistic, or other educational needs of our current student population?
- What resources are available to our team to help us accomplish our goals?
- Does this team have a responsibility to support the professional development of educators in the school or district? If so, what is known about the professional development needs of the teachers we support?
- How will we know when our goal has been accomplished?
- What specific criteria can be set to indicate successful accomplishment of our goal?
  - If we accomplish this goal, will we feel satisfied that our work is done? If not, what additional goals or improvement efforts may be indicated?

Draft and Revise the Mission Statement

Now it is time to take all of the ideas generated during the planning phases above and generate a mission statement that captures the common team vision. This is easier said than done, and you should expect the first draft to undergo revisions before it develops into a clear and concise mission statement to which all team members can commit. Encourage team members not to worry about writing the perfect statement at this point. Instead, use one or more of the strategies listed in Table 2.2 to generate a few short phrases or sentences that can serve as a starting point for team discussion.

During the process of writing and revising the team mission statement, we recommend that teams take the time to critically evaluate whether *all* team members are satisfied with, and committed to, the mission statement. Allow time for discussion and consensus building, because RTI teams will likely work together for the long term. It is better to identify early on what the fears and concerns are of individual team members, and take steps to address any signs of resistance that may hinder team effectiveness moving forward.

The final team mission statement should be one that all members agree (1) is clear and concise; (2) reflects the team's core values; (3) provides the team with a sense of purpose; and (4) connects emotionally with team members as educators, providing motivation to work toward a common goal. Finally, each member of the team should be willing to commit publicly to this mission statement, and agree to use it for guidance in future team activities and decision making. You'll know you've finalized your mission statement when all team members agree that these features are in place.

> The final team mission statement should be clear and concise, reflects the team's core values, provides the team with a sense of purpose, and connects emotionally with team members as educators.

In the context of RTI, it is also worthwhile for district and school leaders to examine the mission statements of teams across the district and/or school. Although some overlap is to be expected, each team should have a somewhat unique purpose and set of

---

TABLE 2.2. Strategies for Developing an RTI-Team Mission Statement

1. Review examples of other RTI-team mission statements.

2. Discuss and list team values and beliefs, purpose, and goal(s).

3. Highlight key words or phrases reflecting team values and beliefs, purpose, and goals that all team members agree are critical to the team's mission.

4. Ask each team member to draft a one- to three-sentence mission statement. Identify similarities in key words or phrases that can form the basis for a first draft of a team mission statement. Discuss differences in words or phrases and consider when revising the draft statement.

5. As a group, collaboratively write one sentence reflecting team values and beliefs, one sentence stating the team purpose, and one sentence stating the team goal(s). Use these three sentences as a first draft of a team mission statement.

6. Consult with members of other district or school RTI teams, your principal, administrators, or other RTI leaders in your district or school for input about the team's purpose. Use this input as a starting point for discussion.

goals. For example, mission statements for a school-level RTI leadership team and a second-grade RTI data team may both include goals of helping 95% of students to meet grade-level benchmark goals, but the two teams may differ in the way they define their role in promoting student achievement. The school-level RTI leadership team may define its purpose as providing teachers with the leadership and resources needed to support student learning through implementation of evidence-based instruction, assessment, and data-based decision-making practices. The second-grade RTI data team may define its purpose as collaborating and using data to identify at-risk students, provide a continuum of academic supports, and formatively evaluate individual student progress to ensure individual students achieve second-grade benchmark goals. By examining RTI-team mission statements from the various RTI teams in a district or school and identifying any duplication in purpose or goals, RTI leaders can prevent redundancy of work across teams and promote efficient use of resources.

DEFINING TEAM MEMBERS' ROLES AND RESPONSIBILITIES

Now that your team has defined its purpose and goals and created a mission statement, you're ready to continue laying the foundation for successful data-based decision-making meetings by developing a team structure in which each member has clear roles and responsibilities. We've all been a part of teams that don't function well, for a variety of reasons. Some teams lack a designated or natural leader, fail to maintain a focus on the topics or issues of highest priority, or struggle to overcome disagreements among team members when decisions need to be made. Other teams fail to develop efficient processes for recurring tasks that should be routine, such as setting an agenda, making decisions (e.g., consensus vs. voting vs. delegating authority to an individual or subgroup), managing time, or taking notes. There are many reasons a team might fail to function effectively or efficiently, but many can be avoided by creating a team structure with clearly delineated roles and responsibilities for team members.

Our experience has been that most teams would prefer to skip the process of defining team member roles and responsibilities, and allow individuals to take on roles and responsibilities more informally. Team facilitators and note takers tend to emerge naturally, and many teams are not comfortable with a more formal meeting structure involving timekeepers or taskmasters. Unfortunately, this lack of structure and clearly delineated roles contributes to inefficient and unproductive meetings. It can also lead to the establishment of a group dynamic in which a few individuals do most of the work and make most of the decisions, while other team members contribute little to group productivity. We believe that RTI teams can promote buy-in and active participation of all staff in the RTI process by proactively designating specific roles and responsibilities to each and every member of the team.

Useful Roles for School-Based Teams

Because there are different types of RTI teams, serving different purposes, within different settings with varying resources and membership composition, the specific roles and responsibilities of individual team members will need to be specified and negotiated by members of each team. These may evolve over time due to factors such as members' availability, interest, skill development, and staff turnover. However, we can predict several general roles that will need to be filled for RTI teams to function smoothly over time. Before we get into identifying specific member responsibilities, let's examine some of these general roles.

Scholtes, Joiner, and Streibel (2003) suggest that organizations may use different labels or combinations of roles for specific team members, but that certain roles and responsibilities must be carried out for any team to be successful. The authors state that to be successful, any team needs members, leaders, data coaches, and sponsors. Each participant is an active team member, working together to accomplish the team's work. Team leaders are individuals who facilitate meetings, maintain notes and records of team work, and serve as a communication link with other parts of the organization. Scholtes et al. describe data coaches as individuals with data-analysis and team-building skills to support the use of specific tools and/ or data for decision making. Sponsors are individuals who may or may not actually be *on* the team, who review the work of the team, identify needed improvements, and support the work of the team.

Delehant (2007) has written more specifically about school-based groups and teams, and has suggested a similar set of team roles that can help groups to operate smoothly. It is noted that not all teams will use each of these roles at every meeting, but some should be considered standing roles to be filled at every meeting. Delehant provides the following team member roles for consideration of school-based teams:

- *Group member.* Actively participates and contributes to team conversations, work tasks, and productivity.
- *Facilitator.* Helps the team to achieve its desired outcome through use of a variety of skills and strategies. The facilitator formally or informally assesses group needs, facilitates examination of issues, decision making, and action planning. This individual manages group processes, ensures member participation and understanding, and may handle logistical details such as scheduling or postmeeting follow-up on assignments.
- *Timekeeper.* Manages time by keeping the team focused on the task or topic at hand, calls attention to the team's use of allotted time for each topic, keeps a record of the amount of time actually spent on specific topics and works with the agenda builder to set realistic time limits for topics at future meetings.
- *Recorder.* Maintains the formal meeting minutes that will become public record, summarizing key discussion points, action items, and team member assignments. The recorder disseminates meeting minutes to group members and other designated individuals.
- *Scribe.* Displays important data and information during team meetings to help focus the group's work and discussion.
- *Process observer.* A member of the group or an outside observer who gathers descriptive information about team functioning and provides feedback to the group about strengths and areas for growth.
- *Agenda builder.* Collects ideas for meeting topics, prioritizes topics, allocates time for each topic, and assigns team members responsibility for specific topics. The agenda builder produces a formal agenda and distributes it to group members in advance of the meeting.

Additional Considerations When Identifying Roles for RTI Teams

The general roles and functions described above are certainly applicable to RTI leadership and data teams. Additionally, RTI teams should consider the types of data-based decision making that will occur when specifying team member roles and responsibilities. Throughout the course of the year, RTI leadership and data teams will use data to answer questions such as:

- What percentage of students in our district/school are achieving grade-level benchmark goals?
- Which students are at risk or struggling academically, and may need additional academic supports to be successful?
- Are individual students responding to interventions as expected, or are instructional modifications needed?

The focus on using data to make these types of data-based decisions will require RTI teams to prepare data reports and graphs in advance of team meetings, include team members with expertise in interpreting relevant data, and implement RTI activities between meetings based on team decisions. These needs should be considered when defining team member roles and responsibilities. In Table 2.3, we've provided a sample list of member roles and responsibilities for RTI teams, selected based on their alignment with the major tasks to be accomplished by RTI teams.

To guide the process of identifying team member roles and responsibilities, it may be helpful to consider your team's current mission statement, along with the skills, expertise, and interests of current team members. Form 2.3 at the end of this chapter can be used to by teams to examine individual members' skills and areas of expertise in relation to the unique needs of RTI leadership and data teams. The roles and responsibilities listed on Form 2.3 are not intended to

TABLE 2.3. Sample Roles and Responsibilities for RTI Team Members

Role	Responsibilities
Facilitator	Sets agenda, facilitates meeting and data-based decision making, assigns tasks for follow-up.
Recorder	Records meeting minutes, disseminates minutes.
Timekeeper	Tracks time allocated and spent on each agenda item.
Taskmaster	Redirects team when discussion gets off topic, observes and provides feedback to team to improve efficiency and team functioning.
Data gatherer	Generates relevant graphs or reports, brings copies to the meeting or disseminates in advance.
Data interpreter	Assists with interpretation of data, identifies data and trends needing further examination by the team.

TABLE 2.4. Sample Roles and Responsibilities for Two Third-Grade RTI Data Teams

School	Team member	Role(s)
School A	Third-grade teacher 1	Facilitator, team member
	Third-grade teacher 2	Recorder, team member
	Third-grade teacher 3	Timekeeper, team member
	Third-grade teacher 4	Taskmaster/process observer, team member
	Reading specialist	Data gatherer and interpreter, team member
	School psychologist	Data interpreter, team member
School B	Third-grade teacher 1	Recorder, team member
	Third-grade teacher 2	Timekeeper, team member
	Data coach	Facilitator, data gatherer and interpreter, team member

be prescriptive; rather, these are provided as a starting point for discussion. Teams may choose to use these roles, combine roles and responsibilities, or create a configuration that matches the mission and strengths of current team members. If your team identifies a lack of specific knowledge, skill, or expertise needed for data-based decision making, reconsider recruiting a colleague with the needed skills to join your team or serve as a consultant to the team on an "as needed" basis. Each standing team member should be assigned a clear role and set of responsibilities, rather than simply an expectation to attend meetings. On smaller teams, individual members may take on multiple roles. Table 2.4 provides examples of how two third-grade RTI data teams with differing composition might structure the roles of team members.

A final consideration related to member roles and responsibilities is the need to reconsider these assignments when your team experiences changes in membership. Changes in team membership most often occur between school years, as team members retire or move on to new teaching positions and new educators are hired to fill their positions. Encourage your team facilitator to welcome new members by providing an orientation to the team's mission, the purpose of the team and its relation to other RTI teams in the school, and the roles and responsibilities of team members. Form 2.4 at the end of this chapter provides a sample "Welcome to the RTI Grade-Level Team!" document that could be completed by the team facilitator or other experienced team member, shared with the new team member(s), and used to guide initial orientation discussions. After a change in team membership, your team should reexamine the previously assigned roles and responsibilities, consider the expertise and skills brought to the team by the new team member(s), and update member roles and responsibilities.

TEAM MEMBER COMMITMENT

At this point, you've identified the relation of your team to other RTI teams in the district/school, selected team members, developed a mission statement, and assigned team member roles and responsibilities. You've made significant investments in establishing your team, and built a strong foundation for effective team collaboration. Before moving on, we recommend conducting a check of team members' agreement with, and commitment to, the decisions that have been made thus far. Form 2.5 at the end of this chapter contains a brief self-assessment for completion by individual team members. Informal group discussions are an alternate strategy for assessing team member commitment, although some individuals may not feel as comfortable identifying concerns or disagreements in a public forum. Results generated from the self-assessment can be used to inform the team of any areas where team member buy-in is low, or where there is a need to revisit decisions made about the team mission, roles, or responsibilities.

Assessing Commitment of Returning Members on Experienced Teams

If you are a member of an existing RTI team, but it has been a few years since the team discussed its purpose, goals, or individual members' roles and responsibilities, revisiting these issues through a quick assessment of team member commitment may assist in identifying any areas needing attention at this time. We recommend examining team member commitment a minimum of every few years, or after experiencing a change in team membership.

Although it may seem tedious to spend time assessing and reassessing commitment to the purpose and goals of a team that has worked together for years when there is much work to be done, sometimes the self-assessment will reveal hidden concerns of team members that can lead to resistance during team meetings. Consider Mr. Jones, a teacher who joined a third-grade data team after a full year of RTI implementation. He did not fully agree with the team's stated belief that all classroom teachers should work together to ensure the academic success of each and every student in third grade. Instead, Mr. Jones preferred to be responsible for his class of 25 students, and expected other third-grade teachers to trust him to do whatever was needed within his classroom to ensure his students' success. However, Mr. Jones kept his disagreement with this aspect of the team's mission statement to himself because he was new and did not want to cause trouble. During data-team meetings, Mr. Jones was reluctant to discuss his students' individual progress and interventions with the team because he did not want to be told how to teach his students, and he did not support the cross-classroom grouping strategies used for reading instruction by the other third-grade teachers. Through a periodic team self-assessment using Form 2.5 at the end of this chapter, Mr. Jones indicated disagreement with the statement "I support the mission of this team," indicating a need for the team to revisit the underlying beliefs and values, purpose, and goals of the team. This new information provided a prompt for the team to engage in further discussion about the mission statement and the role of collaboration in RTI, and build consensus about what collaboration would look like at their grade level.

Of course, there will be times when team members struggle to find common ground on issues related to student learning, teaching philosophies and practices, core components of RTI, behavior management, or related topics. It may be tempting to avoid discussion of these hot topics, but avoidance can lead to lack of buy-in to team goals, or even outright resistance among team members during regular team meetings. Through the process of revising the team mission statement and individual members' roles and responsibilities, teams can often find enough common ground to build consensus about team priorities. Teams may need to seek outside assistance from an administrator or RTI leader within the district when commitment among team members cannot be adequately established.

SUMMARY

In this chapter, we've discussed a series of activities designed to assist with the initial stages of establishing RTI leadership and data teams. After first clarifying the type of RTI team you're on and its relation to other RTI teams in the district or school, it is essential to get the right people at the table, with the right knowledge, skills, and experience. Next, the development of a shared team mission statement can be a powerful step toward ensuring all members are committed to a common purpose, set of beliefs, and goals. Once the team and its mission are established, defining each team member's roles and responsibilities sets the stage for collaborative and productive team meetings.

Now that you've established team member commitment to the mission statement and individual member responsibilities, you are ready to shift the focus of planning from the initial stages of setting up a team to the development of effective collaboration and meeting facilitation skills among team members. In Chapter 3, we continue our discussion of activities that should occur *before* your team begins meeting to focus on RTI decision making, with a focus on preparing for the meeting and establishing routines for collaborative and productive team meetings.

Identifying Team Membership on District and School RTI Teams

List the RTI teams in your district and school. It may also be helpful to draw a picture or organizational chart similar to the one shown here, illustrating the relationship of your RTI team to other RTI teams within the district and school.

Is there a <u>district-level</u> RTI leadership team? If so, describe its purpose and list members:

```
District-Level RTI
LeadershipTeam
├── School A RTI          School B RTI
│   LeadershipTeam        Leadership
│   │                     Team
│   ├── K Data Team       ├── Primary Grades
│   │                     │   Data Team
│   ├── 1st Grade Data    └── Intermediate
│   │   Team                  Grades Data
│   │                         Team
│   └── 2nd Grade Data
│       Team
```

_____

_____

_____

_____

_____

_____

_____

_____

Is there a <u>school-level</u> RTI leadership team? If so, describe its purpose and list members:

_____

_____

_____

_____

_____

_____

_____

_____

What RTI data teams (e.g., grade-level teams, primary and intermediate teams) exist in your school? Describe their purpose and list members:

_____

_____

_____

_____

_____

_____

_____

_____

Developing the RTI-Team Mission Statement

School year: _____

Type of RTI team (district, school, grade level, etc.): _____

Team members: _____

_____

Planning

Discuss and list team ideas for each of the following components of the RTI-team mission statement:		
Values/beliefs. What are our core beliefs and values that will drive our actions and decisions?	Purpose. What is the purpose of this team? Who does it serve? What are our priorities?	Measurable goal(s). What do we hope to accomplish? How will success be measured?

(continued)

Draft RTI-Team Mission Statement

Based on the ideas generated during planning, draft a mission statement that reflects team values, purpose, and goals.

Mission Statement Self-Check

1. Is the mission statement clear and concise?	Yes/No
2. Does it reflect our core values?	Yes/No
3. Does it provide the team a sense of purpose?	Yes/No
4. Does it connect emotionally with us, and motivate us to work toward a common goal?	Yes/No
5. Is each member of the team committed to this mission statement, and agree that it will be used to guide future team activities and decision making?	Yes/No

Final RTI-Team Mission Statement

Based on the results of the team self-check, consider the need for modifications to the draft RTI-Team Mission Statement. Write a final mission statement that reflects team values, purpose, and goals.

Defining RTI-Team Member Roles and Responsibilities

Part 1. Complete the following table to assist with the identification of team members' strengths and areas of expertise related to RTI, and designating team members for specific roles and responsibilities. Write each team member's name at the top of each column, then place an X next to each descriptor that describes each team member. This may be completed as a team, or each team member may self-evaluate his or her areas of skill and expertise.

	Names of team members				
Areas of expertise or skill related to RTI and/or teaming					
Knowledgeable about RTI and/or has expertise with systems-level RTI models and implementation					
Expertise in evidence-based instruction and intervention					
Expertise in assessment for universal screening and progress monitoring					
Expertise in data-based decision making and/or problem solving					
Skilled in creating effective data summaries and displays (e.g., graphs, summary reports)					
Skilled in interpreting data from various sources (e.g., district data system, state assessments, CBM, behavioral data)					
Skilled/effective meeting facilitator					
Skilled in use of technology					
Detail oriented					
Skilled note taker, communicates effectively in writing					
Taskmaster—keeps people on-task and meetings focused					
Consensus builder—brings people together for a common goal					
Skilled in coaching, consultation, or professional development					
Other:					
Other:					

(continued)

Part 2. Considering the individual team member skills and areas of expertise identified above, identify which team members will fill the following roles on your team. Teams may combine two or more roles listed below. Identify any additional roles your team would like to create.

Role and general responsibilities	Team member(s)
Facilitator: Sets agenda, facilitates meeting and data-based decision making, assigns tasks for follow-up	
Recorder: Records meeting minutes, disseminates minutes	
Timekeeper: Tracks time allocated and spent on each agenda item	
Taskmaster: Redirects team when discussion gets off topic, observes and provides feedback to team to improve efficiency and team functioning	
Data gatherer: Generates relevant graphs or reports, brings copies to the meeting or disseminates in advance	
Data interpreter: Assists with interpretation of data, identifies data and trends needing further examination by the team	

FORM 2.4

Welcome to the RTI Grade-Level Data Team!

School year: _____ Grade level(s): _____

Team members: _____

_____

Welcome to the RTI grade-level data team! As a new member of this team, you're joining a group of educators who have invested time in establishing a collaborative team environment where we can work together to promote positive learning outcomes for the students we serve. We recognize that some aspects of our team dynamics and functioning will likely change over time with the addition of new team members with new energy, enthusiasm, and ideas. In the meantime, this form is intended to orient you to our existing mission statement, the purpose of this team and its relation to other RTI teams in the school, and the roles and responsibilities of team members.

Our RTI-Team Mission Statement

_____

_____

_____

_____

Major Tasks of Our Grade-Level RTI Team

1. _____

_____

2. _____

_____

3. _____

_____

4. _____

_____

5. _____

_____

6. _____

_____

Organizational Chart Illustrating District and School RTI Teams

(continued)

Summary of Team Member Roles and Responsibilities

As a new member of the team, we encourage you to consider your skill and expertise in the following areas, and discuss with team members. Identify potential roles and responsibilities that would align well with your professional skills and interests.

- Knowledgeable about RTI and/or has expertise with systems-level RTI models and implementation.
- Expertise in evidence-based instruction and intervention.
- Expertise in assessment for universal screening and progress monitoring.
- Expertise in data-based decision making and/or problem solving.
- Skilled in creating effective data summaries and displays (e.g., graphs, summary reports).
- Skilled in interpreting data from various sources (e.g., district data system, state assessments, CBM, behavioral data).
- Skilled/effective meeting facilitator.
- Skilled in use of technology.
- Detail oriented.
- Skilled note taker, communicates effectively in writing.
- Taskmaster—keeps people on-task and meetings focused.
- Consensus builder—brings people together for a common goal.
- Skilled in coaching, consultation, or professional development.

Existing RTI-team roles and general responsibilities	Team member(s)
Facilitator: Sets agenda, facilitates meeting and data-based decision making, assigns tasks for follow-up	
Recorder: Records meeting minutes, disseminates minutes	
Timekeeper: Tracks time allocated and spent on each agenda item	
Taskmaster: Redirects team when discussion gets off topic, observes and provides feedback to team to improve efficiency and team functioning	
Data gatherer: Generates relevant graphs or reports, brings copies to the meeting or disseminates in advance	
Data interpreter: Assists with interpretation of data, identifies data and trends needing further examination by the team	

Self-Assessment of Team Commitment

Using the following 4-point Likert scale, rate your agreement with the following statements about your involvement with the RTI leadership/data team and commitment to its purpose and goals. This information will be used to inform team planning.

Statement	1 Strongly disagree	2 Disagree	3 Agree	4 Strongly agree
The mission (values, purpose, goals) of this team is clear.				
I support the mission of this team.				
The team includes members with the necessary RTI knowledge, skills, and experience to accomplish our mission.				
Each team member has clearly defined roles and responsibilities.				
I feel prepared to fulfill my roles and responsibilities.				
I agree to fulfill my responsibilities as a team member.				
I have concerns about moving forward with team activities at this time.				

Comments:

CHAPTER 3

Planning for Collaborative Data-Team Meetings in RTI

Productive team meetings do not occur by accident. They are the result of planning, organization, skilled facilitation, and a team culture that promotes positive and collaborative working relationships. In this chapter, we examine how to prepare your team for successful collaboration by establishing routines for productive and collaborative meetings, and then engaging in standard premeeting planning activities before recurring RTI team meetings.

ESTABLISH ROUTINES

Successful meetings begin days or weeks before the actual meetings are held. Once a team is established, and prior to the start of each new school year, teams or designated team members should begin to lay the foundation for well-organized and productive meetings by establishing routines for the decision-making procedures that will be used by the team. By establishing team routines for recurring decision-making activities, productive meeting time can be maximized for team members, just as classroom instructional routines help to maximize productive academic learning time for students. With effective routines, teams will be able to focus on decision making and problem solving, without losing time due to inefficient processes, disorganization, or confusion about the purpose of the meeting.

> **By establishing team routines for recurring decision-making activities, productive meeting time can be maximized for team members, just as classroom instructional routines help to maximize productive academic learning time for students.**

Specific types of data-based decisions (e.g., identifying at-risk and struggling students, grouping students for intervention, evaluating effectiveness of interventions) will be made on a predictable and recurring basis over time. Specific types of meetings will also repeat over time, and teams can improve their efficiency by creating routines for tasks that occur before, during, and after each type of meeting. Helpful routines include (1) adopting consensus-based decision making procedures, (2) establishing predictable meeting schedules, (3) developing standard sets of agenda items and materials for premeeting review, (4) assigning lead topic facilitators for recurring agenda items, and (5) identifying procedures for creating action plans and ensuring follow through. When these routines are established, team members know what to expect and can come prepared to meetings. Team members become comfortable with the meeting format after repeated exposure to consistent routines over time. Time during the meeting is then focused on decision making, rather than negotiating the content, format, or processes to be used during the meeting.

Adopt Consensus-Based Decision-Making Procedures

Because the major role of RTI teams is to *make data-based decisions*, the team must adopt a decision-making strategy and procedures. Before holding meetings, the team should agree on how decisions will be made. The two most common types of decision-making strategies involve voting and consensus. Voting involves each team member casting a vote, and the decision is made based on a simple majority. This is a straightforward approach that most people are familiar with, but it has several drawbacks for decision making in the context of RTI teams. Most importantly, we know that buy-in and consensus building are critical to implementation of RTI practices. If teams use a simple majority voting approach to decision making, there will always be "winners" and "losers," creating division among the team members. This approach does not encourage working together or compromise. Instead, we've seen this approach lead to behind-the-scenes alliance building and triangulation among team members. With voting, individuals who are in the minority may not experience sufficient buy-in to implement the decisions, leading to problems with fidelity of implementation in the broader RTI model.

For RTI-team decision making, we prefer the consensus decision-making strategy described by Schiola (2011), which involves making a decision when all team members can agree to a specific course of action. This approach promotes collaboration and has the potential to increase buy-in and commitment to decisions among all team members. Decision making by consensus does not necessarily require all team members to wholeheartedly support a decision, or to agree that the decision is the best possible course of action. Instead, for a specific action item, a decision is reached by consensus when all members agree to the following:

- "I agree with this decision." Or "Although this decision may not be my first choice, I can live with it."
- "I will publicly support this decision."
- "I will do my part to implement the decision."

In the event that one person disagrees with the position of the rest of the team, Schiola (2011) suggests the facilitator take the steps depicted in Figure 3.1 to reach a resolution. With this approach, one person should not be allowed to hold up the entire group from making a decision.

Your team may also want to consider creating a backup decision-making plan that can be used in the rare circumstance when the team is unable to reach consensus but a decision needs to be made. Consider your context and what resources may be available to your team for assistance in these situations. For example, is there an RTI coach or leadership team member from your school or district who could provide suggestions based on district expectations and/or

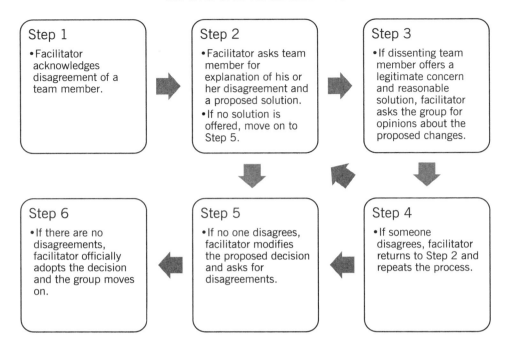

FIGURE 3.1. Steps to resolving disagreements when using consensus decision making.

examples of solutions developed by other teams? Additional options could include making decisions by simple majority voting when consensus cannot be reached, consulting an administrator for input or decision-making authority, or reconvening the team meeting after a 24-hour break to brainstorm additional solutions.

Establish a Predictable Meeting Schedule

One of the most frustrating challenges we encounter related to RTI implementation is when schools invest extensive resources in collecting assessment data and purchasing intervention materials, but teachers are not involved in using existing data to drive decision making at the classroom or grade levels. When it comes to reasons that teachers are not holding regular meetings to analyze assessment data and use data to improve their tiered system of support, the most common challenges we've encountered involve (1) teachers have difficulty finding the time to hold meetings, (2) meeting time is spent discussing topics unrelated to RTI, or (3) teams make non-data-based decisions or make decisions without considering existing data. There are a variety of factors that may create or maintain these challenges, such as competing demands, difficulty scheduling meetings, lack of knowledge or skill needed to interpret and use data for decision making, lack of leadership, lack of team organization, or a school culture that does not prioritize RTI or RTI teaming. To address the challenges related to finding time for meetings, a broader district/school culture must be established in which there is strong administrative leadership that defines RTI and collaborative teaming as a priority, and holds teams accountable for data-based decision making. Using well-planned agendas and meeting facilitation strategies will help to address the challenges related to keeping RTI team meetings on topic.

Knowing that finding the time to meet is a common challenge faced by RTI teams, teams can be proactive about addressing the problem by creating a predictable routine for when and where meetings will be held. It is not sustainable to simply expect teachers to join a new team that meets twice per month without taking something else off their plates. Rather than leaving it up to grade-level teams to find the time to meet twice per month and hoping it actually occurs, administrators and RTI leaders need to rearrange schedules to create specific opportunities for collaboration to occur during the regular workday. It is important to schedule only the number of meetings required to accomplish a specific purpose. Scheduling meetings based on convenience (e.g., every Monday at 3:00 P.M., the first Wednesday of the month at 7:30 A.M.) without identifying the need for each meeting can lead to problems. When too many meetings are set in advance, without an identified purpose, it becomes likely that meetings will be canceled when teachers are busy. And when aren't teachers busy? When meetings are canceled, team members begin to think it is acceptable to cancel future RTI meetings. Instead, the culture needs to respect individuals' time by scheduling only the number of meetings necessary to accomplish the team's tasks, and then protecting and prioritizing the time allocated to team-based RTI activities.

We recommend establishing RTI data-team activities as high priority by creating an annual team meeting schedule prior to the start of the school year. Team leaders can ensure that time will be available for RTI data-team meetings by working with district and/or school administrators to develop a schedule and enlisting the principal's help in protecting the scheduled meeting times from conflict with other activities to be scheduled later in the year. This approach also sends the message that there is important work to be done, and time has been allocated to make sure the team can successfully complete the work. Creating an annual team meeting schedule will likely require planning several months in advance and obtaining support from the school principal. It may involve replacing some traditional ways of doing things with new practices. Consider using one or more of the strategies below when seeking to create a schedule of RTI team meetings:

- Work with the school principal to determine whether all existing faculty/staff meetings need to be held in person. Communicate some topics through newsletter or e-mail, then cancel one faculty/staff meeting per month and replace it with grade-level RTI data-team meetings.

- Create a master schedule in which grade-level teachers share common planning/collaboration time during the school day at least once per month (e.g., students are in "specials" classes). Use this time for RTI data-team meetings.

- Set aside one early release or late start period (or a portion of the release time) per month for RTI data-team meetings.

- Hold "data days" three times per year after each benchmark assessment period, on which substitute teachers are hired to free up one set of grade-level teachers at a time for RTI data-team meetings. The substitute teachers rotate through the school, spending 60 to 90 minutes teaching students at each grade level.

- Consider whether previously existing school teams (e.g., problem-solving teams, multidisciplinary teams, student study teams, prereferral intervention teams, positive behavior support teams) should be reconfigured as the RTI data teams take on responsibility for specific types of decisions. As teams are reconfigured, some teachers may shift time spent on one team to the RTI data team.

Once a team meeting schedule has been established, there should be agreement among team members to prioritize and protect the dedicated team meeting times. Sticking to the calendar of scheduled meetings conveys respect for team members' time and reinforces the importance of the data-based decision making completed by the team. RTI team meetings should not be canceled capriciously, or due to busy schedules. Educators are busy people, and there will always be many demands competing for team members' time. However, if each scheduled meeting is planned to serve a specific decision-making purpose, team members can be assured that the meeting needs to occur for the team to accomplish its purpose.

It will be the responsibility of the meeting facilitator to begin and end the meeting on time, as scheduled. If someone has not yet arrived when it is time to begin the meeting, the facilitator should not wait to begin. Once a routine has been established in which meetings begin and end on time, team members will have reason to arrive prior to the scheduled start time. If a team member arrives late, that person should be responsible for reviewing the meeting minutes at a later date and/or talking with a colleague about any missed agenda items.

Scholtes et al. (2003, p. 3-2) suggest use of "the 100-mile rule." With the 100-mile rule, team members are expected to give their full attention to the meeting once it begins. Colleagues should be instructed not to interrupt the meeting unless the interruption is so important it would occur even if the meeting were held 100 miles away. Similarly, team members should avoid scheduling conflicting appointments and eliminate the possibility of phone call or text message interruptions during the meeting.

Sample RTI Data-Team Meeting Schedule

Figure 3.2 shows an example of an RTI data-team meeting schedule for one school year. This team has a regularly scheduled 1-hour weekly meeting during a common grade-level planning/collaboration period. Approximately twice per month, this planning/collaboration period is used for RTI data-team meetings, with attendance of two additional RTI data-team members (school psychologist and reading specialist). Other weeks, the grade-level teachers use the planning/collaboration period to engage in independent planning or team-based planning for non-RTI-related activities, such as planning fundraisers or grade-level performances.

Prior to developing the annual meeting schedule, the team collaboratively identified the specific purposes for which they would need to meet, based on the team's mission statement and the expectation that all RTI data teams in the school receive coaching throughout the year. Six meeting purposes were identified:

1. Team planning or debriefing.
2. Ongoing professional development and coaching.
3. Screening to identify at-risk and struggling students.
4. Grouping and intervention planning.
5. Evaluating individual student progress in response to interventions.
6. Evaluating effectiveness of instruction across tiers.

When planning the schedule, the team noted that the types of decisions to be made, and the number of meetings needed, varied from month to month. As a result, the team agreed to

Meeting purpose	Aug	Sept	Oct	Nov	Dec	Jan	Feb	Mar	Apr	May	June
Team planning or debriefing	■										■
Ongoing professional development/coaching	■		■		■			■	■		
Screening to identify at-risk students		■			■			■			
Intervention planning		■			■			■			
Evaluating individual student progress			■	■	■	■	■	■	■	■	
Evaluate effectiveness of instruction											■

FIGURE 3.2. Sample grade-level RTI data-team meeting schedule illustrating major purpose(s) of meetings occurring by month.

develop meeting agendas on a monthly basis and combine multiple tasks into one meeting when possible.

As shown in Figure 3.2, this team scheduled meetings immediately after benchmark assessment periods in September, December, and March for the purposes of conducting screening and intervention planning for at-risk and struggling students. The team also holds monthly meetings dedicated to the evaluation of individual student progress between October and May. Meetings dedicated to coaching or other RTI-related professional development for the team was scheduled during months between benchmark assessment periods. Additional discussion of annual meeting schedules and examples of RTI team calendars can be found in Chapter 7.

Develop Standard Sets of Recurring Agenda Items

The types of decisions your team makes will periodically repeat across the course of a school year. When developing your team meeting schedule, you should have identified the major purpose(s) of each meeting. Knowing the purpose of each meeting allows you to identify the specific decisions that will be made at each meeting, and prepare an agenda to keep the meeting focused on those decisions. Common decisions that repeat throughout the year include decisions related to screening, instructional planning, progress monitoring, and evaluating outcomes. Because each of these decisions will involve answering a specific set of questions, using specific data sets or assessment results, teams can improve efficiency by establishing routines for each type of decision. We recommend routines for using standard sets of agenda items, aligned to standard sets of materials for premeeting review by team members in preparation for each type of data-based decision making.

Table 3.1 lists a standard set of agenda items with specific questions to be addressed by RTI teams when making decisions related to screening, instructional planning, progress monitoring, and evaluating outcomes. Figures 3.3, 3.4, and 3.5 provide examples of how these standard sets of agenda items can be used to create standing agendas for repeated use during routine meetings. For example, after each benchmark assessment is completed, an RTI team making decisions related to screening and/or evaluating outcomes could use the agenda in Figure 3.3, making modifications as needed, without having to spend time creating three new agendas during the year.

TABLE 3.1. Routine Sets of Agenda Items for Screening, Instructional Planning, Progress Monitoring, and Evaluating Outcomes Decisions

Agenda items for screening decisions	Agenda items for instructional planning decisions
Identify students needing Tier 2 and Tier 3 intervention. 1. Which students are performing at/above, somewhat below, and substantially below the expected level? 2. Which students need Tier 2 intervention? Tier 3 intervention?	Group students with similar instructional needs. 1. For each student identified as needing Tier 2 or 3 intervention, what are his or her instructional needs? 2. Which students have similar needs? Specify details of interventions for groups at Tier 2 and Tier 3. 1. For each intervention group, what is the intervention plan (i.e., goal, materials, strategies, interventionist, days, time, place, progress monitoring plan)?

Agenda items for progress monitoring decisions	Agenda items for evaluating outcomes decisions
Identify students making adequate progress. 1. Should we continue or fade the intervention? Identify students not making adequate progress. 1. Has the intervention been implemented with fidelity, or is support needed to increase fidelity of implementation? 2. Is lack of progress observed among multiple students in the intervention group, or just one student? 3. Should we make modifications to the intervention at the group level, or for an individual student? 4. What modifications will be made? 5. Do we need to refer any students to the problem-solving team for further consideration?	Evaluate the effectiveness of instruction and intervention across Tiers 1, 2, and 3. 1. At this time of year, what is the expected level of performance for students at this grade level? 2. What percentage of students are performing at/above, somewhat below, and substantially below the expected level? 3. What are areas of strength and areas for improvement within the multi-tier system of supports at our grade level? 4. Are we seeing improvement in student outcomes over the course of this year? Over the last several years? Set goals for improving the effectiveness of the multi-tiered system of supports. 1. Have we met our goal for the percentage of students performing at/above the expected level? 2. If we have not met our goal, what changes (if any) are needed to the instructional supports provided at Tiers 1, 2, and/or 3?

AGENDA

Meeting Title   **Date**   **Time**
RTI Data Team: Benchmark Assessment Review and Screening

Time	Topic	Presenter	Desired Outcome	Action Items
25 mins	Evaluate effectiveness of Tier 1 at grade and classroom levels	Data interpreter	Description of effectiveness of Tier 1 instruction (% of students meeting goals; change over time)	
10 mins	Tier 1 goal setting	Facilitator	Goals set for improving student outcomes at Tier 1	
15 mins	Screening	Team member	Lists of students needing Tier 2 and 3 intervention	
5 mins	Identify responsibilities	Recorder	Document responsibilities for action items	
5 mins	Meeting summary and closing	Facilitator	Meeting ends	

Additional notes:

Prior to meeting, review benchmark assessment reports for your grade and your class (attached). Bring additional relevant data (e.g., program-based assessments, behavior, attendance) to the meeting.

FIGURE 3.3. Sample agenda items for evaluating outcomes and screening decisions.

Assign Presenters to Recurring Agenda Items

Many teams find it useful to assign specific team members the responsibility of presenting a specific type of recurring agenda item each time it occurs throughout the year, and assuming responsibility for identifying any data, reports, or other materials needed for the discussion. For example, a team member who plays the role of data interpreter might be assigned to present all agenda items related to evaluating the effectiveness of instruction, while a team member with expertise in reading interventions may be assigned to present all agenda items related to instructional planning, and so on. Professional development or coaching may be needed initially as team members build new knowledge and skills related to data interpretation, evidence-based interventions, and problem solving, but this would also be true if only one team member were responsible for presenting all items.

There are many benefits to establishing routines for who will present which data and agenda items. Dividing and sharing responsibility for presenting the agenda item and corresponding data for each of the various decision types reinforces the idea that all team members are active participants who play a critical role in the RTI decision-making process. When each member is assigned a specific agenda item, each member must become knowledgeable about at least one aspect of data-based decision making. This shared responsibility builds the team's capacity to sustain practices over time, because the team will not become reliant on one or two team members to lead data-based decision making. Finally, by having a predictable routine for who will present which agenda items, each team member becomes accountable to his or her peers for coming to the meeting prepared and using meeting time productively. Figures 3.3, 3.4, and 3.5 illustrate sample standing agendas with presenter assignments indicated.

AGENDA

Meeting Title   **Date**   **Time**
RTI Data Team: Intervention Planning

Time	Topic	Presenter	Desired Outcome	Action Items
25 mins	Grouping for intervention	Team member	List of students needing intervention, grouped by similar instructional needs	
15 mins	Select and/or modify interventions	Coach	Intervention plan details documented for groups (time, instructor, location, materials, etc.)	
10 mins	Planning for progress monitoring	Facilitator	Progress monitoring plans documented for individual students	
5 mins	Identify responsibilities	Recorder	Document responsibilities for action items	
5 mins	Meeting summary and closing	Facilitator	Meeting ends	

Additional notes:
Prior to meeting, review benchmark assessment reports for your grade and class (attached), and individual student progress graphs for students receiving intervention (see data system). Bring additional relevant data (e.g., program-based assessments, behavior, attendance) to the meeting.

FIGURE 3.4. Sample agenda items for intervention planning decisions.

AGENDA

Meeting Title			**Date**	**Time**
RTI Data Team: Review of Individual Student Progress				

Time	Topic	Presenter	Desired Outcome	Action Items
15 mins	Review student progress graphs for students making adequate progress	Team member	Decision whether to continue/modify intervention; new plan, if needed	
25–30 mins	Review student progress graphs and fidelity data for students not making adequate progress	Team member	Decision whether to address fidelity or modify intervention; new plan, if needed	
5–10 mins	New concerns about student performance	Facilitator	List of students needing intervention and/or monitoring; new plan, if needed	
5 mins	Identify responsibilities	Recorder	Document responsibilities for action items	
5 mins	Meeting summary and closing	Facilitator	Meeting ends	

Additional notes:

Prior to meeting, review individual student progress graphs for students in your class receiving intervention (see data system). Bring additional relevant data (e.g., program-based assessments, behavior, attendance) to the meeting.

FIGURE 3.5. Sample agenda items for individual student progress decisions.

Create Standard Forms for Agendas, Meeting Minutes, Action Plans

We like to keep paperwork to a minimum during meetings, but there are three types of forms that we find essential to helping teams to efficiently accomplish their goals: agendas, meeting minutes, and action plans. Agendas provide a roadmap, or structure, to the meeting itself. Meeting minutes document major team activities, the decision-making process, team decisions, and the rationale for team decisions. Meeting minutes are useful for communication to stakeholders who are not part of the team (e.g., administrators, specialists) and team members who miss a meeting, and to help team members remember details of discussions when there are long periods of time between meetings. Action plans document steps/actions to be taken after the meeting and the persons responsible for each action. Detailed action plans can also be a helpful tool in promoting integrity of implementation of intervention decisions made during the meeting. Action plans may be incorporated into a team's meeting minutes, or recorded on a separate form.

To promote efficiency, we recommend selecting or creating your own forms for agendas, meeting minutes, and action plans prior to the start of the school year. The purpose of creating standard forms is to then use those forms to establish routines for documenting and communicating team decisions so that when meeting facilitators develop the agenda, or meeting recorders take notes during the meeting, they do not need to spend time trying out different recording formats during the year. Similarly, other team members become familiar with specific formats used to document and communicate team decisions, and are able to quickly and easily locate information during or between meetings.

We provide several examples of standard agendas, meeting minutes, and action plan forms in this chapter for your team's use. Form 3.1 at the end of this chapter is a generic agenda template that can be used for any type of RTI meeting. We particularly like this agenda format because it includes an action plan on the same page for ease in recording during a meeting of any follow-up items resulting from specific agenda items. Additional discussion of creating meeting agendas is provided later in this chapter. Forms 3.2 and 3.3 at the end of this chapter illustrate two possible formats for recording meeting minutes. Both include space to document an action plan within the meeting minutes. See Chapter 5 for further discussion of the key components of effective action plans.

Establish Procedures for Ongoing Team Improvement

All teams have their strengths and areas for improvement when it comes to team functioning. Investing time in team development upfront can go a long way in promoting effective and efficient team functioning, yet no amount of planning will prevent problems with team functioning altogether. Over the lifetime of a team there will be ups and downs in member commitment to RTI and team activities, the team will face changing expectations of the school and district, experience changes in membership, and need to deal with conflicts among team members that may be unrelated to the work of the team. RTI teams that take a planful approach to examining team strengths and areas for improvement on an ongoing basis can evolve and meet these and other challenges as they arise.

We recommend that early in the year, *before* problems arise, teams spend time considering what type of data might inform periodic examination of team functioning throughout the year. It is helpful to gather data from multiple sources, using multiple methods, and targeting specific areas of team functioning (e.g., meeting facilitation, using data for decision making, maintaining a respectful climate, record keeping) that your team is most interested in improving. By committing in advance to periodic, routine reflection on team strengths and areas for improvement, these activities become part of the behavioral norms of the group. Then when challenges do arise, it is easier for team members to provide honest feedback to each other because the team has agreed in advance that members *want* feedback. The following strategies are provided as ideas for teams to consider; however, we encourage teams to develop routines that fit their unique needs.

Team Debriefing

Team members are perhaps the best source of information about what is working well and what needs improvement for a specific team. By providing occasional prompts for group members to make suggestions for improving team functioning, buy-in and commitment to the team from individual members can be strengthened. The frequency of team debriefing will likely vary depending on need, how often the group meets, and how long the group has been working together. Some groups may allocate 5 to 10 minutes at the end of each meeting for a quick debrief of the meeting. Other groups may schedule time to debrief about their practices only two or three times per year.

Typically, the group's facilitator would solicit input from team members and lead a discussion about team strengths and areas for improvement. The specific strategies used when soliciting input will depend on the personalities and relationships on the team, and the skill of the facilitator in leading potentially difficult conversations. Form 3.4 at the end of this chapter provides one worksheet that can be used to facilitate this process. When using this worksheet, the following questions are used to generate feedback from team members about general team functioning: (1) What is working well? (2) What is not working? (3) What are suggestions for improving the content or focus of discussion? and (4) What are suggestions for improving meeting facilitation or teaming? The facilitator should carefully consider whether to complete the debriefing activity in the whole-group team setting, or ask individual team members to provide feedback individually. Sometimes allowing individuals to provide feedback anonymously leads to more honest responses. If anonymous feedback is provided, the facilitator should aggregate responses and present the results to the group. Form 3.5 at the end of this chapter is a similar tool teams can use to conduct a sel-ssessment of team functioning during meetings. Other strategies for team debriefing include:

> **By providing occasional prompts for group members to make suggestions for improving team functioning, buy-in and commitment to the team from individual members can be strengthened.**

- Use a round robin approach, in which the facilitator goes around the table asking each team member to list one aspect of team functioning that is working well and one suggestion for the improvement of team functioning.
- Ask each team member to anonymously write one aspect of team functioning that is working well on an index card, and one suggestion for the improvement of team functioning on another index card. Place all index cards in a jar. The facilitator then draws cards from the jar, reading comments to the group for information only or to stimulate discussion.
- Use sentence starters or fill-in-the-blank sentences as the basis for debriefing. Examples of useful prompts include:
  - The most effective strategy we use to keep the team on task is _____.
  - For me, the most valuable aspect of participating on this team is _____.
  - If I could change one thing about the way our team meetings are facilitated, I would change _____.
  - For me, the most frustrating aspect of participating on this team is _____.

- ○ I wish my team members would _____.
  - ○ If I were to describe the greatest impact this team has had on my teaching and/or my students' learning, I would say _____.
- • Include a 3-minute standing agenda item at the end of each meeting dedicated to answering the following debriefing questions: Did we accomplish the goals set for this meeting? If so, why were we successful? If not, what prevented us from meeting the goals, and what should we do differently next time?

Regardless of the strategies used to facilitate team debriefing, the purpose of debriefing is to gather information for the improvement of team functioning. As a result, it is critical that the facilitator uses the feedback provided by team members to lead a discussion about improvements that will be implemented. Debriefing can be a challenging process when relationships among team members have become negative, or when there are one or two team members considered by others to be "difficult" or "resistant" to the team's mission. In these circumstances, it may be useful to ask an administrator, RTI coach, or other skilled facilitator to lead a debriefing session for your team.

Soliciting Feedback from Others

After teams work together for a while, or we serve in a specific role (e.g., facilitator, recorder) for a period of time, we establish habits and become comfortable with a certain way of doing things. We may not realize when our focus has drifted from the original team purpose, our use of data for decision making has become inconsistent, or certain individuals have begun to dominate team meetings. Asking a colleague who is not a member of your RTI team to provide feedback on team functioning can provide team members with a fresh perspective and new ideas for practice. General feedback may be solicited on a periodic, routine basis to proactively collect data to inform team practices. Alternately, feedback may be solicited on a targeted aspect of team functioning in response to a specific challenge faced by the group. Strategies for soliciting feedback from others include:

- • Identify a skilled meeting facilitator in your district/school. Ask this person to observe a team meeting and provide feedback on how to improve team collaboration, data-based decision making, meeting process, and so on.
- • Ask an administrator or RTI leadership team member to review and provide feedback on a draft agenda for an upcoming meeting, to make sure your team is addressing the expected issues and using the appropriate data sets for decision making.
- • Ask an administrator or RTI leadership team member to review and provide feedback on the content of a recent team meeting agenda, minutes, and action plan. Ask the person to examine whether the decisions are based on accurate interpretation of data, appropriate interventions are selected based on student need, and so on.
- • If your team is facing a specific challenge (e.g., lack of follow through on action items between meetings, lack of understanding of a specific type of assessment report), ask a member of a similar RTI data team to provide consultation to your team. Solicit feedback on your team's current practices, and ask for a description or modeling of practices used on the consultant's team.

Additionally, RTI data teams should work closely with administrators and RTI leadership teams to identify the team's needs for coaching and ongoing professional development. During the initial stages of team-based collaboration and data-based decision making, it may not be realistic to expect teams to independently implement team-based collaboration and data-based decision making, even when provided training, procedural manuals, and sample meeting agendas. In some cases, coaches or RTI leadership team members may initially facilitate data team meetings to model effective practices. They may observe or sit in on data team meetings to guide data-based decision making or answer questions that arise. Administrators may provide contingencies to increase the likelihood that teams will accomplish desired tasks and build efficient routines by asking RTI teams to submit a copy of the agenda, meeting minutes, and action plan after each meeting. This initial investment can help to establish routines for high-quality data-based decision-making practices. As teams become more efficient and demonstrate strong team functioning during routine types of RTI meetings, the supports can be gradually faded to providing periodic feedback. Issues of leadership, professional development, and building sustainable practices will be discussed further in later chapters of this book. However, it is important to begin thinking early on about your team's need for initial support and feedback over time in order to establish a team culture and set of routine practices related to ongoing team improvement.

PREMEETING PLANNING

The activities described above related to establishing routines should be conducted once an RTI data team has been established, and then again prior to the start of each school year. After the school year begins, your team should prepare for each and every meeting by (1) identifying the specific purpose of the upcoming meeting, and (2) developing and circulating the meeting agenda prior to the meeting. Depending on the preferences and defined roles of your team members, these tasks may fall under the responsibilities of your team facilitator, or they may be rotated among team members for different types of tasks. It is usually most efficient for the facilitator and data gatherer to always work together to complete premeeting planning tasks, to minimize confusion about who will be completing which tasks. However, some teams have found that it works well for individual members to rotate or share these tasks. For example, the facilitator might complete all premeeting planning tasks for benchmark assessment review meetings, while the reading specialist completes these tasks for intervention planning meetings.

Identify the Purpose of the Meeting

Before each team meeting, premeeting planning should begin by identifying the purpose of the meeting. What decisions need to be made? What are the desired outcomes of the meeting? Your RTI team should already have a good idea of the overall purpose and major goals of the team based on earlier examination of how the team fits within the district's RTI system, and from the development of the team mission statement. Most RTI data teams hold regular meetings for the following purposes: conducting universal screening, instruction and intervention planning, evaluating individual student progress in RTI, and evaluating outcomes at the systems level. Each of these purposes will be discussed in depth in later chapters. The important point here is that preparation for team meetings begins by clearly establishing the purpose of each meeting well in advance of the actual meeting.

Develop and Circulate the Agenda

Creating an effective agenda is one of the most important elements in conducting a productive team meeting. Developing and circulating an agenda in advance of each meeting is important because it communicates information about what will be discussed, who will be discussing each topic, and how much time will be allowed for each topic. This helps participants know what to expect and know how they will be involved. It also allows them to prepare for upcoming discussions and decisions. Second, the agenda provides a structure for the team meeting. It allows discussions to remain focused and on track when adhered to. It also acts as a checklist at the end of the meeting, to ensure all topics were discussed. A clear agenda sets the stage for a productive meeting. It is a necessary tool to use to maximize productivity and ensure important tasks are accomplished.

To promote an efficient and productive meeting, the facilitator or assigned team member should develop and disseminate an agenda several days before each meeting. It is important to carefully consider how many and which topics will comprise the agenda. Specific topics should be identified for discussion, along with a desired decision or outcome for each topic, and an estimate of the time needed for each topic.

Creating an agenda prior to the meeting allows the facilitator to prioritize potential agenda items and consider how much can reasonably be accomplished within the time allocated for the meeting. A common mistake occurs when teams allocate or spend too much time reviewing and discussing the data in assessment reports, without allocating sufficient time to creating an action plan. It is important to create a realistic agenda with sufficient time allocated for both discussion and action planning for each agenda item. An agenda with too many items or too little time devoted to topics can cause frustration among team members, as they may feel rushed to make decisions without adequate discussion or feel discouraged by not getting through all items listed on the agenda. In our experience, two to three primary agenda items is about right for one meeting. If you go beyond three items, distraction and frustration are more likely to set in among team members.

Preparing an agenda in advance of the meeting also allows for the identification of data, reports, or other materials that will be needed for data-based decision making. Selected materials can then be gathered and disseminated to team members, along with the agenda, for pre-meeting review. This level of organization helps ensure that all team members will arrive at the meeting prepared. It also provides individuals who are new to data-based decision making the opportunity to spend sufficient time looking over the data, considering the decisions to be made and desired outcomes for each agenda item, and generating questions to bring to the meeting. There is a steep learning curve when learning to analyze and interpret new types of assessment data at the systems level and individual student level. When first learning these skills, individuals may feel overwhelmed by the quick pace of decision making that occurs in teams with established routines. Having a chance to review the agenda and supporting data prior to the meeting allows each team member to be an informed and active participant during the meeting.

> **Having a chance to review the agenda and supporting data prior to the meeting allows each team member to be an informed and active participant during the meeting.**

Taking time to create and disseminate the agenda in advance of the meeting will pay off during the meeting, because your team can then maximize the allocated time for decision making. The facilitator can begin each meeting with a quick review of the agenda topics, allocated time, and desired outcomes, then quickly move into the first item of business. If an agenda is not developed in advance, precious time is wasted trying to answer questions such as "What are we supposed to be doing this week?" and "Where are those summary of effectiveness reports and worksheets?" and negotiating which items of business take priority over others. We've sat through meetings where the first 10 to 20 minutes were wasted on this type of discussion, and know how frustrating it can be.

During the meeting, the agenda should be used to keep discussion focused and on track. When discussions become sidetracked or focused on a topic that distract the team from the decisions to be made (as indicated by the agenda), teams can "park" the topic in a "parking lot" for further discussion in the future. The facilitator could say, "This is a great discussion about an important issue, but we have gotten off topic and we have a full agenda today. Let's park this issue in the parking lot for now, and come back to it at the end of our meeting, OK?" Teams may keep a list of parked items on a whiteboard, or write topics on sticky notes and place them on a piece of chart paper. When concluding the meeting, the facilitator reviews the list of parked items with the team and determines whether the items should be placed on a future RTI team agenda, added to the action plan as items for follow up by specific persons between meetings, or dropped.

Figures 3.6, 3.7, and 3.8 are agenda examples from schools that were ineffective in their design. In the first example (Figure 3.6), the agenda topics are listed and there is an attempt at an action plan, but more information is needed about who will be responsible for which items and by when. In the second example (Figure 3.7), there is not enough information to even provide a structure for the meeting. Topics are listed and times are provided, but there is no information to indicate the purpose of each topic, the decisions or desired outcomes of the discussion, or how the resulting action plan will be accomplished. In the third example (Figure 3.8), the topics appear to be relevant, but there is little structure to the format. It would benefit from being organized in a different way.

Your team can use the generic agenda template in Form 3.1 for RTI team meetings. Here, an agenda with space for an action plan is provided on one sheet. This is purposeful, as it serves as a visual reminder that a complete agenda is just the starting point. As action items are developed for each agenda item during the meeting, the recorder can complete the action plan as the facilitator leads the discussion. A wide range of agenda templates and styles are accessible online and included with the purchase of common word processing programs. Although agendas may take a variety of forms, effective meeting agendas will always include the following components:

- *Overall meeting purpose.* Include a brief statement of the meeting purpose, or type of meeting to be held (e.g., intervention planning, review of individual student progress).
- *Topic/agenda item.* List each topic for discussion as a separate line item. When listing agenda items, note any handouts, reports, or other materials to disseminate prior to or at the meeting. Always include a meeting summary/closing item at the end of each meeting, allocate sufficient time to review decisions and action items, and set the date and time for the next team meeting.
- *Presenter.* Assign a specific person to be responsible for preparing and presenting the

**Response-to-Intervention
Grade-Level Meetings**

Date: _____

Instructional Area (select one): _____

People Present (list names): _____

Complete?

1. Review student data ☐
2. Determine who is in need of additional support ☐
3. Categorize students based on needs ☐
4. Decide who will run instructional groups ☐
5. Determine how to collect weekly data ☐
6. Set goals for each student ☐
7. Set date to meet in 4 weeks to review student data ☐
8. Complete action plan below ☐

Action Plan
Divide the responsibilities of instructional groups and progress monitoring among those present at the meeting. Each person will be responsible for what is stated below.

Name:

Responsibility:

Name:

Responsibility:

Name:

Responsibility:

Name:

Responsibility:

FIGURE 3.6. Example of an ineffective agenda.

```
┌─────────────────────────────────────────────────────────┐
│              Agenda for September 1st                     │
│  8:45   Coffee and donuts                                 │
│  9:15   Announcements                                     │
│  10:00  Fall benchmarking: Who, what, when, where?        │
│  10:40  Breakout—by grade level                           │
│  11:30  Report from breakout groups                       │
│  12:00  Meeting ends                                      │
└─────────────────────────────────────────────────────────┘
```

FIGURE 3.7. Example of an ineffective agenda.

September 11th Elementary Meeting Agenda	
Participants:	
Topic	**Action Plan**

Interventions professional development for the year	• Set agenda for dates this year
	  ○ Topics
	  ○ Matching instruction to need
	  ○ Progress monitoring
	  ○ Interventions
	  ○ Goal setting
	  ○ Core
	  ○ Phase changes
	  ○ Immediacy of results/actions
	  ○ Scheduling/logistics

DIBELS	• How to use the data • What reports? • What data to focus on? • How to share information with parents
Curriculum	• Will focus on supplementing the core this year • Does it meet the needs of 80% of our kids? How will we address this? • Balance will be between evaluating core this year and supplementing with interventions

Questions/Issues from Meeting

1. How do we address the issue of core?
2. Issues of all kids going through problem solving will end up in special ed. And it takes too long. Need to consider this when planning training.
3. Teachers need support on matching instruction and intensity of instruction to student needs. How to do this?
4. Teachers need a lot of help on writing goals.
5. Logistics of who, where, when intervention groups will occur.
6. Need to emphasize that this takes a while, doesn't all happen in 1 or 2 years. Ongoing change process.
7. Set goals for the year.
8. Fidelity of implementation issues. Talk about this.

FIGURE 3.8. Example of an ineffective agenda.

item and any relevant background information for discussion. The presenter is responsible for identifying the need for handouts, reports, or other materials for the discussion. However, the tasks of creating reports or disseminating materials for review may be delegated to the data gatherer, and the facilitation of decision making may be delegated to the meeting facilitator.

- *Desired outcome.* Each agenda item should be linked to a desired outcome, or result, to be accomplished at the meeting. Examples of desired outcomes may include documentation of a specific decision (e.g., set a team goal, select/modify intervention), or completion of a product (e.g., list students identified as needing Tier 2 or 3 interventions).

- *Time allocated.* For each agenda item, estimate time needed for discussion and decision making based on consideration of the topic content, amount of data to review, and desired outcome. It is better to overestimate the amount of time needed than to list agenda items without providing sufficient time.

- *Action items.* Action items are the follow-up actions for each agenda item that are to be completed after the meeting. Although action items are typically not specified in advance of the meeting, we like to include a reference to action items on the agenda. This provides a prompt during the meeting to identify action items related to each agenda item.

SUMMARY

In this chapter, we've examined steps your team can take to set the stage for collaboration. Because many educators have not received training in meeting facilitation or team-based collaboration, it is important to build knowledge among RTI team members about the basics of preparing for efficient and effective team meetings. We've considered how establishing clear routines for team-based decision making creates predictability and provides structure to group member interactions. We've also discussed how establishing routines and premeeting planning can promote efficient team processes, allowing teams to maximize productivity during the time allocated for meetings. Investing time *before* meetings in the following activities sets the stage for a positive experience *during* meetings:

- Adopting consensus-based decision-making procedures.
- Establishing a predictable meeting schedule.
- Identifying standard sets of recurring agenda items.
- Assigning presenters to recurring agenda topics.
- Developing standard agenda, meeting minutes, and action plan forms.
- Planning for ongoing team improvement.
- Identifying the purpose of each meeting.
- Preparing and disseminating an agenda prior to each meeting.

In the next section of the book, we shift our focus to collaboration and data-based decision making that occurs *during* RTI team meetings.

Agenda and Action Plan Format

AGENDA

Meeting Title   **Date**   **Time**

Time	Topic	Presenter	Desired Outcome	Action Items
_____	_____	_____	_____	_____
			_____	_____
			_____	_____
			_____	_____
			_____	_____
_____	_____	_____	_____	_____
			_____	_____
			_____	_____
			_____	_____
			_____	_____
_____	_____	_____	_____	_____
			_____	_____
			_____	_____
			_____	_____
			_____	_____
_____	_____	_____	_____	_____
			_____	_____
			_____	_____
			_____	_____
			_____	_____
_____	_____	_____	_____	_____
			_____	_____
			_____	_____
			_____	_____

Additional notes:

(continued)

ACTION PLAN

Priorities and Objectives (What are we seeking to achieve?)	Strategies (How will we achieve this?)	By Whom (Name of person responsible)	By When (Date to be completed by)	Key Performance Indicators (How will we measure success?)
_____	_____	_____	_____	_____
_____	_____			_____
_____	_____			_____
_____	_____			_____
_____	_____			_____
_____	_____	_____	_____	_____
_____	_____			_____
_____	_____			_____
_____	_____			_____
_____	_____			_____
_____	_____	_____	_____	_____
_____	_____			_____
_____	_____			_____
_____	_____			_____
_____	_____			_____

Meeting Minutes Format I

Meeting type:	Date:
Facilitator:	Recorder:
Timekeeper:	Taskmaster:
Other members in attendance:	

Agenda Item/Topic:		
Highlights from discussion:		
Decisions:		
Action Item	Person Responsible	Deadline

Agenda Item/Topic:		
Highlights from discussion:		
Decisions:		
Action Item	Person Responsible	Deadline

Agenda Item/Topic:		
Highlights from discussion:		
Decisions:		
Action Item	Person Responsible	Deadline

Meeting Minutes Format II

Meeting Type: _____

Date: _____   Recorder: _____

Team Members Present: _____

Agenda Item/ Topic	Summary of Discussion	Decisions/Action Items (indicate person responsible and due date)
1.		
2.		
3.		
4.		
5.		
6.		

FORM 3.4

Debriefing Team Functioning

Periodically, use this worksheet to solicit feedback from each team member about team functioning. Complete this debriefing worksheet individually or as a group. Use the feedback to identify team practices that should be continued, and team practices needing improvement.

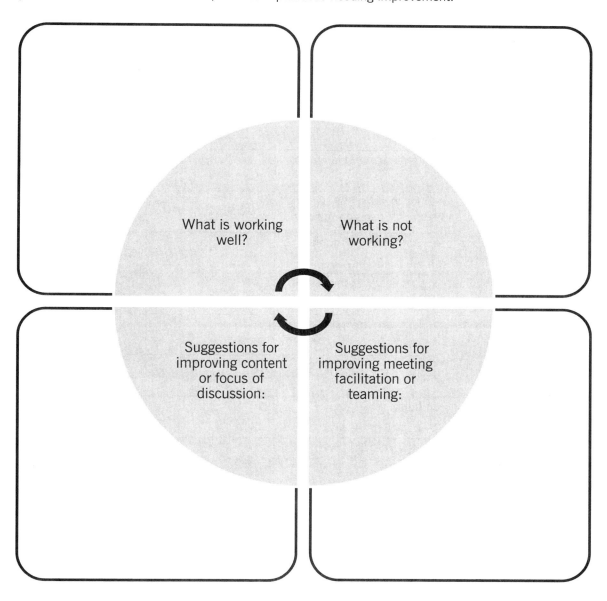

Self-Assessment of Team Functioning during Meetings

Using the following 4-point Likert scale, rate your agreement with the following statements about team functioning during RTI team meetings. This information will be used to inform ongoing team improvement efforts.

Statement	1 Strongly Disagree	2 Disagree	3 Agree	4 Strongly Agree
We stick to our meeting schedule, rarely or never canceling team meetings.				
We begin and end our meetings on time.				
Agenda topics are related to our team's mission.				
Group members are prepared for meetings by bringing relevant data, reports, and so on for decision making.				
We stick to the agenda topics and "park" off-topic items for later discussion.				
We respect the time limits set for agenda topics.				
Meeting minutes and action plans are thorough and accurate.				
All team members actively participate in discussion and decision making.				
We make decisions based on data.				
We maintain positive working relationships and a respectful meeting environment.				
We effectively solve problems that arise during the meeting.				
Our meetings are productive.				
Other:				
Other:				

PART II

DURING THE TEAM MEETING

CHAPTER 4

Data-Based Assessment and Screening Decisions

Collecting screening data is an essential feature of the RTI process. Screening measures are brief assessments that provide predictive information about a child's development in an academic or behavioral area (Compton, Fuchs, & Fuchs, 2010). This allows educators to analyze data on all students three times per year. With this information, decisions can be made regarding who is succeeding with the general education curriculum and who requires instruction beyond the general education curriculum. These data-based decisions encourage a proactive approach, as students are identified and intervened with earlier. RTI has the potential to narrow the achievement gap and reduce the number of referrals to special education by catching children before they fail, because resources can be allocated toward children whose needs are beyond what can be reasonably addressed within general education (Bursuck & Blanks, 2010).

Screening all students also encourages a schoolwide analysis of curriculum and instructional practices. If large numbers of students are identified as "at risk," it signifies that the schoolwide programs and practices are not matched to the students' needs. With this perspective, teams can take a critical look at what is working and what is not on a systemic level. Program can be modified to benefit all students, so more students succeed at a higher rate earlier.

In this chapter we review benchmark and screening practices including how to screen students to identify those who are at risk and how to evaluate grade-level achievement over time. Additionally, information is provided that details how to prepare for meetings where screening data will be reviewed. Finally, we address how to prevent and address common roadblocks during benchmark data review meetings.

REVIEW OF EVIDENCE-BASED BENCHMARK AND SCREENING PRACTICES

Screening measures are used with all students to determine their likelihood for achieving important educational outcomes. When universal screening tools are used, students whose scores fall below a certain criterion score or percentile are viewed as at risk for difficulties (Lembke, McMaster, & Stecker, 2010). In academics, curriculum-based measures are often used for screening. Why use CBM as screening measures? CBM has several advantages over traditional norm-referenced assessment and other informal measures of student performance. Some advantages are listed below:

- Individually referenced (an individual's performance is compared to his or her own performance over time).
- Peer referenced (a student's performance is compared to his or her same-grade peers).
- A tool that can provide teachers with information to make instructional change decisions.
- Highly sensitive to student growth, detecting even small changes in student performance.
- Time efficient (passages require only 1 minute to administer).
- Cost effective (elaborate materials are not needed).
- A method that produces results that are easier to understand than normative tests using standard scores (Deno, Fuchs, Martson, & Shin, 2001).

There are two approaches to using screening data. In the first approach, all students are screened and those students who fall below an identified criterion are placed into Tier 2 interventions (Shinn, 2010). Only after students fail to respond to Tier 2 interventions would they be placed into Tier 3 interventions, according to their progress monitoring data that indicates a "lack of response." The second approach is more proactive, as students' scores allow them to be placed in any tier immediately (Shinn, 2010). Students who fall between the 11th and 24th percentiles would qualify for Tier 2 and students who fall at the 10th percentile and below would qualify for Tier 3. In this approach, students receive the support they need immediately, rather than having to "wait to fail" to receive the appropriate support. When school teams take the time to select and plan for all intervention tiers, the second approach should not be difficult to implement. Thus, we recommend the second approach, as it encourages teams to consider all levels of support and place students accordingly. With all intervention tiers available, students can receive the intervention that is best matched to their needs now, rather than having to wait until their progress monitoring data indicates the severity of the problem.

When selecting screening measures, school teams should consider measures that are reliable, valid, and accurate. Screening measures are defined by two main characteristics: sensitivity and specificity. Sensitivity refers to the ability to accurately identify the students who will encounter difficulty, also known as the true positive rate. When the measure is sensitive to student skills, students will perform at many different levels, indicating a need for different types of support. If the measure is too simple, all students will perform well, making it difficult to determine who really needs support. Specificity refers to the ability to accurately identify the students who will not require additional support, also known as the true negative rate. If the measure is too difficult, many students may struggle, which creates an inaccurate picture that all students need additional intervention. High sensitivity and specificity indicate that the screening battery will accurately identify students in need of intervention. A final consideration for screening is efficiency. Because all children participate in a universal screening model, screening batteries should be brief and easy to administer and score. The measures should not

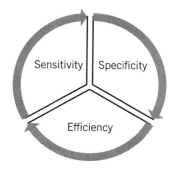

FIGURE 4.1. Features to look for in screening measures.

be too cumbersome to implement, either because they are lengthy, complex, or require too many highly trained individuals to implement the measures. School teams should consider what measures are efficient to implement and score, so that the focus can be on data analysis and intervention placement, rather than data collection. (See Figure 4.1.)

There are three possible outcomes that can result from implementing screening measures. First, screening measures are administered, the data is analyzed, and interventions are implemented. This is the best-case scenario. In schools like this, data collection and analysis and intervention placement is second nature. These schools make all three activities important priorities and leave nothing to chance. In the second scenario, screening measures are administered, the data is analyzed, but interventions are not well planned. Leadership teams review the results and interventions are discussed, but there is no final agreement or action plan to hold people accountable for the next steps. Some educators may try to implement interventions, but because the interventions are not built into the infrastructure, it makes it difficult to follow through with fidelity. In these situations, some students receive support and some may not. In the third situation, the screening measures are administered but the data is not analyzed, which means there is not even a discussion about intervention planning. While time is taken to administer the measures, there is no time devoted to data-based decision making. This is a dire situation. Teams may spend so much time planning and organizing for the logistics of data collection that this becomes the priority, rather than using the data to support students. The team is left with important data that is not used, and students are not provided the interventions they need. As a team, it is important to prioritize the activities so that all facets of the benchmarking process are completed, instead of just one component. Take the time to plan with your team and consider what is needed for all three steps (data collection, analysis, and intervention planning) so that there are measurable outcomes to the process that impact student performance.

PLANNING FOR SCHOOLWIDE SCREENING

There are a number of steps to complete to ensure that screening practices are widely adopted and implemented. School teams should plan to make these decisions before administering the measures, to be strategic in considering different outcomes. With time, planning, and consensus, educators can increase the odds that screening measures and the resulting data are used to improve instruction for students. To support widespread adoption and successful implementation, the following steps are recommended:

1. Create the RTI leadership team to lead the screening process.
2. Select screening measures.
3. Provide professional development to staff.
4. Organize data collection logistics.
5. Analyze and use screening data.
6. Prepare for meetings.
7. Hold regular meetings.

Create the Leadership Team

A leadership team is necessary to lead, plan, and support screening measures adoption and implementation. Without administrator support and a leadership team, there is little chance that RTI will be implemented at an advanced level. Leadership is vitally important because it leads the school on a path of new thinking and new actions, some that will be easy and some that will be difficult. Administrators and leadership teams must keep the long-term vision of RTI in place as they balance the short-term actions that must be taken now to achieve the goals. They can paint an attractive picture of the desired future state of the school, but they must balance this vision with steps that can be taken today (DuFour, DuFour, Eaker, & Karhanek, 2004).

The leadership team will meet regularly to plan for implementation, provide professional development to teachers, organize the schedule and measures for administration, and facilitate data entry and analysis. By taking the lead with these activities, schools are in a better position for data analysis and planning for student support. A leadership team dedicated to RTI adoption supports the change process because they take on the burden of learning the content, facilitating the process, and supporting educators in their new work. The RTI team is responsible for creating a school RTI implementation plan, monitoring the plan consistently, and identifying and finding the needed resources to support these new school activities (McDougal, Graney, Wright, & Ardoin, 2009).

Because RTI teams are tasked with keeping the vision while managing the current actions, there is significant responsibility allocated to this team. This leadership team should not be considered as just another committee that staff members will serve on for a couple years before moving on to the next committee. This is a long-term commitment, one that will require team members to have a deep understanding of RTI and a dedication to the work that is required to make this happen. Because of the importance of this team, we recommend using Form 4.1 at the end of this chapter as a planning tool for considering who should be involved. This tool should be used to consider the size of the school, its instructional needs, and staff skills and expertise. Use the tool to consider who will bring what skills to the team, how the team will operate, and how members will support long-term implementation.

Select Screening Measures

There are a number of screening measures available for administration. While much of the focus around screening is on academics, the area of behavior is growing as well. The same principles that we use to evaluate academic performance can be applied to behavior. Behavioral screening measures can be administered to all students, students can be organized into three tiers, and Tier 2 and Tier 3 interventions can be selected to support behavioral performance. Once interventions are in place, students can be progress monitored and intervention effectiveness and student growth can be evaluated.

The leadership team should take time evaluating the strengths and weaknesses of the systems to determine what measures will be valid, reliable, and have high social validity for their school. Social validity refers to the social or applied importance of the screening measures that are selected. If the selected screening measures have high social validity, the staff will see them as useful and worthy of administration. If the measures have low social validity, the staff will not view the measures as necessary, and the extent to which they are used will be negatively affected. It is important that the measures do what they're designed to do, and it's of equal importance that the measures are accepted among the staff so that the data is used.

The National Center on Response to Intervention (NCRTI, 2012) provides a chart on progress monitoring tools that are available. The chart is a useful reference as it specifies how tools fare on many dimensions including the reliability and validity of the performance-level score, the reliability and predictive validity of the slope, sensitivity to student improvement, the rates of improvement specified, and the end-of-year benchmarks. The tools can be filtered by subject and grade and the vendors of the tools have provided implementation information that includes the cost of the tool, what is needed to implement it, and how the tool is intended to be used. The leadership team can use this information to select measures that are reliable, valid, and will be useful for students and helpful for staff.

Provided next is a brief description of the main screening systems available. The information is designed to provide a brief overview of the systems, who they are intended for, and what measures are included. The authors of this book have no affiliation to the systems below. Rather, information is provided to give teams a place to start when selecting a system for benchmarking.

AIMSweb

AIMSweb (2012) is a benchmark and progress monitoring system. The system offers many curriculum-based measures. These include oral reading fluency, Spanish oral reading fluency, maze-CBM for reading comprehension, tests of early literacy, Spanish early literacy, spelling-CBM, written expression-CBM, tests of early numeracy, math computation and math facts, mathematics concepts and applications, and behavior. Schools can choose to purchase the Complete Pro package or purchase smaller packages of the measures.

They offer a specific RTI component that allows teams to review student data and plan interventions by providing a documented summary of RTI activities of who did what, when, and with what outcome. They also provide specific instructional placements tied to Pearson curricula, and a browser-based scoring system that uploads data automatically. General information is provided regarding how AIMSweb can be used with the Common Core State Standards. In the area of behavior, AIMSweb includes the Behavioral and Emotional Screening System (BESS), which is a quick screener for emotional and behavioral issues. They also include a measure of student social skills against grade-level expectations in two areas—prosocial behavior and motivation to learn—using items taken from the Social Skills Improvement System (SSIS) Performance Screening Guide. See *www.aimsweb.com*.

Dynamic Indicators of Basic Early Literacy Skills (DIBELS)®

The DIBELS Data System (2012) is a web-based database that schools and districts can use to enter student performance results and create reports based on scores. Included within the DIBELS package are DIBELS (*Dynamic Indicators of Basic Early Literacy Skills*), 6th edition; IDEL (*Indicadores Dinámicos del Ṕxito en la Lectura*) for native Spanish speakers; DIBELS Next; easyCBM Math; and one local or state outcome measure. DIBELS Next is a new edition of DIBELS that includes new measures and new benchmark goals. EasyCBM® Math provides math numbers and operations, geometry, and algebra; assessment scores are automatically entered as the student takes the assessment online.

The Data System tracks and measures progress at the student, class, school, and district levels. Reports are available at the student, class, school, district, and project levels. Benchmark reports include histograms (distribution of scores), district norms, box plots (percentiles over time), individual student profiles, class list reports (student name, scores, percentiles, and instructional status), and scatter plots. A useful feature are the "Summary of Effectiveness" reports, where teams can evaluate if students moved from different tiers of support throughout the year. This informs teams whether the instruction is effective or needs to be changed.

Teams can also create individual progress monitoring graphs to see how students are responding to additional instruction and intervention. On the website, they provide video demos and example reports for schools. The DIBELS Data System (2012) is operated by the Center on Teaching and Learning at the University of Oregon. See *http://dibels.uoregon.edu*.

EasyCBM

EasyCBM was designed by researchers at the University of Oregon as part of an RTI model. The project began with a grant from the federal Office of Special Education Programs in 2006 and has expanded to schools in Oregon and throughout the country. The system offers many curriculum-based measures including measures of alphabetic principle, phonics, fluency, vocabulary, and comprehension. The math tests are based on the National Council of Teachers of Mathematics (2012) Focal Point Standards in Mathematics and include three test types per grade. Each of the math tests comprises 16 items.

EasyCBM offers two versions, for the teacher and the district. The teacher version contains progress monitoring measures so teachers can measure their students over time. The district version contains both screening as well as progress monitoring measures. The screening measures are designed for use three times per year (fall, winter, spring). The progress monitoring measures are designed for more frequent use including every month, every 2 weeks, or every week. Information is provided that encourages teachers to select the measure and grade level that will be most sensitive to showing growth for a particular student. Reports can be created at the group and individual levels, and there is a tab for intervention planning as well. See *www.easycbm.com*.

Behavioral and Emotional Screening System (BESS)

The Behavioral and Emotional Screening System (BASC-2 BESS; 2012) is a brief, universal screening system for measuring behavioral and emotional strengths and weaknesses in children and adolescents. There are teacher forms, student self-report forms, and parent forms. Each form ranges from 25 to 30 items and takes about 5 to 10 minutes of administration time. The BESS provides an assessment of a wide array of behaviors that represent both behavioral problems and strengths, including internalizing problems, externalizing problems, school problems, and adaptive skills. Reports are printed for individuals and groups and provide information about specific responses, percentile rankings, and a behavior classification. They also provide Spanish-language versions of the parent and student self-report forms. See *www.pearsonassessments.com*.

Direct Behavior Rating (DBR)

DBR is a quick rating that is provided by a teacher on a specific behavior for a student in a specified time period. It is called the DBR because it is *direct*, meaning that the ratings are recorded immediately after an observation period. The *behavior* refers to specific behaviors like academic engagement or disruptive behaviors. The *rating* can be conducted repeatedly to gather information over time. It is a simple, inexpensive, and flexible way to provide frequent feedback about behavior. After the rating is provided, the information is shared to inform behavioral decision making. DBR also serves dual purposes by acting as a progress monitoring tool and a behavior intervention. While the DBR can be used to monitor behavior in response to an intervention, it can also act as an intervention tool to teach and reinforce expectations regarding behavior. For example, the DBR can be used to rate academic engagement in language arts class. If Avery is being monitored using the DBR, her teacher would rate her academic engagement and also share the results with Avery. Positive results would be tied to a positive reinforcement component. The benefits of also using it as an intervention component include the ability to provide immediate and consistent feedback, student awareness of behavior is promoted, students are encouraged to take responsibility for their behavior, and communication between the adult and student is increased. See *www.directbehaviorratings.com*.

School-Wide Information System (SWIS)

SWIS is a web-based information system that uses office referral data to design schoolwide and individual student interventions. It is an information system that is designed to collect and summarize information used for decision making. It is a web-based computer application that allows easy collection, summary, and storage of office referral data. SWIS provides the capability to evaluate individual student behavior, the behavior of groups of students, behaviors occurring in specific settings, and behaviors occurring during specific time periods of the school day. Specifically, SWIS can monitor the number of office discipline referrals per month, type of problem behaviors leading to office referrals, locations of problem behavior events, problem behavior events by time of day, and the students contributing to office discipline referrals. Custom graphs and reports can be generated to note these patterns and be used to select behavior interventions. See *www.swis.org*.

Provide Professional Development

After an RTI team has been created and screening measures selected, professional development should be planned to get all staff on board. Professional development is essential to the adoption of new practices and it must be designed with purpose. Part of the RTI team's responsibility can be to provide training for the rest of the teachers, so that staff understand the intention and outcomes of screening all students.

Planning professional development carefully and strategically is important so that the objectives are achieved and learning occurs for teachers that is worthwhile and meaningful. Too often teachers are subjected to professional development that does not match their needs or is poorly executed. How many times have you sat in a training and started grading or getting other work done because it did not feel worth your time? We would guess more times than you can count. Unfortunately, professional development is often poorly designed and poorly implemented, so little new learning occurs.

First, training should be relevant to all participants and they should walk away with new skills. The National Staff Development Council (NSDC, 2012) has developed standards for professional development that are organized into three categories. These can assist schools in creating a framework for staff training. First, there are context standards. These address what components should be in place in the environment to support sustained and continuous staff learning. These include learning communities, leadership, and resources. Staff must have the opportunity to meet in small groups, be provided guided leadership, and have adequate resources to perform their job functions.

The NSDC (2012) also provides process standards, or what should occur during the process of professional development. Process standards include data-driven practices, where performance and growth is measured over time. There should also be a focus on how the professional development is designed as well as how it promotes collaboration among staff. Are educators encouraged to work together? Are there opportunities to share and learn from one another? Do activities promote collaboration rather than individual growth? These are questions that should be considered when designing a process for professional development.

Finally, the NSDC (2012) provides content standards. These designate what should be covered in staff training. First, the content should promote equity, so that it prepares educators to understand and appreciate all students. It should also promote quality teaching, so educators are provided with research-based instructional strategies to assist students in meeting academic standards. Finally, family involvement should be considered so that teachers have the knowledge and skills to involve families and other stakeholders appropriately. We encourage RTI teams to visit the NSDC website to gather additional resources and information (*www.nsdc.org*).

Once the RTI team has considered the NSDC standards, they can begin to plan for their professional development sessions. Form 4.2 at the end of this chapter can assist RTI teams in planning professional development. The following categories are on the first page of the planning form: review of past learning, stage of learning, learning objectives, content, activity, assessment (see also Figure 4.2). Presenters should first consider the outcome and what content will help achieve the outcome. The purpose should be targeted toward two to three main objectives, so that participants can focus on the important goals. Any more than that, and too much information will be covered. Any less, and it may seem like time could have been used more effectively.

After the outcomes are identified, the learning hierarchy should be considered in planning the professional development for staff. The hierarchy has four stages: acquisition, fluency, generalization, and adaptation (Haring, Lovitt, Eaton, & Hansen, 1978). Acquisition occurs when learners are learning how to complete the target skill correctly but are not yet accurate or fluent in the skill. The goal in this phase is to improve accuracy. In this stage, learners have little

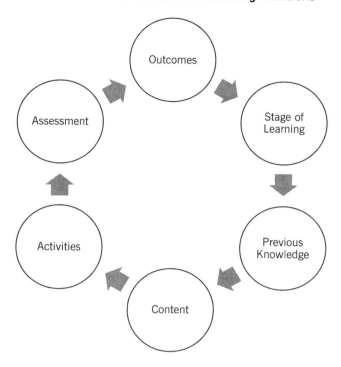

FIGURE 4.2. Components of professional development.

knowledge or experience with the skill, so the objective is to improve learner skill acquisition. Significant time should be allocated to this stage, because although most professional development only covers a topic once, what we know about adult learning is that we have to hear it multiple times and practice it multiple times before it becomes part of our repertoire.

In the fluency stage, the learner is able to complete the target skill accurately but works slowly. The goal of this phase is to increase the speed of responding. At this point, the staff in your school will have heard about RTI for a while now, are familiar with the main components, but still have some questions regarding the details. As trainers, it is the job of the RTI team to provide additional practice opportunities so that staff have the opportunity to become fluent with the material so there are no questions or concerns. This includes providing review of past content at each session, answering any lingering questions, and addressing issues as they arise.

With the generalization stage, learners are accurate and fluent in using the target skill but do not typically use it in different situations or settings. The goal of this phase is to get learners to use the skill in the widest possible range of settings and situations. At this point, staff are fluent with RTI, understand the "what" and "why," and have been engaging new practices for a while now, so much so that they aren't new anymore. In this stage, the goal is for staff to understand how intervention groups can also be set up for math or behavior, for example. Or how screening practices can be adopted for the middle or high school levels. Presenters should provide a list of examples to highlight modifications as well as ask participants to create a list on their own.

The last stage, adaptation, refers to learners who have mastered the skills but are not yet able to modify or adapt the skill to fit novel task demands or situations. The goal is to identify elements of previously learned skills that can be adapted to the new demands or situations. In this stage, the team is working with very advanced participants, ones who have been making RTI work well for a while now. These staff have gained consensus, adopted new practices, made changes as necessary, and have continued to refine the process so that it best supports students in their school. At this point, staff need to be presented with new potential situations, to determine how they would adapt their current RTI practices as needed, depending on the issue. The training here would focus more on discussion and problem solving, rather than establishing new skills by presenting content the entire time.

Next on the planning form is the previous content that should be reviewed. Reviewing previous content is important to assist teachers in becoming more familiar with the core concepts. Instead of hearing about schoolwide screening once, they should hear about it multiple times. What's necessary is sustained practice, which is regular, ongoing review or use of the target material (Willingham, 2009). With this, staff have the chance to develop deep understanding of the material by working through it multiple times. Without this, staff only develop a cursory understanding, which can lead to problems in building consensus or mastering efficient implementation later. The RTI team can facilitate review by creating activities, games, or brief assessments that allow participants to remember what they learned in the previous session, which primes their background knowledge and prepares them for new content.

The content that will be covered in the session should be considered next. The content will vary depending on participant previous knowledge, the amount of consensus among the group, and the goal for the school year (Are we just trying to collect screening data three times this year or do we also want to organize systematic Tier 2 interventions as well?). The content will be determined by the team at the start of the year, as each professional development session should be planned out. As training occurs throughout the year, the team should assess how the staff perceives the information and what is successful and what needs to be changed. With this informal progress monitoring information, the content may change, as participants may need more information or practice with a certain objective. The goal is to foster deep understanding rather than to just get through the content as scheduled. Taking a step back and slowing down may be the best course of action for some schools, as addressing all the issues and questions now is better than having to address them later.

Presenters are also encouraged to consider what activities will support sustained and improved learning. Activities should be selected so that they (1) allow participants to practice newly learned skills, (2) increase their understanding through discussion, or (3) provide enhanced learning activities through demonstration. It is common for presenters to forgo activities for longer presenting. Unfortunately, participants may learn some from being talked to, but they will learn more when they do something with the information. Likewise, trainers should thoughtfully select activities so that they complement new learning. Activities should not be selected simply because they seem appealing, but rather selected to achieve a learning outcome, and a positive byproduct is that variety is infused throughout the presentation.

How learning is assessed is another component of the training to consider. To measure participant learning, presenters should consider the goals of the training, the content that was covered, and what measure will best inform the trainers about participant learning. Too often, professional development sessions provide information with no measurement of objectives. Assessments should be used to determine the overall learning of the group, as well as individual needs. This information can be used to plan follow-up sessions. Presenters can then tailor their follow-up sessions according to staff needs, rather than moving along a training schedule that is not addressing the critical issues.

On the second page of the planning form, we encourage teams to consider what presentation method is best for the professional development. There are many formats available and they each have strengths and weaknesses. Often, the decision is based on what technology is already available and what teams are familiar with. While more traditional methods like Microsoft PowerPoint and Apple Keynote work well, there is the chance that teams may fall victim to "death by PowerPoint" (Reynolds, 2008). Unfortunately, it is common for presenters to create many slides that are full of text that is difficult to read. Presenters may feel effective in that they covered a lot of information. Participants, on the other hand, leave the training wondering if they really learned anything. Teams are encouraged to explore newer methods like Prezi and Slide Rocket that assist trainers in focusing more on the main points and less on frivolous text. Because the point of using a presentation technology is to make the training more engaging, use it to do just that. Include images, videos, and simple statements that will be memorable, so that participants walk away with a message. Inundating participants with too much information may feel like the right thing to do, but it actually increases frustration and discourages learning.

Finally, the third page provides a sheet to plan for what activities to include in the presentation. Variety is key, so that participants are experiencing something new every 20 minutes or so. Going longer than that will reduce participant learning, because it is difficult to pay attention for extended periods of time. Teams can think about what videos will drive the point home. Also, there are games, role plays, practice activities, discussions, and work-time options to consider. Work time is a powerful option, because it allows participants to practice new skills, share out, and have the whole group learn from one another. We encourage teams to incorporate work time into every professional development session, as teachers have little time to get the work done otherwise.

Organize Data Collection Logistics

After planning the professional development, the RTI team should organize the screening administration process. While the process includes many details, it is one that becomes easier over time. With time allocated to planning, the team can organize the specifics, communicate the plans to teachers, and increase chances of an efficient process. The main considerations are below.

First, the size of the student population should be considered. The student population will directly affect the number of data collectors needed for benchmarking. Put simply, more students will require more data collectors. Fewer students will require less. A school with a student population of 200 students will require a different number of data collectors than a school with a student population of 600 students. The RTI team should consider how many students there are so that an adequate number of data collectors can be trained on the measures. By determining this beforehand, teams can ensure that all measures are administered within a couple of weeks.

Next, the RTI team has to review who has been trained in data collection and who is available to administer the measures. Ideally, enough data collectors were trained initially and were tested to check for interobserver reliability. If more data collectors are needed, the team should consider when they can be trained. Second, the team should determine how many data collectors are available during the benchmark period. There may be a number of teachers who were trained, but they are unable to administer the measures because they have to teach during that time. The team can consider getting substitutes to cover the classrooms if it is within the budget. If this is not an option, other data collectors need to be considered for their availability and the time they can allocate to the administration process.

Third, the RTI team should plan for materials organization and collection. The benchmark booklets, administrator materials, writing utensils, and clipboards should be available and ready. If the school is collecting their data using computers, the computer lab should be scheduled. The "where" and "when" should also be decided. Administration should occur in quiet places, where students can concentrate and data collectors can clearly hear student responses. Options include the library, the lunchroom, the gymnasium, or empty classrooms. Data collectors should know where they're going, be set up in their space, and have students come to them one by one to minimize transition time. Often, administration occurs wherever it can take place, which includes the hallway, the back of the classroom, or other spaces that are not as ideal for testing situations. Testing should be prioritized so that it occurs in quiet places. Finally, the schedule for data collection resides with the RTI team and what works best for all teachers involved. Students should be pulled as quickly as possible to minimize disruptions to instruction. Consideration should be given to what times of the day work better for different grade levels. These are decisions that can be made using Form 4.3 at the end of this chapter.

Analyze and Use Screening Data

When using browser-based scoring on a laptop, tablet, or other device, data entry is an automatic task. As the student reads the test and gives oral responses, data collectors are able to score the responses on screen and the system will score the test and upload the results automatically. This is beneficial because data collectors can score directly on the device screen, a timer is built in, and a final score is calculated automatically. This minimizes the need for data entry, as it is already in the system, allowing teams to move forward with data analysis more quickly.

When using paper-based scoring, there is the additional step of data entry afterward. This additional step can make things difficult. Schools can get caught up in the administration of the measures, rather than data analysis. Once administered, there is a chance that data will not be utilized, or worse, not even be entered in a system for analysis. It is of importance then, that the RTI team plan for what to do after benchmarking so that the data is used effectively in a timely manner.

After the measures have been administered to all students, a member of the RTI team can enter the data into the database. Data should be entered carefully and checked for accuracy. This is a common place for errors, so it is recommended that two people be used for this process. One person can read the data, the other person can enter it into the system, and then both people can check the data afterward. Data entry can also be a lengthy task depending on the size of the student population, so using two people for data entry can greatly reduce the time required.

A benefit to using many of the screening systems available is the wide variety of data analysis features and reports that are available. The reports vary in their purpose and design, and should be selected based on what questions the team is trying to answer. The number and types of reports presented to grade-level teams should be selected based on their experience with them. If teams are new to the formats, focusing more attention on fewer reports will be helpful to increase understanding. If teams are experienced with the data system, more information can be presented because there is greater fluency with the material.

Data are analyzed at the individual, classroom, grade level, and whole-school levels. The RTI team, along with the administrator, can first view the data as a whole. How is the school doing overall? Is the core curriculum meeting students' needs in all grade levels? The percentage of students who should be successful with the core curriculum should be approximately 80%. This means that 80% of students are at benchmark with the screening assessments and performing well on the end-of-unit tests. There will always be students who require more instruction than the core curriculum to be successful. The percentage of students who require support at this level should range from 10 to 15%. Finally, there are students who require extensive instruction and assessment that is of higher intensity and greater duration. The percentage of students who require support at this level should range from 5 to 10%.

> **Determine who will enter the data into the database before benchmarking takes place so it can be done immediately after data collection. Plan the data review meetings before benchmark administration as well, so that they are in the calendar and data can be analyzed soon after it is collected.**

If the data from your school indicate that the number of students requiring core, supplemental, and intensive instruction are similar to the guidelines set above, then the core curriculum is working. It is meeting the needs of most of the students, and fewer students are requiring supplemental and intensive support. If the data from your school indicate that you have larger percentages of students who require supplemental and intensive instruction, then this may be an indication that the core curriculum is not working for your students. Classroom data is also analyzed to determine what individual students will be placed in tiers of support. The RTI team should review the data and determine whose needs are met with the core instruction and who needs Tier 2 and Tier 3 support. Adding to or "beefing up" the core curriculum may be more efficient than setting up multiple intervention groups if data indicate that many students are in need. (See Figure 4.3.)

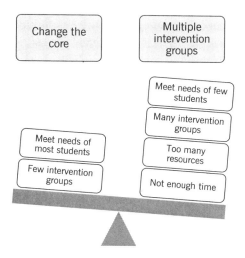

FIGURE 4.3. Change the core curriculum or schedule multiple intervention groups?

Schedule Data Review Meetings

First, it is important to schedule the data review days so that they occur immediately after data collection. With the data in hand, educators can begin to make decisions about which students need what support, and action can then occur swiftly and efficiently. Without scheduled meetings, data sits, decisions are made later, and students lose time in receiving necessary interventions. Thus, scheduling the meetings so they occur soon after data collection is an important first step.

"Data day" meetings allow grade-level teams to review, analyze, and use the data. These meetings provide a format for discussion as the team discusses the groups of students, who should be placed where, and the resulting action plans for each grade level. Essential members of the team include the administrator, grade-level teachers, the school psychologist, and other support staff involved in the intervention process. The administrator typically acts as the facilitator, guiding the meeting in the specified time. The administrator should provide a structure for the meeting and ensure that action plans are completed at the end of the meeting. The grade-level teachers provide input about their students to discuss in relation to the data. They offer what they know, agree to the groups that their students are placed in, and understand the importance of checking in about their students' progress over time. The school psychologist should also be involved, to assist with reviewing and analyzing the data. The school psychologist can assist with reviewing the data beforehand, sending out reports to all grade-level teachers, and ensuring that everyone has the information they need to make decisions about students. Finally, support staff should be involved to assist as needed. The reading specialist may help review the data and plan for interventions. The counselor may participate in data review as well. The special education teacher can offer additional insight about students who may already be receiving services. As a team, each role is important, as every member provides something worthwhile to the team.

Scheduling the meetings and determining the where and when depends on team member availability. There are a few options to consider and the pros and cons are reviewed here. First, all grade-level team meetings can be conducted on 1 day, where substitutes rotate in and out of classrooms. Each grade-level team can participate in the meeting for a selected amount of time, where the administrator and school psychologist are present throughout the whole day. The pros are that the data is reviewed in 1 day, decisions are made, and students receive support quickly. The cons are that the administrator and school psychologist need to be present the whole day, which may be difficult to schedule and/or commit to given other responsibilities. Second, teams can decide to divide the "data day" into 2 half days, where a few grade levels review their data one morning and the rest of the grade levels review their data the following morning. This provides for more flexibility, as all teams are not meeting in 1 day. The pros are that the administrator and school psychologist are not committed to 1 full day. This may work better for scheduling and also supports optimal performance, as they are more focused on each day. The cons are that this may also inhibit scheduling for the administrator and school psychologist, depending on availability. Finally, grade-level teams may meet on different days throughout the same "data review week." During this week, the administrator and school psychologist will meet with all grade-level teams on different days. The pros are that this can support more focused discussion, as one or two grade-level teams are discussed each day, so the other team members can direct their focus well to each team. The cons are that it may be difficult to schedule. Teams should select the schedule that works best for them, so that all students can be discussed in a timely manner.

In the meeting, the team will first review what percentages of students fall into each tier. This provides an initial view of the data. Next, goals can be set for students so they can make progress and move to the next benchmark level. In Tier 1, after goal setting, the team lists whole-class instructional strategies that teachers can use throughout each day. This is the brainstorming period, as many ideas are offered. After brainstorming, the team analyzes and rates the listed strategies according to the extent to which they are evidence based, practical, and available or according to the feasibility of their creation (Kovaleski & Pedersen, 2008). Finally, the team selects which strategies to implement during the next intervention period. In Tier 2 data analysis, these students are identified and goals are set. Tier 2 strategies are selected based on their evidence base and their specificity to target certain skills. In Tier 3 analysis, students for Tier 3 are identified by the same process described for Tier 2. These students need the most intensive supports, so planning for specific interventions according to need may be more involved than Tier 2 planning. Form 4.4 is provided at the end of this chapter to guide teams in creating their intervention plans.

For students placed in Tier 3, teams may choose to more formally go through the "problem-solving process." The problem-solving process is comprised of four major steps and allows teams to specifically document what the issue is, why it is happening, what will be done about it, and what the next options are depending on effectiveness of the intervention. This may be helpful because a problem-solving model is a systematic approach that reviews student strengths and weaknesses and identifies evidence-based interventions that match specific needs. While there are many variations of this process, the following questions guide the general process:

- Is there a problem and what is it?
- Why is the problem happening?
- What can be done about the problem?
- Did the intervention work? (Reschly & Tilly, 1999)

Problem identification is the first step. In this phase, teams work to identify if a problem exists and if it warrants additional assessment (Shinn & Hubbard, 1992). The guiding questions are "What is the problem?" and "What is the discrepancy between what is expected and what is occurring?" The premise is that problems affecting student performance do not exist exclusively within the learner, but occur as the result of an interaction between learner characteristics and the demands of the setting. Dependent upon the intensity and severity of the problem, this step requires analysis and assessment to clearly define the problem, identify why it is occurring, and indicate the solution with the highest likelihood of success. In this stage, teams will work to define exactly what area the student needs to improve, so that they have a clear idea of what additional information is needed.

The second step is *problem analysis*. Once the problem is defined, teams will ask the questions "Why is it happening?" and "Is this a skill deficit or a performance deficit?" To answer the "why" question, teams need to designate the school psychologist or other qualified team members to gather additional data on the student. With this information, more specific details are gathered on strengths, weaknesses, and skill patterns. This information can be used to select an appropriately matched intervention.

The third step, *plan development*, is where the team decides what intervention will be best for the student and how it will be implemented. In this step, the guiding questions are "What are we going to do about it?" and "What are the goals?" The team will decide the plan, document the plan, and schedule a follow-up meeting to review progress. This plan might be informal for lower-intensity problems, but needs to be clearly written with specific detail for more severe problems. A goal should be set and plans for how to evaluate effectiveness should be established. At Tier 3, interventions are not activities intended to put students into settings or placements; rather, they are activities requiring a range of resources designed to improve student performance.

The last step of the problem-solving model is *plan evaluation*. Data gathered during the problem-solving process are used to make decisions regarding the best educational strategy for a student. These decisions are based on a trend of student performance over time, during the application of the intervention, rather than on any one measure of student performance. Here teams will review the data, determine if it worked or something needs to be changed, and make plans accordingly. This is an important part of the process, because it allows for teams to make the necessary changes and continue to support the student over time.

RULES, ROLES, AND REGULARITY

Effective teams do many things. They have established ground rules, roles, and processes for decision making. They function with a purpose in mind and stick to a structure, but provide flexibility when needed. They allow for all participants to be heard, while supporting the facilitator. Effective teams are well-oiled machines that rarely break down. And when they do, there is a solution that is selected by the team that allows the team to move forward, even if everyone does not agree. Effective teams function because time and thought is put into planning and holding the meeting, rather than assuming that everything will just fall into place. It is a dangerous assumption to believe that because we are all on the same team we will be able to function effectively. The reality is that people come to the table with different knowledge, experience, agendas, and philosophies that will create difficulties if not handled well. With planning, structure, and accountability though, teams can function well by addressing the goals and achieving the outcomes in a way that is demanding yet supportive. In this chapter, we discuss the importance of establishing ground rules and assigning roles.

Establish Ground Rules

Ground rules can either be established by the facilitator, who then explains and discusses each one, or decided by the team as a whole. It is up to the facilitator to make this decision and it should be based on the team's experience and knowledge with RTI and meeting facilitation. Being presented with the ground rules makes the meeting experience more formal, and this may be necessary if the team is prone to side conversations, disagreement, or unbalanced participation. The facilitator may decide to present the ground rules to establish leadership, so there is a clear facilitator in the room who is always acknowledged. The facilitator may also decide to have the team create the ground rules as a team-building activity. This will encourage people to be respectful and work together as they decide what team norms will be accepted by all members. In this situation, the facilitator should establish clear rules for this discussion, encourage participation, and have a process for decision making.

Ground rules are important because they establish norms for behavior that otherwise would not be established, may not be assumed, and some may adhere to and some may not. Because participants come to the meeting with various past meeting experiences, there will be a range of behaviors that are displayed and it is an important first step to establish what is OK and what is not OK when participating in the meeting. The following are a list of sample ground rules that may be used in a meeting:

- *Everyone participates.* Seemingly obvious, it actually makes a big difference when it is stated at the start of the meeting. It reminds people of the group effort.
- *Different opinions are OK.* Contrary views usually need to be encouraged. The goal is to have all issues discussed in the meeting, rather than after the meeting behind closed doors.
- *We will start on time and end on time.* Respecting peoples' time is one way to show them that their participation is vital, but that their other responsibilities will be acknowledged and respected as well.
- *Side conversations are discouraged.* This encourages everyone to actively listen and participate regarding the item at hand.
- *No laptops.* One team member may have a laptop to take notes, but other team members will focus their attention on the discussion, rather than their laptop. Some school teams have decided to do this to encourage participation, because all team members were bringing laptops, which greatly limited the discussion.
- *Respect is the focus.* No personal attacks. Challenge ideas, not people. When discussions venture toward disagreement, there is a tendency to attack others when people feel under pressure. The facilitator should encourage a focus on ideas, rather than individual people.
- *Parking lot.* The parking lot is used to hold ideas that are important and need to be discussed, but do not fit into the current agenda. They will be addressed at a future meeting.
- *Decision-making process.* We will use a process for making decisions that is identified ahead of time (voting vs. consensus). Decisions may not be made at every meeting, but when they are, a designated process will be used.

Roles in Meetings

Assigning roles can also help meetings move along, as people have specific action items to complete. When roles are designated, more productivity ensues. When roles are not designated, there may be less investment in the meeting. Assigning a role is assigning a duty: Members have to pay attention, complete their task, and as a result, are more engaged in the meeting overall. There are three main roles for meetings: facilitator, recorder and timekeeper.

Facilitator

The facilitator is an important role in the meeting, if not the most important role. A facilitator can ensure that all agenda items are addressed, allow all people to be heard, and guide the creation of action plans for after the meeting. An effective facilitator will do all of these things and more. He or she will also allow for flexibility, if some issues need more discussion. He or she will show leadership from the beginning, so the meeting is structured and clear. And he or she will address team members afterward who were either unhappy or unengaged with the meeting. An ineffective facilitator will forgo any of those activities. Without keeping a brisk pace that allows for all agenda items to be addressed, the meeting can be less productive, or worse, make some people feel that their items were less important than others. Without facilitating the development of an action plan, there will be no substantial follow-up to the meeting. And without addressing team members who are upset or disengaged, the team will function ineffectively because there are not commonly shared values. Form 4.5 at the end of this chapter is a planning sheet for facilitators to use as they plan for meetings.

Establishing leadership from the beginning is an important first step. Send an e-mail invitation, attach the agenda, and alert anyone who will have a major role at the meeting. Make sure that the meeting date, time, and place are clearly designated in the e-mail, so team members can show up and be ready on time. Remind members of the purpose and importance of the meeting. Any additional documents should be attached to the original e-mail, so that participants come prepared with handouts.

Watching the clock is also a task for the facilitator with the help of the timekeeper. Starting on time shows respect for the team members who are present. It also teaches late members that the meeting will not wait for them. They should respect the time scheduled and show up on time. If the facilitator decides to wait for late team members, they have been taught that they can be late and thus, there is no incentive for changing their behavior. Ending on time is equally important, so that members can accomplish other daily tasks.

Showing flexibility is one of the most important tasks for the facilitator. While it is important to follow the agenda and address all items, it can be difficult to determine if some items will need more time. There may be an issue that arises that needs to be discussed more. Or a participant asks an important question that needs to be addressed. It is during these times that the facilitator needs to read the situation and make the decision to spend more time on that item/question or not. There are times when the new discussion may take precedent and there are times when it should be discussed and then the meeting moves on. To assist in making this decision, the facilitator should have prioritized the list of agenda items beforehand. With a ranking in mind, the facilitator can more easily make a decision about what should be allowed more time and what should be quickly addressed.

Finally, it is important to support equal participation in meetings. This works on both ends. The facilitator should have a strategy to deter individuals who sidetrack the meeting. This goes for people who talk, joke, or interrupt too much. This goes for people who distract others with side conversations. And this goes for people who bring up unrelated topics for discussion. These individuals need to be told politely that they need to pay attention, focus on the topic at hand, or wait until someone else is finished talking. The following statements are examples that facilitators can use to rein in the discussion:

- That's a good point, but we need to finish this item first. Let's write that down to remember to discuss it later.
- I appreciate your perspective. Let's give Suzanne and Barnie a chance to share their ideas as well.
- Mark, thanks for adding some humor to the situation but we need to move on now so we can create an action plan.
- Chris, can I have your attention? Thanks.
- I am going to wait until everyone is ready to review the data and talk about individual students before I move on.
- I know we may have many students who are struggling but let's break it down into small groups to see what we can do about interventions.
- We have 15 minutes left. Let's focus on the task at hand so we can achieve all of our goals for today.
- Maggie, I think Brian wasn't finished. Brian, would you like to continue your point?

Each of the above statements is respectful, in that they are clear, direct, and include a positive note. We tend to respond much better when we are given positive feedback first, before given corrective feedback. Is this absolutely necessary? Many facilitators would argue no. Their stance is that they are running the meeting, the meeting should be important enough in itself, and individuals should pay it the appropriate amount of attention and respect. And this is true. However, by adding a piece of positive reinforcement as well, the individuals will be more open to change, because you've given them a reason to change. If the meeting is simply run based on rules, strict adherence to guidelines, and punishment, the individuals will pay attention, but not because they want to, because they feel like they have to.

What's important about these statements and questions is that they are asked politely, with respect and minimal emotion. As a facilitator, this is easier said than done. When individuals are frequently interrupting or joking on the side, it is easy to feel annoyed or frustrated by their behaviors. You may feel disrespected because the meeting content does not appear important to them. And here is the simple reality. People are busy, their minds are in other places, and the meeting may not be a priority for them. With that in mind, it becomes less personal and more about the meeting structure. With enough structure and a response for those who are disengaged, the meeting becomes about the work, and less about the people. If we focus on the work, we are less likely to become preoccupied with the idiosyncrasies of the individuals. Practice saying those statements without emotion. Direct the focus toward the work.

Inevitably there are individuals who represent the opposite end of the spectrum. There are those who are quiet and offer little. There may be a variety of reasons for this including feeling ignored, feeling unsafe to share their opinions, or they have "checked out" because they do not feel the meeting will go anywhere. If multiple participants appear disengaged, this is a sign of a larger issue that needs to be addressed. This calls for some critical conversations about what is working with the meeting format and what is not. On the other hand, if a few participants have a quiet disposition or tend to "check out" on a regular basis, it is the role of the facilitator to encourage their participation as well. "Don, what do you think about this?" or "Juliana, do you know what you're going to do?" are simple questions that can encourage more participation. Finally, the structure of the meeting can be such that each person is required to respond to each agenda item before moving on. With this structure, each person participates for a specified amount of time, and he or she is given the opportunity to make a statement or ask a question. Regardless of the meeting structure used, or the individual personalities of the participants, facilitators can organize a productive meeting by using a prioritized structure with built-in flexibility that encourages participation.

Recorder

The recorder (a.k.a the secretary, note taker, the one with the laptop open [the only one]) is an important role because he or she keeps notes for the meeting and ensures information is available to create a viable action plan. A common misconception is that an engaging discussion and productive meeting will yield productivity later. There are times when the meeting is productive and beneficial to many participants. Great conversations are had, and all of the agenda items are addressed. Someone took brief notes. There is no action plan. The note taker will e-mail the notes later. After the meeting, everyone leaves and goes back to their classroom. And then nothing happens. There was a fruitful conversation, everyone left feeling productive, and then no further action occurs. Note taking is important for this reason. It provides a record of what was discussed and provides an outline for next steps.

There are many formats that can be used to take notes during a meeting. The notes should be comprehensive, yet concise and explicit. They should be tied to the agenda items, provide a nice summary of the meeting, and allow for meeting participants to sign up for action items at the end as part of the action plan. With a specified structure, the note taker can easily take notes, record important items, and fulfill his or her meeting duty easily. Some items to address in note taking include the following:

- Date of the meeting
- Type of meeting
- Participants
- Purpose of the meeting
- Topics discussed
- Decisions made
- Action items and who is responsible for each
- Follow-up meetings and what needs to be addressed in those

Taking notes using a sharing platform like Google Docs allows note takers to easily share their notes with others immediately after the meeting. Other meeting participants can view and modify the document as allowed.

Timekeeper

The timekeeper has an important yet simple role. With a timekeeper, the facilitator gains additional assistance to keep the meeting on track and address all agenda items. Without a timekeeper, the facilitator is left to engage in this task on his or her own, which can be a lot to navigate when there is much to coordinate with the meeting. The timekeeper should familiarize him- or herself with the specified times for each agenda item beforehand and bring a device to adequately monitor the time. There are a variety of ways timekeepers can keep the time for each agenda item. Three of them are discussed here.

First, the facilitator may allow great flexibility for each item, as there is a lot to discuss and he or she does not know how much time each of the items will take. Maybe it is the first time that these items are being discussed or maybe there are a number of important issues to address. With this approach, the timekeeper may do infrequent check-ins to remind everyone where they're at in the meeting. This may be a check-in midway through like "We've covered three items and we have five to go. We have 1 more hour." This can help the facilitator to prioritize and make a decision based on what has already been covered and what still needs to be addressed.

Second, the timekeeper may adhere to the agenda with more attention, so that the time lengths are strictly followed. This may be because there is a lot to cover in the meeting, participants tend to get offtrack, or a lot of structure may be needed for a meeting with many team members. In this situation, the timekeeper can provide 5-minute warnings, 2-minute warnings, or whatever the facilitator decides is best for keeping people on track. Because these are stricter timelines, they may be more difficult to follow, so it requires a keen adherence to make this effective.

The last timekeeping option that is mentioned comes from Toastmasters, the public speaking organization (*www.toastmasters.org*). Using a green, amber, and red light system, the timekeeper can alert people to what time is left for discussion on a particular item. Toastmasters offer an actual lighting system that can be purchased, but sheets of paper with each light color can be used as well. The color green indicates that there is ample time to discuss the issue and the meeting is still on track. This will be used until the time is getting close to nearing the end. At this point, the color amber can be used. This signifies that the time is reaching the end, and the discussion should be finishing up soon. Red is used to indicate that it is time to finish the conversation and end the topic. Using a lighting system such as this can be helpful because it provides three stages for the discussion, instead of an abrupt warning.

Hold Regular Meetings

Regular meetings will be helpful for the RTI team as they plan the implementation of screening measures. During these meetings, teachers can begin to plan the large-scale administration process. These meetings should occur regularly, so that plans can be made and orchestrated well. Without regular meetings, there is less accountability, which leads to less planning and less work getting completed. Moreover, irregular meetings increase the chance of issues during the benchmarking period.

Depending on the time of year, there will be a different purpose and agenda for each meeting. Although some meetings will be similar in nature as teams plan for each administration, other meetings will look different because of the time of year. During the fall, winter, and spring, teams should meet to finalize plans for benchmark administration. Subsequently, after each of the benchmark periods, teams should meet to review the data and complete a self-analysis of the overall administration. During the fall and winter, teams will review the data and plan for tiered interventions. In the spring, data will also be reviewed, interventions planned, and additionally consideration should be given to summer ideas for parents. Figures 4.4–4.6 illustrate meeting outlines for each time of the year.

Before Administration

1. Secure administrator support.
2. Train data collectors.
3. Plan logistics including where administration will take place and when.
4. Meet with the screening team to review procedures.
5. Determine who will organize the materials for administration.
6. Determine who will input the data into the database after administration.
7. Schedule follow-up days for students who are absent.
8. Schedule data day meetings to determine tiers of intervention support.

After Administration

1. Enter the data into the database.
2. Print out whole-school, grade-level, and classroom summaries.
3. Meet to review the data as a leadership team and plan for grade-level meetings.
4. Facilitate grade-level data day meetings.
5. Place students into tiers of support.
6. Implement interventions.
7. Progress monitor interventions.

FIGURE 4.4. Meeting outline topics for discussion: Fall (August–November).

Before Administration

1. Plan logistics including where administration will take place and when.
2. Meet with the screening team to review procedures.
3. Determine who will organize the materials for administration.
4. Determine who will input the data into the database after administration.
5. Schedule follow-up days for students who are absent.
6. Schedule data day meetings to determine tiers of intervention support.

After Administration

1. Enter the data into the database.
2. Print out whole-school, grade-level, and classroom summaries.
3. Meet to review the data as a leadership team and plan for grade-level meetings.
4. Facilitate grade-level data day meetings.
5. Ensure that students are placed in appropriate tiers of support.
6. Implement interventions.
7. Progress monitor interventions.

FIGURE 4.5. Meeting outline topics for discussion: Winter benchmarking period.

Before Administration

1. Plan logistics including where administration will take place and when.
2. Determine who will organize the materials for administration.
3. Determine who will input the data into the database after administration.
4. Schedule follow-up days for students who are absent.
5. Schedule data day meetings to determine tiers of intervention support.

After Administration

1. Enter the data into the database.
2. Print out whole-school, grade-level, and classroom summaries.
3. Meet to review the data as a leadership team and plan for grade-level meetings.
4. Facilitate grade-level data day meetings.
5. Ensure that students are placed in appropriate tiers of support.
6. Implement interventions.
7. Progress monitor interventions.
8. Secure evidence-based summer enrichment ideas for parents.
9. Schedule meetings with parents to provide summer activities that support reading.
10. Secure dates in early fall to meet and review spring data and plan for fall administration.

FIGURE 4.6. Meeting outline topics for discussion: Spring benchmarking period.

PREVENTING AND ADDRESSING COMMON ROADBLOCKS DURING BENCHMARK MEETINGS

There are a number of roadblocks that can occur during meetings. The following is a list of common roadblocks and matched solutions:

- **Roadblock 1:** Data are not available on all students.
  - *Cause:* Data may have not been entered, analyzed, or printed on all students.
  - *Solution:* Increase accountability for data entry, analysis, and document preparation for meetings. Determine who will be responsible for these activities, check in, and follow through on preparation.

- **Roadblock 2:** There are too many students in need of intensive support.
  - *Cause:* The core curriculum is not effective for most students.
  - *Solution:* Supplement the core curriculum instead of purchasing multiple interventions for each grade level. Select evidence-based strategies to use with all students in general education and purchase a few programs for those students who are discrepant.

- **Roadblock 3:** One teacher has the majority of students in need of additional support in his or her class.
  - *Cause 1:* How students were placed in classrooms at the beginning of the year.
  - *Solution 1:* Place those students in appropriate intervention groups. Provide the teacher additional evidence-based instructional strategies to use in the classroom.

- o *Cause 2:* The teacher is experiencing difficulty with teaching.
- o *Solution 2:* Assess the cause. Determine what needs to be changed (training, motivation, ongoing support). Check in frequently with the teacher.

- **Roadblock 4:** Too much time devoted to organizing documents at the beginning of the meeting.
  - o *Cause 1:* Documents are not properly prepared ahead of time.
  - o *Solution 2:* Prepare properly for the meeting. In addition to the agenda, make sure that any documents that need to be reviewed or that require a response are distributed with the agenda. Having these documents ahead of time will signal participants that they should do some preparation themselves.

- **Roadblock 5:** The meeting participants stray from the agenda and start talking about *related, but separate* issues.
  - o *Cause 1:* There is no progress checker assessing where the group is at and keeping people on track.
  - o *Solution:* State your purpose for the meeting. Keep the goal of the meeting in mind as you prepare the agenda. Then, make sure that the purpose of the meeting is clearly stated. It is important to tailor the agenda so that no point is left too broad. If you keep your agenda focused on the topic at hand, it is likely that the discussion will stay on topic as well.

- **Roadblock 6:** The meeting participants stray from the agenda and start talking about *unrelated* issues. There is more frequent aimless drifting and random discussions.
  - o *Cause 1:* There is no plan or process for sticking with the agenda.
  - o *Solution:* Rein in the discussion. Make sure that the goal of the meeting is reiterated at the beginning of the discussion and then hold people accountable. Nothing is more frustrating than listening to people go on about something that has no bearing on the agenda. Limit discussion as needed so that everyone gets an opportunity to share without dominating the conversation.

- **Roadblock 7:** Meetings start later than scheduled.
  - o *Cause 1:* The facilitator is not providing reinforcement to those who are present and establishing accountability for those who are absent.
  - o *Solution:* Start meetings on time. Show respect for those who arrive on time by starting the meeting punctually. If you consistently start on time, chronic latecomers will eventually get the hint and they should begin to conform to your schedule.

SUMMARY

In this chapter, we've examined steps your team can take to plan for schoolwide screening. We've provided planning checklists, descriptions of screening measures, considerations for data collection, and information detailing how to review and analyze the data. We've also provided information on how to plan for professional development so that staff are adequately trained. The problem-solving process is also included because we believe in the importance of using this model to address all student needs proactively and efficiently. Finally, we reviewed how to organize and facilitate effective benchmark data review meetings. During the meetings, we encourage teams to:

- Establish ground rules for discussion.
- Assign roles so that each member contributes.
- Schedule and hold regular meetings.
- Prepare for common roadblocks that occur during benchmark data review meetings.

In the next chapter, we review the considerations for intervention selection and planning and discuss how to facilitate those meetings.

RTI-Team Planning Tool

Questions	Answers	Action Plan		
		Item	Person Responsible	By When?
SCHOOL DEMOGRAPHICS				
What other school committees exist? How many are there?				
How frequently do these committees meet? What is the time commitment?				
Which teams are effective? Which teams are less effective? Why?				
How involved is the administration in these teams? Where does administration need to be involved? Where can they be less involved?				
SCHOOL NEEDS				
How many individuals would be needed for the RTI team?				

(continued)

94

RTI-Team Planning Tool *(page 2 of 3)*

Questions	Answers	Action Plan		
		Item	Person Responsible	By When?
Is there a similar team in existence that should be incorporated into the RTI team? Why or why not?				
How much time can the administrator devote to the RTI team? Will this be enough?				
What will the expectations be of the RTI team? The time commitment? How will staff members be compensated for their time?				
STAFF MEMBERS' AREAS OF EXPERTISE				
Schoolwide screening				
Progress monitoring				
Evidence-based interventions				

(continued)

RTI-Team Planning Tool *(page 3 of 3)*

Questions	Answers	Action Plan		
		Item	Person Responsible	By When?
Leadership experience				
Differentiated instruction				
Meeting facilitation				
Providing professional development				
Communication skills				
Action plan development				

Professional Development Planning Outline

Step 1. Complete the planning form. Consider the purpose for each session, how it will be achieved, and how it will be practiced and assessed.

Date	Review of Past Learning	Stage of Learning At what stage is most of the audience (acquisition, fluency, generalization, adaptation)?	Learning Objectives	Content	Activity	Assessment

(continued)

Professional Development Planning Outline *(page 2 of 3)*

Step 2. Consider how you will present the content. What will be meaningful for participants? How will they be engaged? What format best suits the audience needs?

Presentation Tools	Notes
Microsoft PowerPoint	
Apple Keynote	
Prezi	
Slide Rocket	
Zoho Show	
280 Slides	

(continued)

Professional Development Planning Outline *(page 3 of 3)*

Step 3. Consider how you will present the content in a way that is engaging and meaningful. What activities best support learning?

Activities	Purpose: Why use this activity?	Planning Notes
Introduction (getting to know you)		
Videos		
Role play		
Games		
Practice activity		
Data review		
Audience participation		
Small-group discussion		
Large-group discussion		
Sharing news items/quotes/statistics		
Providing time to work		

FORM 4.3

Benchmark Planning Form

Component	Planning	Notes
Students	How many? _____	
Time required per student	_____ minutes	
Assessors	How many needed? _____	
Total time required	_____ days	
Materials	• Student materials • Benchmark booklets • Clipboards • Writing utensils • Stopwatches • Others?	

(continued)

Benchmark Planning Form *(page 2 of 2)*

Component	Planning	Notes
Logistics	Where and when by grade level: Grade level _____ : Where? When? Grade level _____ : Where? When? Grade level _____ : Where? When? Grade level _____ : Where? When? Grade level _____ : Where? When? Grade level _____ : Where? When?	

Group Intervention Form

Student Names: _____

Target Skill: _____

Teacher Name: _____

Start Date:	Instructional Procedures:	Times per Week:
School District/Building:		Length of Session:
Data Indicating Need:	Materials:	Progress Monitoring Plan:
Person(s) Responsible for Analysis:		
Behavioral Incentives:	Person(s) Responsible for Intervention:	Decision-Making Rule:

Facilitator Responsibilities

Responsibility	Helpful Hint	Planning Notes
Establish leadership	Start on time, reward those on time, talk to those who were late, state the purpose, respond to comments, summarize, and hold people accountable.	
Prepare properly for the meeting	Documents e-mailed ahead of time, review data, plan for how long discussion items will last, have a backup plan for items not addressed, summarize main points, be ready to answer questions.	
Watch the clock	Assign a clock watcher.	
Show flexibility	Follow the agenda but if a topic seems important and people want to keep talking about it, do a check-in. "It seems like we've gotten off topic but that this is an issue we need to address. Are we OK with discussing this for the next 15 minutes?"	
Keep everyone focused	Deter side conversations, provide variety, use the board, require participation.	
Follow up on the action plan	Assign people to each task, follow up on due dates, establish accountability.	

CHAPTER 5

Data-Based Intervention Planning Decisions

One of the primary goals of RTI is to provide multiple tiers of intervention to prevent the emergence of early learning difficulties. With multiple tiers, many students' needs can be met efficiently. With few tiers, only some students are receiving the support they need. In this chapter, we review considerations for selection and delivery of interventions. We also discuss the importance of creating action plans at intervention planning meetings and provide a list of common roadblocks at these meetings and how to address them.

Intervention tiers relate to instructional placement. Where should students be placed and how will that tier meet their needs? A framework for instructional placement comes from Shinn and Walker (2010). They provide guiding Big Ideas related to using an RTI framework. First, no single tier solves all problems. There are some students whose needs will not be met by general education and they require additional intervention to be successful. Second, a well-designed multi-tiered system will have tiers of increasing intensity. Some schools function with three tiers and some function with four, but all should have multiple levels of support. Shinn and Walker (2010) point out that the number of tiers is less important than ensuring that all students, students who are more at risk, and students with chronic longstanding problems receive support. Finally, the third idea they offer is that effective interventions at a lower-level tier will reduce the need for interventions at subsequent tiers. If an effective evidence-based program is being used at Tier 1, this will reduce the need for the number of students who require intervention at Tiers 2 and 3. The emphasis is on providing a powerful program so that student needs are met efficiently.

This proactive schoolwide approach swifts the focus from individual student problem solving to a larger focus on all students. In the past, schools would engage in individual problem solving that promoted the problem identification, plan analysis, plan development, and plan evaluation steps for any student who was struggling. While this provided support to some students in need, it was a time- and resource-intensive process for any student who needed support. These schools are changing to schoolwide application of problem solving because better assessment measures have been developed to use at a system level, and because it is more efficient and beneficial to provide resources and support to groups of students with similar needs rather than individually (National Research Center on Learning Disabilities, 2012).

In this approach, students are viewed as being part of a group. They receive evidence-based group interventions as needed, are monitored individually, and are considered part of a tier. Benchmark students meeting expected level of performance who are given the core instructional program need no further assessment or intervention. These students are considered to be established in the skill area at the level expected. Approximately 80–85% of students would be expected to meet benchmark levels of performance without interventions (Sugai & Horner, 1999; Simmons, Kame'enui, & Good, 2002). Strategic students not meeting expectations need some type of adaptation or modification of the core instructional program. These students are considered to be emerging in the skill area being assessed. Approximately 15–20% of the students in a school may need strategic interventions to meet expectations (Sugai & Horner, 1999; Simmons et al., 2002). Intensive students who are not meeting expectations need highly differentiated instruction. These students are considered to have skill deficits in the area being assessed. Approximately 5–10% of the students in a school would be expected to need intensive interventions (Sugai & Horner, 1999; Simmons et al., 2002).

Tier 1 is often referred to as the core curriculum or universal instruction. Tier 1 should be provided to all students. Tier 2 is referred to as supplemental or secondary intervention and is provided to some students. Tier 3 is known as intensive or tertiary intervention and is provided to an even smaller group of students who need individualized support. The three tiers are differentiated by what specific program is being used and who it is delivered to. More importantly, they are also differentiated by (1) the duration of the instruction, (2) the intensity and specificity of the curriculum and instruction, (3) the balance between whole-class versus small-group instruction, and (4) the frequency of progress monitoring (Parker, Fleischmann, Loughlin, & Ryan, 2010).

The *duration* of the instruction varies from tier to tier and is an important feature that can be changed to increase intervention intensity. In the area of reading this is most widely researched, and it is recommended that students receive 90 minutes of core reading instruction per day (Vaughn Gross Center for Reading and Language Arts at the University of Texas at Austin, 2005). For students who are in Tiers 2 and 3, they require an additional 30 to 60 minutes of instruction per day. Many schools opt for the 120-minute reading block, so that they can easily find the time for students who need additional support, rather than struggle to find it during other times in the day. This way, students whose needs are met at the core level then have time for additional enhancement activities during this block of time. For students who require more than the 60 minutes, it is easily built in.

The *intensity* and *specificity* of the curriculum and instruction refers to the design and outcomes of the program. The program delivered at Tiers 2 and 3 should be evidence based, highly scripted, and targeted toward the instructional skills that students need to improve. Teams can use the What Works Clearinghouse (n.d.) website as a tool to review what programs have sufficient evidence behind them (*http://ies.ed.gov*). The What Works Clearinghouse has summaries of the research that has been conducted on intervention programs. The website provides information on effectiveness and provides ratings of each program. We recommend using the

What Works Clearinghouse as a starting point to determine what evidence is behind programs. Other websites also have ample resources for evidence-based strategies and interventions (see Figure 5.1). Teams can use these to gather additional ideas and strategies. *Highly scripted* refers to programs providing the teacher script so that there is little room for deviation. This ensures that all students get what they need, and that the program is delivered as intended. Finally, *targeted toward the instructional skills* means that the programs directly teach the skills the students need to improve. If a student needs to improve his or her math computation skills, he or she will receive a math computation program, not a math application program. If a student needs to improve his or her spelling, then he or she will receive a spelling program, not a writing program focused on grammar.

Next, the balance *between whole-class and small-group instruction* should be considered. This refers to how much time students will spend in different size groups. Students receiving instruction at the core level will be exposed to both whole-class and small-group instruction, because each are beneficial in the general education classroom. Students placed at Tier 2 will receive additional small-group instruction. Students in Tier 3 will also receive additional small-group instruction, and the instruction may take place with even smaller groups. Small groups promote more enhanced learning, because as the group becomes larger, there is less individualized attention.

Finally, the *frequency of progress monitoring* will change at each tier because students who are performing below the benchmark will need more monitoring to ensure their growth. Essentially, these students have to make more growth than their average-performing counterparts, because teachers are trying to close the gap between them and their peers. For students performing at the benchmark level, their progress monitoring is three times per year, when the benchmark measures are administered. For students identified as "some risk," they are progress monitored monthly, to determine if they are making progress on a monthly basis. For students identified as "at risk," they will be monitored on a weekly basis to ensure that each week there is some growth.

- What Works Clearinghouse
  http://ies.ed.gov/ncee/wwc

- Evidence-Based Intervention Network
  http://ebi.missouri.edu

- Direct Instruction and Intensive Intervention
  www.sradirectinstruction.com

- Florida Center for Reading Research
  www.fcrr.org

- Collaborative for Academic, Social and Emotional Learning (CASEL)
  www.casel.org

- Intervention Central
  www.interventioncentral.org

FIGURE 5.1. Internet resources on evidence-based interventions.

REVIEW OF EVIDENCE-BASED INTERVENTION PRACTICES

Modifying Group Interventions within the Grade-Level Continuum

After students are administered screening measures, teams often place students into corresponding tiered grade-level groups. In other words, there is a Tier 1, 2, and 3 program for each grade level. The assumption is that students in different grades will be working on different skills. This is true for the core group. But probably not true for Tiers 2 and 3. A fifth-grade student reading at the third-grade level will benefit from a Tier 2 intervention that targets third-grade skills. That intervention should be categorized by its skills focus, not its grade focus. Just because it's a "third-grade program" does not mean only third-grade students should have access to it. Imagine that a few students in third grade are struggling with phonics, while most of the other students flagged by the schoolwide screening process were third-grade students who need to increase their fluency with oral reading. Does that mean the students struggling with phonics should receive the fluency intervention because that is what most of the struggling students in third grade need? Absolutely not. The students struggling with phonics can easily be placed with the second-grade students who are also struggling with the same phonics skills. Each student then is receiving the instruction precisely matched to his or her needs.

Grouping students by skill level rather than by grade level is a more efficient way of providing support. A student in first grade very likely could need to work on the same skills as a student who is in second grade and both of their needs would be met by the same intervention. Because they are in different grades does not necessarily mean they need to work on different skills. They may need to improve the same skills. And if so, placing them together in skills-based groups rather than grade-based groups is the best approach. This also allows schools to be more efficient with their time and resources. Implementing two phonics interventions across two grade levels may not be necessary, if students struggling all need to work on the same skill. In this situation, the school now only has to find fewer interventionists, instead of placing interventionists at each grade level. Additionally, the school may need to purchase fewer teacher copies of the program, because fewer interventionists are needed. (See Figure 5.2.)

Making Groups Dynamic

Once students are placed in groups, they will receive the specified instruction and their progress will be monitored over time. The progress monitoring component is important, as this is the marker that defines whether the instruction is effective, or if a modification needs to be

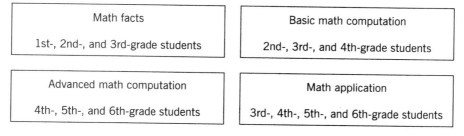

FIGURE 5.2. Students of different grade levels in the same intervention groups.

made. Progress monitoring will inform the team about growth and allow the team to make swift decisions about what to do next. Without this information, teams have to wait until the next benchmark period, which is 3–4 months away. This is too much time to wait for the students who are in Tiers 2 and 3, thus the importance of weekly or monthly progress monitoring. Progress monitoring is discussed more in Chapter 6, but it is addressed here briefly to highlight the importance of how using these data make the intervention groups dynamic. They change over time because students change over time. As a result, the groups are frequently changing based on student need. The group membership changes often and students are not considered "Tier 2" for the rest of the year if the data indicates otherwise.

This is equally important for students who are found to be at the benchmark level. While they do not need to be progress monitored monthly or weekly, they do need to be administered the screening measures three times per year. Some schools fail to recognize this importance and fall victim to the idea that if the students were at benchmark level in the fall, it is likely they will stay at that level throughout the year. While this may be true for some students, it is not true for all. To believe that all students who screen in the benchmark category initially will stay there is a big risk and a faulty assumption. When the screening measures themselves do not take more than a few minutes to administer, it makes sense to administer the measures to *all* students three times per year.

Consider the following school. School A is an elementary school, grades K–6, with a population of 550 students. School A is beginning to administer schoolwide CBM measures for benchmarking three times per year. The principal is supportive of the data collection process and believes it will allow students to receive adequate support. The decision is made to administer benchmark measures to all students in the fall, and just the "some-risk" and "at-risk" students in the winter and spring. The principal believes that most students who are at benchmark in the fall will stay in the category, even if they are on the cusp of being "benchmark" and "some risk." If they fall down to the "some-risk" category, she explains that they still aren't *that* low, so they will probably be fine. However, this is not her primary reason for only assessing all students once, instead of three times per year. The primary reason is more about consensus and teacher adoption than efficiency. The real story is that the principal knows that the curriculum coordinator and the teachers at her school are not supportive of the new benchmarking process. The district is immersed in a "balanced literacy" approach and this makes a focus on "fluency" difficult for many educators. Option one would be to make modifications to the process to satisfy people, even though it does not consider the students first and it puts them at risk. This is what she chose because she did not want to burden the teachers and wants to start things "slowly." The other option would be to spend time building consensus, supporting teacher adoption, and increasing understanding. With increased knowledge and a commitment to the students, there will be a refocus of priorities.

Considerations for Selection, Delivery, and Fidelity of Interventions

Essential to this process is building the infrastructure first, and placing students second. Without the system in place, there is no place for students and they are left in each classroom, as general education teachers struggle to provide them individual support. Therefore, building the infrastructure becomes our important first step. Building the infrastructure means building the intervention block, so that the time for intervention delivery is built into the school schedule. With this in place, interventions can easily occur without having to squeeze time from other parts of the day.

Tier 1 is defined by core instruction that can be provided whole-class plus small-group work where students are placed according to their level. Tier 2 is provided to students in small groups in addition to core instruction. Tier 3 can also be provided in small groups, or be provided individually to students, in addition to core instruction. Core instruction could occur for 90 minutes per day. If a student was receiving Tier 2 intervention as well, an additional 30 minutes of instruction would be provided. For a student who did not make progress in Tier 2, the student would move to a Tier 3 intervention where an additional 30 minutes would be provided in even smaller groups. This totals 2½ hours per day and can be difficult to manage. If the school schedule is reformatted to build in intervention time, it will be easier to schedule the time needed. Form 5.1 at the end of this chapter is an intervention planning map to assist teams in assessing what programs they have in place and which programs need to be filled in to complete all of the tiers for each area.

Considerations for Selection

Intervention selection is one of the most important and most difficult steps of the RTI process. Interventions that are evidence based, targeted specifically to student needs, and frequently monitored can result in positive outcomes for students. The decision to select interventions is difficult though, not only because of the varying needs of students but also because of the varying resources, philosophies, and educator skills that make up a school's constitution. As Merrell and Buchanan (2006) state, "It is simply not realistic to think that most systems will be able to provide the best intervention needed to solve particular problems, or that such intervention efforts, even if possible, will be delivered with fidelity across situations" (p. 4). There are many issues surrounding implementation related to planning and logistics that often impede the progress of well-meaning schools. The following is a list of questions that school teams should consider when selecting interventions:

- Does the intervention have evidence to support its effectiveness?
- Does the intervention match the instructional philosophy of educators in the school?
- Does the school have enough resources (personnel, time) to implement the intervention effectively?

To start, an intervention must be evidence based. Evidence-based interventions (EBIs) are treatments that have been proven effective (to some degree) through outcome evaluations. This means that when implemented with integrity, the intervention is likely to be effective in changing the target behavior. The What Works Clearinghouse (*http://ies.ed.gov/ncee/wwc*) is an initiative of the U.S. Department of Education's Institute of Education Sciences and is one of the largest sources of information on EBIs. They pull together many studies that have been conducted on intervention programs and review the results using meta-analysis procedures. What results is a website complete with intervention effectiveness ratings, improvement indices, and a descriptor regarding the extent of the evidence available. They review intervention programs in the areas of academic achievement, career readiness, dropout prevention, early childhood education, literacy, math, teacher incentives, and many more. It is an excellent resource for curriculum coordinators and leadership teams investigating new programs.

Another resource for teams is the University of Missouri's Evidence-Based Intervention Network (*http://ebi.missouri.edu*). Their goal is to provide educators a resource for simple interventions that can be done in most classes with little resource commitment. Unlike large group interventions you might find on the What Works Clearinghouse (n.d.), these are interventions that a teacher or leadership team can select and try out with a target student demonstrating a common problem. They provide a number of academic and behavior interventions organized by the type of problem the student is experiencing (e.g., in academics, some of the interventions would be organized under the "The task is too hard for the student" category). They also provide resources on RTI, English language learners, and the problem-solving process.

We encourage teams to start there. Spend some time reviewing the information on their websites and determining what interventions have evidence behind them that is suitable to your team. Next, go to the publisher websites and look for research studies that document effectiveness. Call the publishers to solicit this information as needed. With the data in hand, schedule a meeting to discuss the pros and cons of the interventions. If they've been determined to be effective for students, will they work with your student population? Can the teachers easily implement them? Do they match the instructional philosophy of your school? And finally, are the costs reasonable? Finding and reviewing the evidence behind interventions is a crucial first step. Teams should make selecting EBIs an important priority. And then, it is also important to consider planning, logistics, and feasibility. Just because an intervention is evidence based does not mean it will be implemented with fidelity. Teams should consider what educators need to make interventions happen.

A helpful model for school teams to plan for intervention selection is the RE-AIM framework. Developed originally by public health researcher Glasgow and his colleagues (Glasgow, 2002; Glasgow, Lichtenstein, & Marcus, 2003), Merrell and Buchanan (2006) use it to provide a framework for determining intervention impact after selection. School teams can walk through each step to determine if the intervention they are considering will be accepted, feasible, and implemented with fidelity.

RE-AIM stands for reach, efficacy, adoption, implementation, and maintenance (see Figure 5.3). *Reach* represents what percentage of students will be exposed to the intervention. If the intervention has a high reach, many students will be impacted, where if it has a low reach, fewer students will be impacted. This step should be reviewed in terms of how many students need to work on specific skills. If a large percentage of students need to improve their alphabetic principle skills and an alphabetic principle intervention is selected, then the intervention will have a large reach. If a phonemic awareness intervention is selected instead, the intervention may have a smaller reach, as fewer students need to work on that skill. *Efficacy* stands for the intervention's success rate when it is implemented as intended. This step represents the "evidence-based" characteristic that is frequently mentioned when discussing intervention selection. Does the intervention produce positive outcomes for students? Is it successful when implemented with fidelity? Essentially, does it do what it is intended to do? *Adoption* represents whether the intervention will be adopted fully by staff. If the intervention differs significantly from current practices and requires new task demands that take time, it is less likely to be adopted by educators in the school. If the intervention is similar to current practices and educators have the skills

> **Reach:** How many students will be impacted by the intervention?
>
> **Efficacy:** Is the intervention successful when implemented?
>
> **Adoption:** Will the intervention be adopted by educators?
>
> **Implementation:** Will the intervention be implemented as intended?
>
> **Maintenance:** Can the intervention be implemented over time?

FIGURE 5.3. RE-AIM framework.

to implement it, it will be more likely be adopted by staff. This step is critical, as even the most evidence-based intervention will fail to be implemented if it not accepted and adopted fully by staff. *Implementation* refers to the consistency and quality of the intervention implementation in real-world settings (Merrell & Buchanan, 2006). If the intervention is implemented as it was intended, then the implementation fidelity would be considered high. If the intervention was implemented with some modifications, the fidelity decreases. If the intervention is implemented with many changes, then the fidelity is considered low. Often, modifications are made because educators find parts of the intervention not relevant, too redundant, boring, or they believe these parts are not useful for students. Although some of these beliefs may hold true, it is a significant risk to take to make modifications to interventions. When followed as intended, the intervention is indeed "evidence based" and has a chance to produce positive outcomes for students. Without following the intervention as designed, it cannot be referred to as "evidence based" anymore, because deviations from the structure and implementation have occurred. The last step, *maintenance*, refers to how the students are affected over time. Is student skill acquisition and behavior change maintained over time? This dimension can also be evaluated at the systems level, where educators assess whether the intervention has been maintained through the practices of adults, and if it has become part of the system (Merrell & Buchanan, 2006).

INSTRUCTIONAL APPROACH

For many students who are struggling with learning basic skills, a direct instruction approach is necessary to assist them in remediating the deficits. Direct instruction is an instructional approach that forms the basis of some programs that can be used with students in Tiers 2 and 3 (see Figure 5.4). When direct instruction is used, the teaching is explicit and clear. Skills are broken into their component parts, so that students can learn each subskill before moving on. Direct instruction is also known by the following design features: concepts are broken down into manageable steps to help students possess appropriate preskills and prior knowledge; clear, concise language is used so students grasp concepts the first time they are presented; skills and steps needed to complete tasks and ensure understanding are modeled by teachers; guided

Skills broken down into steps	Clear language	Teacher modeling	Guided practice	Multiple examples	Ongoing assessment

FIGURE 5.4. Features of direct instruction.

practice is provided to support student learning; multiple examples are provided in a carefully planned sequence to build independence; and continuous assessment is incorporated to monitor student learning (National Institute for Direct Instruction, n.d.).

The phases of direct instruction teaching include orientation, presentation, structured practice, guided practice, and independent practice. Orientation is the first stage where teachers introduce the purpose of the lesson, connect the purpose to student prior knowledge, and help students to understand the focus of the lesson. Presentation is defined by explicitness, where teachers identify a strategy for students and model exactly how to use it. During this phase, teachers demonstrate exactly what to do and how to do it and frequently check for understanding. In the structured practice phase, teachers use new but related material to demonstrate again how to use the strategy and give students an opportunity to demonstrate their learning. In the guided practice phase, students have more responsibility in applying the strategy to the new material and the teacher checks for participation and understanding of all students. In the independent practice phase, students work individually to apply their new skills to new material. The benefits of this approach are that teachers constantly have information about student knowledge of the concepts, additional examples and lessons are provided to students who need them, and the explicit approach promotes maximum understanding in students because there is no guesswork.

How direct instruction is delivered is also an important feature of the program. Direct instruction lessons are delivered by teachers in a way to catch and keep students' attention throughout the entire class. In these programs, teachers do the following: give placement tests so students begin at an appropriate level, follow scripted lessons to ensure consistency, use quick pacing and group responses to keep all students engaged, implement planned correction procedures to prevent errors from becoming learned habits, and provide positive reinforcement to motivate students (National Institute for Direct Instruction; n.d.). These characteristics are important because research indicates that average-performing students need to practice a skill approximately 24 times before gaining mastery (Marzano, Pickering, & Pollock, 2001)

WHY DOES DIRECT INSTRUCTION WORK?

Direct instruction is effective for many students because of four main reasons. First, students are placed in an instructional group at their skill level. Before students begin the program, each student is tested to find out which skills they have already mastered and which ones they need to work on (National Institute for Direct Instruction, n.d.). Students are grouped according to similar skills, which assists students in working together and learning from each other as they are exposed to new content. Second, the program is designed to ensure mastery of the content. Skills are introduced gradually, which gives students a chance to learn new skills thoroughly. Only 10% of each lesson contains new material. The remaining 90% of each lesson's content is review and application of skills and concepts introduced in earlier lessons (National Institute for Direct Instruction, n.d.). Third, these programs are designed to accommodate these different rates of learning. Because students master the material at different rates, some will require additional practice and others don't require as much practice and can advance more quickly. If students need more practice with a specific skill, teachers can provide the additional instruction within the program. If students demonstrate that they already possess the skills covered in a lesson, students can be moved to a more advanced placement (National Institute for Direct

> - National Center on Response to Intervention
>   *www.rti4success.org*
> - National Center on Intensive Interventions
>   *www.intensiveintervention.org*
> - National Institute for Direct Instruction
>   *www.nifdi.org/15*
> - What Works Clearinghouse
>   *http://ies.ed.gov/ncee/wwc*
> - RTI Action Network
>   *www.rtinetwork.org*
> - Evidence Based Intervention Network
>   *http://ebi.missouri.edu*

FIGURE 5.5. Internet resources on instructional approaches.

Instruction, n.d.). Finally, these programs are field tested and revised before publication. They are tested with a wide range of students and revised based on feedback from the field before they are published. (See Figure 5.5.)

Considerations for Delivery

After interventions have been selected, the next part of the process is to examine how best to support implementation. Implementation can be defined as the act of accomplishing some aim or executing some order. There are many actions that need to occur to ensure interventions can be delivered as they were intended. Because of this, there are multiple issues that arise when programs are implemented, and more often than not, changes are made rather than adhering to the programs. Described often as the "research-to-practice gap" (Carnine, 1997; Gersten, Vaughn, Deshler, & Schiller, 1997; Greenwood & Abbott, 2001; Kennedy, 1997; Robinson, 1998), it is a persistent issue that needs to be addressed in each school.

The common assumption is that once teams select evidence-based interventions, those designated to implement them will do so with fidelity. *Delivering the interventions should be straightforward. Delivering the interventions should be easy. Delivering the interventions should be like second nature.* These assumptions are based on the following beliefs: Interventions are scripted, so it is simple to follow the lessons. Educators were trained in the interventions, so they will learn them quickly. Finally, interventions will increase student success, so all educators will agree wholeheartedly to delivering them. What we know however, is that adopting new behaviors requires investment, time, training, and ongoing support. Without these components in place, the delivery of interventions is at risk for fragmented implementation.

> **To support teacher adoption and implementation, it is helpful to present short lessons in grade-level meetings. Trainers can pick one strategy to share and demonstrate it with live modeling or videos.**

The following six levels of implementation (adapted from Fixsen, Naoom, Blase, Friedman, & Wallace 2005) provide teams a way to assess their current placement and set goals for where they want to go. Teams can use these steps to determine their baseline and determine what to do next. The first stage is known as *exploration*, where the team is actively considering a change. In this stage, individuals are thinking about the importance of delivering interventions for students. To arrive at this stage, there is some basic knowledge and awareness that teams must have. This may come from initial trainings on intervention selection and delivery in the RTI process. During this stage, teams should determine the match between their needs and their resources so they can determine to move forward or not. A needs assessment is helpful at this point. A needs assessment is a tool teams can use to assess their needs, how to address them, and the amount of resources needed to address them. There are many needs assessments available related to RTI (see Figure 5.6).

The second stage of implementation is known as *installation*. In this stage, teams are preparing for the delivery of interventions. This is the most difficult step, as it requires significant change for many individuals. Each individual has a different knowledge base, skill set, and investment in the new process. This is where the "rubber meets the road" (Fixsen et al., 2005) and actual implementation needs to occur. For real change to occur here, there must be determination and skill. Skill can be provided by the trainings and practice sessions. The determination must be fostered by administration as they provide ongoing encouragement and appreciation for the new behaviors that the teachers are demonstrating. Unfortunately, most attempts to implement innovations fail during this stage because the requirements for successful implementation are both poorly understood and inadequately supported (Fixsen et al., 2005). There must be understanding of systems change first, and time should be spent fostering this understanding before any real change takes place. It is necessary to spend this time upfront, instead of losing time later due to inadequate implementation. If organizations can survive the initial challenges, completion of the initial implementation stage may require from 9 to 24 months (Fixsen et al., 2005). This is also important to remember, because with an understanding that there will be bumps in the road, there will be more patience and more dedication to fixing issues as they arise instead of judging them as "mistakes."

The third stage of implementation is known as *initial implementation*, where teams are actively engaged in implementing and supporting RTI. This step is exciting as actual changes

- National Association of State Directors of Special Education
  www.isbe.state.il.us/rti_plan/default.htm
- RTI Action Network
  www.rtinetwork.org/images/Colorado_School_RtI_Fidelity_Rubrics_2.pdf
- Illinois State Board of Education
  www.isbe.state.il.us/rti_plan/default.htm
- Indiana RTI Inventory
  www.indstate.edu/blumberg/presm/docs/Guidelines-for-Completion-Indiana-RTI-Inventory-and-Needs-Assessment-Screener.pdf
- RISS Project in Maine
  http://usm.maine.edu/smart/mainerti/files/RISS%20District%20Needs%20Assessment%20and%20Planning.pdf

FIGURE 5.6. Internet resources on RTI-related needs assessments.

occur, individuals are renewed in their commitment as they see changes in students, and it seems like this movement can be promising. It is often filled with a positive outlook among staff, as they start to see real changes. These changes may be small, they may be big, and regardless, they should be celebrated. Because individuals need positive reinforcement, administrators and teams should take the time to recognize and reward the successes as they arise. This is also important because there will likely also be issues. Implementation requires making changes to the organizational capacity and organizational culture, which is a lot to consider (Fixsen et al., 2005). With these potential pitfalls, teams will need to address them head on, determine acceptable solutions, and solidify action plans that allow progress to move forward.

The fourth stage is *full implementation*, where intervention delivery and data analysis become part of regular practice. It is integrated into practitioner and organizational practices, policies, and procedures (Fixsen et al., 2005). At this point, RTI becomes fully operational, it is being used with all students, and it fits seamlessly into the typical school day. This is the ideal goal, where RTI is completely understood, it is implemented with full fidelity, and the infrastructure is completed and supported by all. Fixsen et al. (2005) state that in their estimation, "few attempts to implement innovations ever reach the full implementation stage" (p. 5). This is because there

> **Incorporating accountability is important so staff follow through with the adoption. Checking in at the following meeting or using administrator observations can be powerful motivators for learning new skills.**

are so many smaller changes in structure, support, attitude, investment, commitment, and continued learning that must take place. For those who do reach full implementation stage, the process from the exploration stage to the point of first achieving full implementation may take 2 to 4 years.

The fifth stage is *innovation*, where individuals learn more about RTI and the conditions under which it can be used with fidelity. At this point, implementation is up and running, things have been going smoothly, and staff are at a point where they can take a step back and reflect on what is working, what is not working, and what can be improved to make the intervention delivery more effective. There are opportunities to refine and expand the delivery of interventions, which is an exciting place to be. Innovations are made that impact students, teachers, and administrators. The process becomes more efficient, better designed, and changes, both big and small, improve the whole process. As Fixsen et al. (2005) state, "The advice from successful purveyors is 'first do it right, then do it differently'" (p. 50).

The final stage is *sustainability*, where the administrator and team work to ensure the continued use of RTI. The goal during this stage is the long-term survival and continued effectiveness of implementation in a changing educational context. Critical to this stage is having a keen awareness of the changes that have occurred and that will occur again. Being able to anticipate the needs, address them, and keep changing over time is a skill that requires much commitment, observation, and adept awareness. The administrator and team should work closely together to be a large set of eyes and ears where they can come together, discuss the issues, brainstorm solutions, and select action plans that will address the needs effectively and efficiently. With a team approach, a shared vision, and an ongoing commitment to being honest and evaluative, the team can support the school in continually moving forward to address student needs and help to ensure their continued success. (See Figure 5.7.)

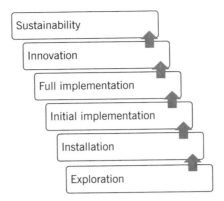

FIGURE 5.7. Phases of implementation.

Considerations for Fidelity

Fidelity is defined by *Merriam Webster's* (2012) dictionary as exactness, or "exhibiting strict, particular, and complete accordance with a standard." *Fidelity* can also be defined as the delivery of instruction in the way in which it was designed to be delivered (Gresham, MacMillan, Beebe-Frankenberger, & Bocian, 2000). A team can select an evidence-based program that has been proven to work, and unless it is implemented as intended, the students will not make positive growth as intended. Teams need to consider both "what works" and what will actually be implemented. As Shinn and Walker (2010) state, "The most effective program or practice will not yield the expected outcomes in the absence of a high quality application" (p. 11).

This relates to the idea of acceptability. Teams may peruse the What Works Clearinghouse website, review research on programs, and ultimately select effective programs that will *not* be implemented. People will go through a "cost–benefit" analysis, where they weigh the trade-off between what it takes to learn and execute the new program with what the perceived benefits are. As such, it is important for teams to consider the following when selecting new intervention programs:

- It fits easily into current school routines.
- It is consistent with educator values.
- It solves a high-priority problem.
- Time and effort costs are reasonable.
- Teachers feel like they have the skills and resources to implement the program. (Shinn & Walker, 2010)

If any of the above criteria are lacking, there are risks to implementation with fidelity, and that can cause many issues with seeing an actual increase in student performance. Form 5.2 at the end of this chapter has been designed from the criteria provided by Shinn and Walker (2010) to act as a rubric for teams selecting new intervention programs to purchase.

Why is fidelity important? Because it often suffers due to lack of investment, time, or training. Educators struggle to implement new programs when the rationale has not been established, they do not understand the "why," or sufficient information about effectiveness has not been provided to them. If there is not enough time to implement the program, teachers may have bought into it, but there is simply not enough hours in the day to execute it. It has not been identified as a priority and so other classes and programs still rank higher. Or there may not have been enough training. There may be an investment, there may be enough time to implement it, but teachers were inadequately trained on how exactly to implement the program. The assumption may be that they received a 1-day training and that should be enough. It may be enough, with follow-up and accountability. It may not be enough, because they were trained once in the fall and program implementation began in the winter. With too much time in between, not enough opportunities for practice, or some teachers were missing from the initial training in the first place, there are many reasons why lack of training can dramatically impact program effectiveness.

Consider the following situation: The special education teachers in the district were trained in Reading Mastery in the early fall of the school year. With RTI in place, one of their new roles at the elementary level was also to act as Tier 2 interventionists for 45 to 60 minutes during the school day. During this time, they would work with students identified as Tier 2 and teach Reading Mastery. At the district training in the fall it was made clear that this was one of their new responsibilities. Also described at the training was evidence of its effectiveness, videos were shown displaying what it looks like when implemented, and practice opportunities were provided. After the training, teachers went back to their respective schools and began the school year. At School A, the principal set regular monthly meetings where Tier 2 students' data would be reviewed, decisions would be made, and there would be conversations about the actual implementation of the program. Teachers would discuss what was working, what could be improved, and they were given the opportunity to brainstorm and learn from each other. At School B, the monthly meetings were scheduled but sometimes they occurred, and sometimes they were canceled due to other priorities. When they were canceled, teachers were happy to have the additional time to get other work done. The principal did not schedule follow-up meetings but instead recommended that teachers get together on their own time to discuss the Tier 2 students' progress. As a result, some teachers would meet and some would not. Sometimes the data were reviewed and sometimes they were not.

Most disturbing about School B was that one teacher decided not to implement Reading Mastery at all. She decided that her Tier 2 students needed more of the general education curriculum and with more opportunities for practice, they would perform higher on their monthly curriculum-based oral reading fluency timings. So she provided them more opportunities to learn about and practice the general education program. They did not receive Reading Mastery at all. And things were going along swimmingly, until the administrator finally noticed that her data were lower than the other teachers implementing Reading Mastery. In his initial meeting with the teacher, she explained that she thought she was giving the students what they needed. They seemed to be doing "better." She also explained that she was unclear about the requirement to implement Reading Mastery. She thought it was optional, depending on how each teacher though their Tier 2 students were doing. She believed her students were making progress, thus she didn't see a reason to implement a new program when the general education curriculum was working.

There are many issues with the above situation. The tendency may be to blame the educator, because she did not adhere to the requirements expected of her. This is true. She made a grand mistake by disobeying district expectations, she put students at risk for not making progress, and she ignored what other teachers were doing with their Tier 2 students. Instead of blaming the teacher though, it is more productive to place fault on the system, one that did not provide ongoing support, required little accountability, and provided no consistent format for monitoring how things were going. What should have happened was that the administrator should have made the monthly Tier 2 meetings a priority, so that they always occurred and they were viewed as a constant. Teachers should have been given time to review student data and check in about program implementation. The administrator should have scheduled observations of teachers implementing Reading Mastery, and using a fidelity checklist, provided teachers feedback about what was going well and what could be improved. The special education director should have also scheduled observations or a visit where teachers met to discuss program implementation. Finally, student progress at the Tier 2 level could have been celebrated at staff meetings to bring attention to the teachers doing the hard work. According to the teacher, she thought she was doing what she was "supposed to be doing." Unfortunately, without reinforcement and accountability, she put students at risk rather than giving them the opportunity to make additional progress.

This scenario is described to highlight the importance of expectations, monitoring, and reinforcement for school staff, not just the students. Many of us have been in situations where we thought we were going to engage in a new behavior, but other priorities, lack of time, and lack of investment were barriers. Are we at fault? Yes, because we are ultimately responsible for our own behavior change. Do we have a higher chance of succeeding when there are supports in place? Absolutely. It is naïve to think that adults will engage in a new behavior simply because they've been trained. Just like students, we vary along a continuum. Some educators will engage in new practices simply because they've been told to. Some educators will engage in new practices with support and maintenance over time. Some educators will not engage in new practices unless there are consistent supports in place to maintain the new behavior. Instead of assuming that teachers will easily engage in new behaviors and risk having them not, assume that teachers will not engage in the behaviors, and supports are essential to the change process. With this assumption, fewer students are at risk for inadequate teaching practices and more likely to be given the chance they need.

The National Research Center on Learning Disabilities (2012), in a document on fidelity, describes the importance of proactive measures to support teachers. They recommend the following:

- Link interventions to improved outcomes (credibility).
- Definitively describe operations, techniques, and components.
- Clearly define responsibilities of specific persons.
- Create a data system for measuring operations, techniques, and components.
- Create a system for feedback and decision making (formative).
- Create accountability measures for noncompliance.

With this in mind, Form 5.3 is provided at the end of this chapter. It is a checklist designed to assess and support intervention implementation. Not specific to an intervention, it is a general form that should be used by administrators and school psychologists to support, monitor, and improve fidelity. With the information in hand, teams can follow through on issues that need to be addressed and make plans to support their implementation.

For teams interested in monitoring fidelity with specific interventions, there are many resources available online that support observation and monitoring. Teams can select a tool based on what interventions are being implemented, conduct regular observations, and provide feedback to teachers. Heartland Area Education Agency (2008) in Iowa provides a number of instructional integrity checklists that can be found at *www.aea11.k12.ia.us/idm/checkists.html*. These include both direct observation and permanent product checklists. The website for Oregon Response to Intervention (n.d.) also has a number of useful checklists. These can be found at *http://oregonrti.org/node/33*. Their focus is primarily on reading programs. Another useful website is the St. Croix River Education District (n.d.) available at *www.scred.k12.mn.us*. They also offer a number of tools that can be used to evaluate intervention programs.

Teams should select the monitoring tool that applies to their program and use it consistently over time to monitor implementation. Using the tool is important but scheduling and holding the feedback meetings with teachers is also important. This is a step that is often ignored, because once students are placed and interventions are up and running, it is easy to become preoccupied with other responsibilities. It is comforting to assume that interventions are implemented as they were intended, and easy to believe that everyone is doing what they are supposed to. And this may well be true. And it may not. It is a risk to take to assume that everything is happening as it was planned, because we may become less diligent over time. If check-in meetings are built into the school year schedule initially, they become "constants": meetings that are predictable, consistent, and a common occurrence that staff become accustomed to. These meetings will be welcomed if there is a culture of support, rather than judgment. An important task for the principal and leadership team is to approach fidelity from a supportive standpoint, rather than a policing standpoint. The team should work to create a culture that supports honest evaluation and reflection, and celebrates successes and growth instead of focusing on mistakes. It should never be used to force change, but rather to support people as they change their behaviors over time. With this perspective, monitoring fidelity then becomes less of a chore, and more of an opportunity to provide feedback and celebrate what is working.

Form 5.4 at the end of this chapter is a format for delivering feedback to individuals implementing interventions. Principals can use this to structure a conversation that is productive, supportive, and goal-oriented. The form is designed around the following ideas with regard to what characteristics should define feedback. Feedback should be understandable. It should be kept clear and simple so that recipients can easily understand the content. Second, it should be focused. If there is too much information, it quickly becomes overwhelming and is easy to ignore. By addressing only one or two issues instead of a "laundry list" of problems, the conversation becomes more tailored to what is occurring and what may need to change. Third, it should be specific. Hearing "Great job with that lesson" informs someone that he or she did something well, but he or she would have little idea regarding what exactly went well. The feedback should contain details and specific examples. It should be personalized and be precise. Fourth, it should be substantive and focus on what is really important. The comments should be meaningful and address what is relevant ("I like how you provided five examples because you realized that with only three examples, the students were still unclear" vs. "Next time, be sure to make eye contact with each student the same exact number of times"). Fifth, the feedback should be objective and provided in quantifiable terms. This allows the person to identify the baseline and determine the amount of growth needed to reach the goal. Finally, the feedback should be behavior focused, which means its focus is on the behavior to be changed, not the person. Instead of "I don't like the way you started the lesson," which focuses more on the person, the feedback could be changed to "Let's review the start of the lesson again and see what questions you may have," which focuses more on the behavior. (See Figure 5.8.)

Consider School E. School E is an elementary school that has been attempting to engage in the RTI process for a few years now. When asked, they would say they are "doing RTI." They refer to intervention implementation and schoolwide screening data that they collect three times per year. During an initial observation, you would be able to see interventions being implemented and screening data would easily be provided. On a cursory level, the school is engaging in some "RTI-like" practices and they are seeing growth in student performance. They see initial gains in student performance and are pleased with how students are responding to the interventions. This appears to be a good starting point except that they have been "doing RTI" for a few years now. They should be further along in their process and be to a point where they are meeting regularly to review progress monitoring data in data day meetings, fidelity checks of the interventions are occurring regularly, the core curriculum is evaluated using all schoolwide data, and the administrator is leading the RTI leadership team in meeting regularly to review progress and make plans for the next steps of the systems change process. Unfortunately, none of the above actions are occurring. As a result, the interventions are at risk for problems of fidelity, students may not make as much growth because their progress is not monitored, and teachers feel like they are fumbling for ideas on what to do because there is little administrator or leadership team involvement. At best, some teachers are trying to continue to implement interventions. At worst, interventions are not occurring anymore. And in some classrooms, this is what was actually happening.

One of the most glaring issues at this school is the lack of administrator support. At first, during Year 1 of RTI adoption, it appeared that he was supportive of this initiative. It was included on schedules for professional development days, it was mentioned in staff meetings, and interventions were being purchased for teachers to use. Additionally, there was a team created to collect the schoolwide data three times per year, a few teachers were selected to input

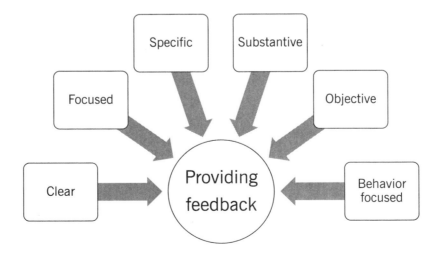

FIGURE 5.8. Characteristics of feedback.

the data into the system, and a team of graduate students assisted in analyzing the data with the RTI leadership team. It seemed like the school was off to a good start. And then other priorities got in the way. The administrator would remove RTI from the professional development days, as there were "other priorities" that needed to be addressed with teachers. He stopped talking about it as much in staff meetings. And once interventions were purchased and teachers were trained, he never talked about the interventions unless asked. Data continued to be collected three times per year yet there was little done with the information. It was noted that some students were improving, but for those students remaining at the "some-risk" or "at-risk" levels, not much was done to modify their interventions or increase the amount of progress monitoring.

When we ask the teachers what could be improved, many of them wish they had more administrator praise and support. It appears that the administrator rarely acknowledges the work that teachers are doing. For those students who are making growth, the teachers receive little praise. The administrator states "That is what should be happening" and shows little appreciation. For the teachers whose students continue to struggle, the administrator provides reprimands without recommendation. Teachers are left feeling like something needs to change, but are given no direction for what to do next. Perhaps the most egregious act that the administrator engages in is providing feedback that attacks the person rather than the behavior. Instead of "Let's think about what you can do to improve the intervention lessons," many of the comments sound more like "It seems like you're not giving this all you can, and it makes you appear lazy." With these types of comments, teachers feel hurt, unmotivated, and wonder what to do to improve their teaching practices.

This school's situation is described to highlight the importance of administrator support throughout the RTI process. Without direction, praise, guidance, and specific feedback, educators are left wondering how to make RTI "work" when there is no incentive and a highly punitive approach. In a situation like this, there is little chance for systems change. What the administrator doesn't realize is the magnitude of the negative impact he is making and how he is inhibiting the change process. In the end, the teachers are affected, but ultimately student progress is stalled. When the teachers lack the tools and support they need to move forward, the students consequently cannot move forward.

THE ACTION PLAN

It is important to prepare for the meeting by organizing the data, bringing copies for all participants, and bringing copies of planning forms that take inventory of what interventions are available at your school. First, use a planning form to organize all students in Tiers 2 and 3. Once students are organized into tiers, the second planning form should be used to place them into appropriate intervention groups.

In Chapter 4, we discussed the importance of establishing ground rules and assigning roles. In this chapter, we discuss the importance of including an action plan in the meeting. Creating an action plan at the end of the meeting is an essential and important step to moving the team forward. It can be argued that this is the most important step, because without a plan, there is little likelihood for action. How many times have you participated in a meeting, felt productive, and then left without knowing what to do next? Or you knew what to do, but other job responsibilities quickly got in the way afterward? Without a clear plan that targets goals, has built-in progress monitoring and accountability, and an established timeline for action, the team runs the risk of accomplishing less work.

Consider School A. School A's district is in the planning stages of RTI adoption and administrators and school team leaders are attending trainings all year to learn about the process. The administrator at School A has a special education background and understood the importance of data collection. He wanted to start the process sooner, so with his school psychologist and counselor, he decided that the team would screen all students three times per year to collect and analyze the data. The school psychologist and counselor worked with the special education teachers (who also were trained in CBM) to form a team to assess all students. The team used AIMsWeb (2012) and were provided with reports that categorized students according to need. After fall administration, the administrator knew the next step was to schedule meetings with each grade-level team to review the data.

The meetings were scheduled over 2 days, with each grade-level team participating in the meetings for 2 hours. The school psychologist, counselor, and one special education teacher were present at each meeting. The counselor took notes, the school psychologist completed group-intervention planning forms, and the administrator facilitated. The special education teacher collaborated with the grade-level teachers regarding high-risk students. The conversations were targeted, focused, and rich with insight. The administrator was happy with the process, thinking that he was able to get his school ahead of the curve in the RTI process.

In reading this scenario, it sounds like an effective process overall. Data was collected and analyzed, meetings were scheduled to determine intervention planning, and discussions occurred in the meetings centered around student needs and appropriately matched interventions. So what is missing? The action plans. There were no formal action plans completed at the meeting. So the teams were left with great discussions that didn't result in any change. Some interventions were implemented, some were not. Some students were progress monitored, and some were not. Some teachers checked in with the team and some did not.

Was it the school's first time engaging in the data day process? Yes. Are there some difficulties that will be encountered the first time? Yes. Yet an action plan is an easy fix. It is a form that allows for planning with vision, accountability, and check-ins to support educators as they engage in this new process. Rich discussions are invaluable, because they address the heart of the issues, build collaboration and camaraderie, and solidify the team process. But without action, they don't assist students in improvement. A specific action plan that is paired with a rich discussion is the ideal goal. With both of these components, teams move forward in a way that is efficient and powerful, because student needs are met through purposeful teacher action.

There are a few steps to follow when creating action plans for the team. (See Form 5.5 at the end of this chapter for a general meeting outline.) First, determine the goals for the team. Consider what you want to accomplish, what needs to be done to facilitate intervention planning, and how the team will know when the goals are accomplished. Next, prioritize the goals. Which goals are most important and absolutely necessary to complete? With this information, you can determine what comes first and what should come next. Draft a plan of goals in sequential order. The team might have to come up with a series of preliminary goals that they need to accomplish in order to arrive at their final goal. Next, take one of the preliminary goals and begin to brainstorm all of the actions that need to occur to accomplish that goal. Once the actions are determined, the team can begin to set objectives that are specific, measurable, and achievable. They should be easily identifiable and measurable, so teams can ensure that progress can be measured.

Next, prioritize these tasks. Which things are more important than others? Which intermediate steps must be done first before moving onto other steps? What different strategies are appropriate to each step? Timelines should be created next, where deadlines are set that are realistic but also encourage productivity. With a data day meeting in September, the goal should not be to set up the intervention group by November, as too much time has passed and students have been without the additional instruction they need. Finally, create mechanisms for accountability. The facilitator and team should consider what needs to be done to ensure each participant is engaging in his or her specified responsibility. Clear deadlines should be established, a team member may be assigned to check in with other participants, and clear evidence of action should be presented at the next meeting. The basic steps to creating an action plan are listed below:

1. Determine the goals of the team.
2. Prioritize the goals. What should be completed first? What can be completed later?
3. Select a preliminary goal and brainstorm actions to complete the goal.
4. Prioritize the actions. What should be completed first? What can be completed later?
5. Create a timeline for the actions.
6. Determine mechanisms for accountability.

The action plan should be monitored frequently so that the interim activities can be completed. This should be a designated role of one of the participants. With this role, the team understands that someone will be a "progress checker" who checks in with them regarding their responsibilities with the action item before the next meeting. The "check-in" is expected because it is part of the team's normal procedures. It becomes less threatening because it is more about the work and less about the people. Without this established role, someone may randomly decide to "check in" and at best it is unexpected and at worse it is threatening and people respond negatively. With someone established in this role, it becomes a part of regular team activity, which makes it predictable and expected. A process should be followed to inform individuals of team functioning and how accountability will be established. The process can follow these steps:

1. The progress checker checks in with each person by the established deadline.
2. The progress checker tracks who has completely, somewhat, or minimally accomplished the action item.
3. The progress checker informs the facilitator of each individual's progress.
4. The facilitator checks in with those individuals who have not accomplished all of the item to determine why.
5. The facilitator has each person explain his or her item and his or her progress on it at the next meeting.

At the next meeting, the action plan should be reviewed, to determine what was accomplished and how it shapes the team's next steps. If all of the action plan items were accomplished, then it is time to move forward with the next steps. In this scenario, it is important to acknowledge the work and celebrate progress and successes, to motivate the team as it continues to move forward. If one or two action plan items were not accomplished, then a process should be followed that allows the team to address why there was difficulty and what to do next. If two or more action items were not completed, this is a sign that there is a larger issue that has not been addressed. It is up to the facilitator to determine why progress has been halted on so many items, what is needed to remediate these issues, and how the team can move forward knowing that there is still previous work that needs to be accomplished.

There are a number of reasons why multiple action items may not be completed. For teams struggling with action item completion, complete Form 5.6 at the end of this chapter. Determine who and why, and consider the next steps using the ideas provided.

PREVENTING AND ADDRESSING COMMON ROADBLOCKS DURING INTERVENTION PLANNING MEETINGS

There are a number of roadblocks that can occur during meetings. The following is a list of actions that can be taken to address common roadblocks:

- **Roadblock 1:** There are too many students in Tiers 2 and 3 and not enough interventions.
  - *Cause:* Data are not analyzed ahead of time. Resources may need to be reallocated.
  - *Solution:* Determine how many students need support, what instructional skills they need to improve, and group accordingly. Assess how many interventions can be purchased and determine evidence-based instructional strategies to use to support students as well.

- **Roadblock 2:** There is confusion regarding how students should be placed into intervention groups.
  - *Cause:* Not enough data on students.
  - *Solution:* Collect more data on students. A benchmark screening is a good starting point but more data is needed to determine what skills a student needs to improve. Collect additional data to target the correct area and look for patterns in skills.

- **Roadblock 3:** There are concerns about following through with intervention implementation.
  - *Cause:* There is little to no accountability built into the action plan.
  - *Solution:* First, ensure that there is a clear action plan with an individual designated to check in regarding responsibilities. Second, discuss the importance of everyone following through so that the check-in meetings run smoothly. Determine reinforcement and accountability procedures for both possible outcomes.

- **Roadblock 4:** The group always seems to run out of time just as the important decisions are about to be made.
  - *Cause:* There is poor time management.
  - *Solution:* Create an agenda and stick to it. But also build in some flexibility. When

creating your agenda, realize that it is possible you may not get through everything. Prioritize your agenda and put less pressing items toward the end. Then, if time is running short, you can table those items until the next meeting.

- **Roadblock 5:** Participants are frequently looking at the clock at the end of the meeting.
  - *Cause:* The meeting has gone overtime, or is approaching the end and there is still a discussion occurring.
  - *Solution:* End on time, or even early. No one enjoys an open-ended meeting that has no clear conclusion. Set an ending time and then stick to it. Avoid putting "miscellaneous items" or "other business" at the end of your agenda. These phrases simply invite random or irrelevant discussions that use up time.

- **Roadblock 6:** Participants want more time to discuss a topic.
  - *Cause:* The topic is evoking thoughts in participants and not enough time was allocated to the topic on the agenda.
  - *Solution:* Show flexibility as the facilitator. While prepared agendas are useful, important discussions can arise and as the meeting chair, it is wise to recognize when it's necessary to stray from the prescribed format.

SUMMARY

In this chapter, we've reviewed a number of evidence-based intervention practices. Considerations for selection, delivery, and fidelity were discussed so teams are prepared to implement the interventions that will be effective for students in their schools. Because using schoolwide data to select interventions and implement them with fidelity is the crux of the RTI approach, we also reviewed the importance of finding EBIs, supporting fidelity of implementation, and planning for intervention delivery. Finally, the importance of an action plan after each meeting was highlighted, as well as common roadblocks to avoid during intervention planning meetings. In the next chapter, we review how to plan for progress monitoring, data reviews, and what should occur during these types of meetings.

Intervention Planning Map

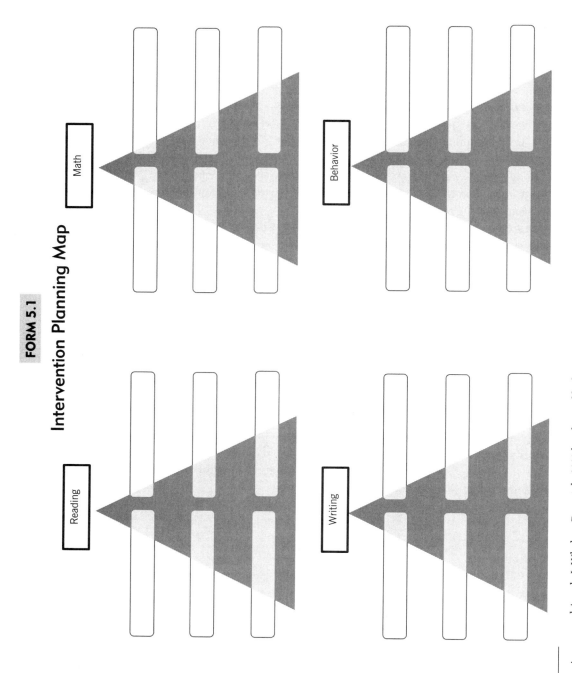

Math

Behavior

Reading

Writing

Evaluation Criteria for Tier 2 and Tier 3 Interventions

The RTI team will review new interventions based on the criteria below after it has been determined that the intervention is evidence based. To complete the rating form, a survey should be created to administer to teachers first. The survey will address educator values, the time and effort required, and the skills and resources needed (see below). After administering the survey and reviewing the results, each RTI member will rate the intervention individually below. Then the team will meet to discuss the ratings and create an average score for each dimension. Interventions must receive a _____ or higher to be accepted.

Criterion	3	2	1	0
The intervention fits easily into current school routines	No modifications to the schedule, interventionists, and/or grouping needed. Fits easily into current school routines.	Minor modifications to the schedule, interventionists, and/or grouping needed. Fits easily into current school routines.	Modifications to the schedule, interventionists, and/or grouping needed, but the changes can be made. Does not easily fit into current school routines, but the changes are possible.	Significant modifications to the schedule, interventionists, and/or grouping needed. Does not easily fit into current school routines.
The intervention is consistent with educator values	Teacher survey results indicate that 90% or more of teachers agree with the teaching philosophy behind the program.	Teacher survey results indicate that 80–90% of teachers agree with the teaching philosophy behind the program	Teacher survey results indicate that 70–80% of teachers agree with the teaching philosophy behind the program.	Teacher survey results indicate that 70% or less of teachers agree with the teaching philosophy behind the program.
The intervention solves a high-priority problem		The intervention is matched to a high-priority need in the school.	The intervention is somewhat matched to a high-priority need in the school.	The intervention is not matched to a high-priority need in the school.
The time and effort required to implement the intervention is reasonable	Teacher survey results indicate that 90% or more of teachers agree that the time and effort required to implement this program is reasonable.	Teacher survey results indicate that 80–90% of teachers agree that the time and effort required to implement this program is reasonable.	Teacher survey results indicate that 70–80% of teachers agree that the time and effort required to implement this program is reasonable.	Teacher survey results indicate that 70% or less of teachers agree that the time and effort required to implement this program is reasonable.
Teachers feel they have the skills and resources to use this intervention	Teacher survey results indicate that 90% or more of teachers agree that they have the skills and resources to implement the program.	Teacher survey results indicate that 80–90% of teachers agree that they have the skills and resources to implement the program.	Teacher survey results indicate that 70–80% of teachers agree that they have the skills and resources to implement the program.	Teacher survey results indicate that 70% or less of teachers agree that they have the skills and resources to implement the program.

Reviewer notes:

Providing Feedback

Directions: Use an integrity tool that is matched to the intervention being implemented. Conduct an observation and determine what is going well and what could be improved. Use that information to complete this form. This form can be used to provide feedback to the person in a conversation.

Steps	Notes	Questions
Step 1: Thank the teacher for allowing you to observe the lesson.		
Step 2: Provide three positives about the intervention implementation.		
Step 3: Provide one or two "needs to be improved" about the intervention implementation.		
Step 4: Check for understanding.		
Step 5: Set an expectation for follow-up.		

Tier 2 and Tier 3 Interventions: Supporting Ongoing Intervention Fidelity

After interventions have been adopted, this form can be used to address issues of implementation. As an RTI team, go through each item. Answer yes or no to the questions. If the answer is no, list the reason why, and fill in ideas for a potential action plan. List who is responsible for each action and follow-up dates for long-term planning.

Component	Guiding Questions	Yes or No?	Explanation for "No" Answers	Action Plan		
				Item	Person Responsible	Due Date
Role designation	Has role been clearly designated so that interventionists are clear about their responsibilities?	Yes No				
Initial training	Were interventionists initially trained on the intervention?	Yes No				
Ongoing training	Have interventionists been provided opportunities to get trained again? Are there ongoing opportunities for learning?	Yes No				
Skills	Do interventionists have the skills to implement the intervention?	Yes No				
Resources	Do interventionists have the resources to implement the intervention?	Yes No				

(continued)

Tier 2 and Tier 3 Interventions: Supporting Ongoing Intervention Fidelity *(page 2 of 2)*

Component	Guiding Questions	Yes or No?	Explanation for "No" Answers	Action Plan		
				Item	Person Responsible	Due Date
Time	Do interventionists have the time to implement the intervention?	Yes No				
Collaboration	Do interventionists have the time to collaborate and discuss the intervention?	Yes No				
Accountability	Is accountability built in so that interventionists have to demonstrate what they are doing?	Yes No				
Reinforcement	Is reinforcement provided to interventionists who are implementing the intervention?	Yes No				
Meetings	Are meetings held regularly to support interventionists?	Yes No				
Fidelity checklists	Are fidelity checklists used to monitor implementation over time?	Yes No				
Student progress	Are progress monitoring graphs reviewed regularly to determine progress?	Yes No				

Meeting Outline

Procedure	Items to Address	Action Plan		
		Who	Action	By When?
Review benchmark data	What percentage of student needs are being met by Tier 1?			
Set goals for students	What goals need to be set for individual students who are on the borderline of Tier 1 and Tier 2?			
Brainstorm instructional strategies to enhance core instruction	What strategies have worked for teachers before?			
Analyze instructional strategies to enhance core instruction	Which strategies are evidence based? Easy to implement? Effective and efficient?			
Select instructional strategies to be used in the classroom	Are we in agreement that these are the strategies we've selected?			
Plan logistics of the instructional strategies	How much time does each strategy take? How often will teachers implement the strategies?			
Follow up on implementation	What is going well? What needs to be improved?			

Action Item Completion

Directions: Complete this form if follow-up meetings have occurred and action items have not been completed. Use it to address the issues and formulate a plan.

Issue	Who?	Why?	Ideas	Action to Resolve It
Confusion about how to address the action item			• Schedule meetings to clarify confusion. • Provide ongoing support and follow-up. • Offer more time for collaboration.	
Lack of skills to address the action item			• Provide additional trainings. • Provide time to practice. • Offer more time for collaboration.	
Disagreement about the importance of the action item			• Meet with the individual to have a clarifying conversation. • Discuss pros and cons of action items. • Aim for consensus.	
There is little motivation to complete the action item by the due date			• Consider the accountability system. Is it enough? • Consider the reinforcement system. Is it enough? • Speak with the person individually to find out more.	
There is not enough time to complete the action item, given the person's other responsibilities			• Remove another responsibility so he or she can focus on the current one. • Assist the person in prioritizing. • Assign the task to another person.	

CHAPTER 6

Data-Based Progress Monitoring Decisions

Progress monitoring is ongoing assessment that is used to assess students' performance and evaluate the effectiveness of instruction. When used consistently, educators are able to understand a student's response to an intervention. Teams can focus on what to do next to help students, instead of focusing on what was just done. Progress monitoring allows teachers to estimate rates of improvement, identify students who are not demonstrating adequate progress, and compare the efficacy of different forms of instruction to design more effective, individualized instruction. This helps students to learn more because teachers have a better sense of what to do and when to do it.

Data collected from progress monitoring can be used to determine if the intervention is working, if it is not working, or if more data is needed before a decision is made. It allows teams to make decisions about students efficiently, because changes can immediately be made once the data is reviewed. Without this information, it is difficult to determine if the intervention is truly working and if the student is benefiting from the instruction. It becomes a guessing game that is difficult to play without any real data. The U.S. Department of Education, National Center on Response to Intervention (2012) indicates that there are several benefits to engaging in this practice. These include:

- Accelerated learning because students are receiving more appropriate instruction.
- More informed instructional decisions.
- Documentation of student progress for accountability purposes.
- More efficient communication with families and other professionals about students' progress.
- Higher expectations for students by teachers.
- Fewer special education referrals.

Accelerated learning occurs because students are receiving the instruction they need. If data indicate the intervention is not working, it can immediately be changed. The intervention can be changed to a more intensified version or a different intervention that is more instructionally matched. In either case, students are able to receive an intervention that is more effective for their needs. *More informed instructional decisions* refers to teachers having the tools they need to make decisions about students. With progress monitoring data, we have a good understanding of whether the intervention is working or not. Without it, we don't have information to make that decision. It may seem like a student is improving, but it will be difficult to tell if he or she is making real gains that will impact his or her performance. *Documentation for accountability purposes* refers to how teams can show the actual progress that students are making to parents, administration, and the school board. Progress monitoring graphs will demonstrate how students are improving due to the curricular and instructional changes initiated by the school. *More efficient communication with families and other professionals* refers to how graphs can be easily communicated and shared with others. Teams are not going through multiple examples and documents to show progress, rather they can communicate with one graph. These graphs are easy to understand and powerful in what they convey. *Higher expectations for students by teachers* is something that can have a powerful impact on student performance. When teachers have higher standards for students, student performance increases. Because teams set ambitious goals on progress monitoring graphs, teachers will have higher standards, which impacts student performance in a positive way. Finally, *fewer special education referrals* addresses the fact that with interventions in place, fewer students will need special education to remediate their deficits. The interventions are addressing student needs, thus special education will not be needed for some students. We encourage RTI teams to review the list of benefits above and after they have engaged in progress monitoring, indicate which benefits they have seen in their schools. These are powerful reasons for progress monitoring, and once schools start to see the positive effects, it will be easier to continue the process.

In this chapter, we discuss progress monitoring practices. A review of best practices for progress monitoring students is provided. We cover how to prepare for progress monitoring meetings and what documentation is needed for a successful and efficient meeting. Next, goal setting is discussed, and information regarding how to set goals for individual students is covered. Information regarding how to examine RTI using data-based decision making is also examined, as well as modifying interventions for individual students when necessary. Finally, we address how to prevent and confront common roadblocks in progress monitoring meetings.

REVIEW OF EVIDENCE-BASED PROGRESS MONITORING PRACTICES IN RTI

The purpose of progress monitoring is to monitor students' response to core, supplemental, and intensive instruction. It is used at all tiers to monitor student progress and depending on student need, may be used more or less frequently. While many believe that progress monitoring is used only to evaluate progress, it can be used for additional purposes as well. The National Center on Response to Intervention (*www.rtiforsuccess.org*) provides the following questions to consider when using progress monitoring data:

1. Are students meeting short-term goals that will help them reach their long-term goals?
2. Are students making progress at an acceptable rate?
3. Does the instruction need to be adjusted or changed?

First, progress monitoring is used to determine if students are meeting short-term goals that will allow them to meet their long-term goal. These data allow educators to assess whether the student is making adequate progress based on the intervention that is being provided. Using data-based decision-making rules like trendline analysis, student progress is compared to the goal line that was established for the student. More information on trendline analysis is provided later in the chapter. For now, take a moment to review the graph in Figure 6.1. You can see that the student's trendline, which is modeled after her data, is approaching the goal line. This is a positive outcome because the student is making so much growth that she will be able to reach her goal in the specified time. Using progress monitoring data this way allows teams to evaluate student progress in relation to the goal.

Second, progress monitoring data can be used to estimate the rates of improvement. With this information, the student can be compared to peers. The RTI team can answer the question "Is the student making enough progress to catch up to peers?" This is an important question, because it addresses the gap between the student and where he or she needs to be. And this question is most often ignored. Often with progress monitoring data, we focus on the first question, "Are they meeting their short-term goals?" Meeting the short-term goals is a good first step,

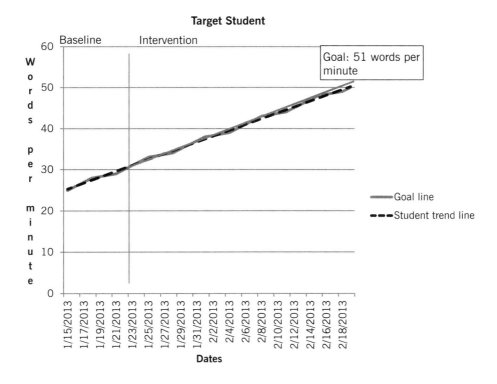

FIGURE 6.1. Positive response to intervention.

but it may not be enough. With students who are performing below the norm, it is not enough just to make progress. These students need to make so much progress that the gap is closed. In Figure 6.2, the student who is discrepant is making great progress. Her performance improves weekly and she is clearing gaining new skills. If you take a moment to view a comparison peer's trendline however, you will notice that he is making progress as well. This is a good thing for him. For our struggling student, we should not be 100% pleased with this outcome. Although it is important to recognize and celebrate her success, we need to make a change to the instruction so that it accelerates her growth. She is making good progress, and so are her peers, so essentially, she may not catch up to them. In Figure 6.3, there is a low-performing student who was initially discrepant from her peers. She was struggling, so an intervention was put in place. She has made significant growth, so much so that she has actually caught up to her peers. This is our ideal outcome. This is the goal for all RTI teams intervening with students. And yet it can be difficult to do without the appropriate instruction. To accomplish this result, we need powerful, carefully matched instruction. This is why selecting evidence-based interventions that are matched to student need is so important.

The third way that progress monitoring data is viewed is by determining whether the intervention is working. The same data is used, the same decision-making rule is used, but the purpose for viewing the data is different. Here we want to identify the intervention or instructional approach that led to the greatest improvement in students. We can compare the effectiveness of different types of instruction and determine what works best for our student population. Essentially, the focus changes so that the instruction is evaluated using student data. We are still evaluating student progress, but to answer a different question. "Is our instruction working?" We can alter the curriculum and we can alter the instruction, which can lead to significant improvements for students. Based on the decision-making rule we choose to use, the RTI team can review student graphs to determine next steps. First, it can be determined that the inter-

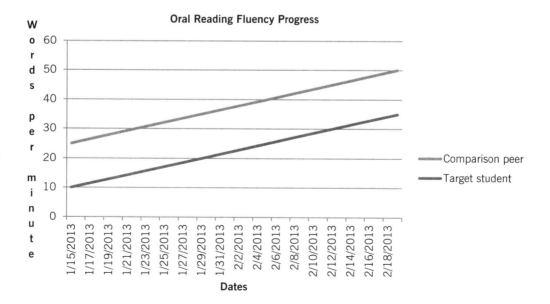

FIGURE 6.2. Student makes progress, but does not catch up to peers.

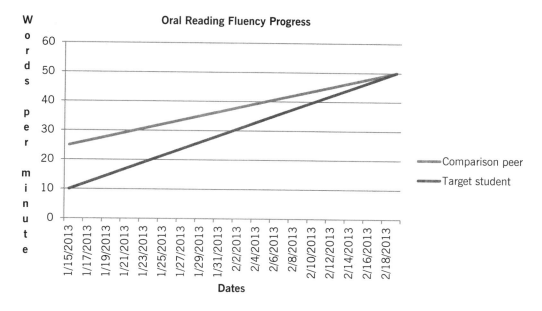

FIGURE 6.3. Student catches up to peers.

vention is successful. Because it's working and the student is making progress, the team can decide to *continue* implementing the intervention because it has worked so well for the student. The team may also decide to *fade* the intervention, because the student has done so well that support may not be needed any longer. Second, the data may indicate that the student is still experiencing difficulties and has not made adequate progress. In this situation, the team may decide that the intervention is matched to student needs, but the student needs a more intensive form of the intervention. For example, the student may be receiving the appropriate intervention, but only for 30 minutes three times per week. Because the student is struggling, the team decides to *intensify* the intervention and provide it to the student for 45 minutes five times per week. The team will continue to collect data, monitor progress, and determine whether the specified changes made a difference. The third option is similar to what was just described, but a different course of action is taken. In this case, the student is still struggling and his or her data indicates he or she needs additional support. The intervention does not appear to be working, because he or she is making minimal progress. The team may decide that the intervention was not well matched to the student's needs and *change* it entirely. The student may have been receiving a reading fluency intervention when in fact he or she really needed to work on phonics. Instead of intensifying the current intervention, the team changes it completely to an intervention better matched to his or her needs. The team would know this through additional problem analysis data that they collect, identifying patterns of strengths and weaknesses in the student's reading skills.

Selecting Progress Monitoring Measures

There are a number of progress monitoring measures that are commercially available. Before teams select measures, we would like to encourage them to review the differences in the two types of measurement: mastery measurement (MM) and general outcome measurement (GOM; L. S. Fuchs & Deno, 1991; L. S. Fuchs & Fuchs, 1999). MM is what many teachers are familiar with. Educators will teach a skill and then test it to determine if students have acquired that skill. For example, a teacher may teach two-digit by two-digit multiplication for a week and then test students on it the following week to determine who has acquired the skill and who needs additional teaching with the skill. This is helpful because it provides great instructional utility to teachers. They can determine which students have gained certain skills and modify their instruction accordingly.

GOM refers to a broader type of assessment, where students are assessed on general domains of skills. In GOM, students are administered standardized measures that have been validated by research (Deno et al., 2001; L. S. Fuchs, 1986; L. S. Fuchs & Fuchs, 1999, 2004). The measures are more reflective of a general outcome in reading, math, and writing. These measures act as indicators because they are broad domains that have been shown to be vital to school success. These measures provide educators a way to determine whether students are making adequate progress with important academic skills. GOMs also have the most evidence behind them regarding their use, therefore we recommend using them to monitor and assess students over time.

To select progress monitoring measures, RTI teams can use the resource provided by the National Center on Response to Intervention. The chart was created by their Technical Review Committee and offers information about the rigor, cost, and implementation requirements of the tools. The tools listed on their website are not necessarily endorsed by them, rather they were submitted to be reviewed. The center issues calls for new submissions for progress monitoring tools every so often and updates to the site will be posted accordingly. We encourage teams to use this tool because of the rigor behind the review process and the amount of information available on the site. With this information, teams can make a decision about the most appropriate progress monitoring tool for their school.

In the area of behavior, teams have a number of tools available to them. The Behavioral and Emotional Screening System (BASC-2 BESS; 2012) is a brief, universal screening system for measuring behavioral and emotional strengths and weaknesses in children and adolescents. It is easily used for behavioral progress monitoring. The direct behavior rating (DBR) can also be used to measure behavioral progress. It is a quick rating that is provided by a teacher on a specific behavior for a student in a specified time period. Finally, the School-Wide Information System (SWIS; 2012) is a web-based information system that easily can be used to track office referral data over time. It is a web-based computer application that allows for collection, summary, and storage of office referral data.

It should also be noted that the National Center on Intensive Interventions (*www.intensiveintervention.org*) is soliciting a call for behavioral interventions and behavioral progress monitoring tools. After the interventions and progress monitoring measures have been submitted, the center will review the tools using a standard process. The reviews are conducted by four Technical Review Committees made up of national experts who together have developed rigorous evidence standards to guide the review process. Information on tools and programs will be disseminated through the center's various technical assistance activities and through their website. This will be a great resource for teams interested in learning more about the effectiveness of various interventions and progress monitoring tools.

Frequency of Progress Monitoring

As soon as a student is identified as at risk for achievement deficits by the universal screening measure, his or her progress should be monitored (Fletcher, Lyon, Fuchs, & Barnes, 2007). We recommend that RTI teams progress monitor students in Tiers 2 and 3, so that timely decisions can be made about the effectiveness of interventions. The frequency (e.g., monthly, weekly) of progress monitoring students in Tiers 2 and 3 can be decided in part by how sensitive the skill is that is being measured. For example, teaching letter naming is comparatively easier with more immediate results than developing a student's reading comprehension. Thus, more frequent measures would be used with letter-naming interventions than with comprehension skills interventions (Florida Center for Reading Research, 2012). However, general guidelines exist that make decision making around the frequency of progress monitoring easier. D. Fuchs and Fuchs recommend that progress should be monitored frequently, at least monthly, but ideally weekly or biweekly (2006). If your team decides to use the DIBELS (2012) or AIMSweb (2012) progress monitoring systems, they recommend monitoring students at the supplemental level monthly and monitoring students at the intensive level weekly. The progress monitoring system would look like Figure 6.4. We recommend that teams follow these guidelines, so that data can be collected on all students regularly and modifications can be made to the instruction as needed.

Goal Setting for Individual Students

Goal setting is one of the most important steps in the progress monitoring process. With a goal, we know where we need to go. Without a goal, progress may be made, but we won't know exactly where we are headed. Goals provide an end point, progress monitoring data allow us to know if we're getting there, and then we can make changes to our path accordingly. As Roland Good, one of the creators of DIBELS, states, the system is "GPS for educators" (personal communication, May 15, 2006). It gives us a way to monitor whether we are headed in the right direction, and if not, we need to turn that boat around.

Consider the following students. Avery and Sam are both sixth-grade students at the same middle school. This middle school has recently begun collecting screening data on sixth-, seventh-, and eighth-grade students to determine who needs additional reading support before they go on to high school. The screening data have been collected for 2 years now, so it is still a fairly new process. Some teachers have adopted the process more than others, and the RTI leadership team is continuing their efforts to train and support all teachers in this new approach. Avery and Sam are both struggling a bit in reading. Their screening results indicated that they are considered in need of supplemental support. As a result, both Avery and Sam are receiving

Tier	Frequency of Progress Monitoring
Tier 1	Three times per year
Tier 2	Monthly
Tier 3	Weekly

FIGURE 6.4. Frequency of progress monitoring.

an additional half hour of reading instruction per day. Both are making progress, but Avery is making more progress than Sam and continues to do well, while Sam's progress is encouraging, but slow. What's the difference? Avery is in Mr. Dodd's classroom and as part of the additional half hour of reading instruction, Mr. Dodd has his aide progress monitor twice per month. Avery has her own graph, with a goal set for June that would have her performing as high as typical peers. Using the goal line and the four-point decision-making rule, the aide knows that Avery is making good progress. Avery's last four data points were above the goal line, so with the help of Mr. Dodd, the aide increased the goal and Avery continues to do well. Avery is proud of her progress and her parents were happy when Mr. Dodd showed them the progress monitoring graphs with ambitious goals that clearly demonstrated her growth.

Sam is in Mr. Trimble's class. Sam is also making good progress. He is benefiting from the additional half hour of instruction per day and seems to be enjoying the work. Mr. Trimble set up a progress monitoring graph, but then forgot to include a goal and didn't make progress monitoring a priority. Mr. Trimble has told his aide not to worry about the progress monitoring because he believes the aide will be able to tell from her observations how Sam is doing and what Sam needs to work on next. And this may be true. The aide may have a sense of how Sam is doing overall and will likely have some ideas regarding what Sam needs to improve. But without a graph and without an established goal, how do we know if Sam is truly making progress? The aide has no data to show by how much Sam is responding. So while he looks like he is performing better, there are no objective data to indicate this. Unfortunately, Sam may be ready for more intensive work with higher expectations, but without the data, Mr. Trimble and the aide do not know to do this. So Sam makes some progress, but not as much as Avery, because without ambitious goals, we don't push students as much. Mr. Trimble owes it to Sam to set high goals and monitor progress. But if Mr. Trimble doesn't know how to do that or why it's so important, the RTI leadership team owes it to Mr. Trimble to train and support him as he learns this new approach.

To write appropriate goals for students, there are two concepts to understand. First, the components of goals, or how they should be written. Second, the process for choosing the goal itself, or finding a criterion that is ambitious yet realistic for the student. Writing goals is not just about selecting a number for a student, but a systematic team decision that considers where a student needs to be and what resources are available to get him or her there. Goals speak to both the rate of progress we need to see as well as the intensity of the instruction. Set a goal too low and the student will never catch up to peers. Set a goal too high and it looks like the student is making insignificant progress when he or she may be doing well. Goal setting is an important part of what we do to help students and it is an important team decision to make.

Allowing all participants to be involved with goal setting can increase the chance that the goal is appropriate, ambitious, and reasonable.

A goal is comprised of five main components: time, student, behavior, criterion, and conditions. Time refers to when the goal is being set for in terms of weeks or months. The student is the one in consideration and the behavior is what we would like him or her to do (read orally, compute math problems, write a total number of words, stay in his or her seat). The criterion refers to the number, or the goal itself. The conditions or materials refer to the environment or with what materials the student will accomplish the task. The following examples include all five components:

Reading

- By May 15, 2013, Charlie will read 140 words per minute when given a sixth-grade oral reading fluency probe for 1 minute.
- By May 20, 2013, Aven will read 90 words per minute with 95% accuracy when given a second-grade oral reading fluency probe for 1 minute.
- In 20 weeks, Laticia will read 50 words per minute when given a first-grade oral reading fluency probe for 1 minute for 3 consecutive weeks.

Math

- In 16 weeks, Alejandro will compute 20 problems correct when given a second-grade math computation probe for 2 minutes.
- By June 8, 2014, Smith will complete 25 multiplication math facts when given a third-grade math facts probe for 1 minute.
- By June 1, 2014, Tevon will complete 15 math application problems when given a seventh-grade math application probe for 7 minutes.

Written Language

- In 20 weeks, Mark will write 20 correct writing sequences when given a story starter with 1 minute to think and 3 minutes to write.
- By June 1, 2013, Alexander will write 40 total words when given a story starter with 1 minute to think and 3 minutes to write.
- In 15 weeks, Reese will write 30 words spelled correctly when given a story starter with 1 minute to think and 3 minutes to write.

Behavior

- By June 5, 2014, Juliana will be rated as "on task" on her behavior-monitoring form 90% of the time during her morning classes (language arts, math, and PE).
- In 20 weeks, Chase will earn a 4/5 on the behavior-rating form when rated by his math teacher during math class.
- By May 1, 2014, Cassandra will earn a 5/5 on the prosocial skills behavior-rating form when rated by her teacher during science and social studies.

Once the team has adopted the structure for goals, they can move to selecting the criterion itself and following a process to determine how to select ambitious but realistic goals. There are three ways to do this. First, the team can use local norms to determine where the student should be performing at the end of the year. In this approach, the first consideration is determining where the student is currently performing at his or her grade level. This is known as the baseline and it is established by collecting three scores and taking the median. If the student can perform adequately with grade-level material but just needs to make additional progress, then the goal can be written for his or her current grade-level material. For example, if the student is in third grade and is reading at the third-grade instructional level but performing lower than peers, the goal can be set within grade-level material. If the student is reading 90 words per minute and the team feels he or she should be reading 110 words per minute by the end of the third-grade year, the goal can be set at 110 on third-grade-level materials.

For many students who struggle however, it is often that they are not performing adequately at their grade level and the team will need to sample back with lower grade-level passages. To do this, administer lower grade-level passages in descending order until they find the grade level where the student is at in the instructional level. This is the cornerstone of the goal-setting process, so teams can select what grade-level material will be most appropriate. For example, if the student is in fifth grade and is reading at the second-grade level, the team will monitor using second-grade passages and use the established goal for second grade at the end of the school year.

Second, the team can use the exact same process as described above but decide to use national norms instead of local norms. In this instance, the team will use the national norms for spring to determine where all students should be performing at the end of the year. For example, the team will find the corresponding number that represents the 50th percentile for the spring national norms. If that number is 160 words per minute, the team can decide to set the goal to be 160 words for a springtime goal.

Third, teams can use established growth rates that have been determined by research. Using these growth rates, teams can do simple math to determine where a student should be performing at the end of the intervention. Deno et al. (2001) summarized the different growth rates found by researchers. They provide an informative table that includes growth rates to consider. For example, if the growth rate for oral reading in third grade is one word per week, the team would take the student's baseline (e.g., 50 words per minute) and add the product of 1 (one word per week) × 15 weeks (the length of the intervention). The equation is 50 + 1(15) = 65 words per minute. That would be a reasonable goal for an intervention that occurs for 15 weeks.

The final option is to use an intraindividual framework. The team can calculate the student's typical rate of growth. To do this, collect at least eight data points. Next, find the difference between the highest and lowest score. Divide that number by the number of weeks the data was collected and multiply it by 1.5. This is the student's growth rate. Take the growth rate and multiply it by the number of weeks until the end of the year, which will be the length of the intervention. Finally, add this number to the baseline and that will be the goal for the end of the year. For example, the student's eight CBM scores were 20, 22, 19, 25, 23, 24, 25, and 20. The difference between the highest and lowest score is 6 (25–19). Divide this number by 8 (because there are 8 weeks of data) and multiply it by 1.5: (6/8) × 1.5 = 1.125. Let's say there are 20 weeks until the end of the year. Multiply 1.125 × 20 = 22.5. This represents the expected growth. Now, we will add this number to our baseline score (which, if we take the median of all of the baseline data points, is 22.5). So add 22.5 + 22.5 = 45 words per minute. This would be the goal for the end of the year. Figure 6.5 summarizes all of the goal-setting options.

Examining RTI

Examining a student's response to the intervention is the crux of an RTI approach. It is an important step that all too often is forgotten because teams get caught up in organizing the logistics of intervention implementation. In this section we will review important concepts around evaluating interventions and determining whether they were effective for students. Before we address graphing, the importance of intervention fidelity is discussed.

The first question teams should ask before evaluating the data is "Was the intervention implemented as planned?" This is an important question because it determines whether the

Using End-of-Year Benchmark Goals

The end-of-the-year benchmark goals on a measure of oral reading fluency are as follows:

First grade	50 words per minute
Second grade	100 words per minute
Third grade	120 words per minute
Fourth grade	130 words per minute
Fifth grade	135 words per minute
Sixth grade	139 words per minute

Bryn is a sixth-grade student. She is reading at the fourth-grade level. She is receiving a Tier 2 intervention and the team wants to monitor her progress in oral reading fluency. The team decides to use the end-of-the-year established goals. She will be monitored at her instructional level (to answer the question "Is she making progress with the intervention?") and she will be monitored at her current grade level (to answer the question "Is she catching up to peers?"). The team sets her fourth-grade goal at 130 words per minute and sets her sixth-grade goal at 139 words per minute.

Addison is a third-grade student. He is reading at the second-grade level. He is receiving a Tier 2 intervention in reading and the team wants to monitor his progress using oral reading fluency. The team decides to set the goals using end-of-the-year established benchmarks. They monitor Addison on second-grade-level probes and set the goal for 100 words per minute and they monitor him on third-grade-level probes and set the goal for 120 words per minute.

Growth Rates

Shoshanna is a third-grade student. She is currently reading 50 words per minute. Shoshanna is receiving a Tier 2 intervention and the team wants to select a goal to monitor her progress in oral reading fluency. The team uses established growth rates and sees that on average, she should be making 1 word-per-week growth. It is the beginning of January and the goal will be set for the end of the year in May, which is 20 weeks from now. The calculation would be:

Baseline + # of weeks (growth rate) = goal
50 + 20(1) = 70 words per minute

Charlie is a fifth-grade student. He is currently reading 65 words per minute. Charlie is receiving a Tier 3 intervention and the team wants to select a goal to monitor his progress in oral reading fluency. The team uses established growth rates and sees that on average, he should be making .5 words-per-week growth. It is the beginning of October and the goal will be set for the end of the year in May, which is 32 weeks from now. The calculation would be:

Baseline + # of weeks (growth rate) = goal
65 + 32(.5) = 81 words per minute

Tiandra is a seventh-grade student. She is currently reading 80 words per minute. Tiandra is receiving a Tier 3 intervention and the team wants to select a goal to monitor her progress in oral reading fluency. The team uses established growth rates and sees that on average, she should be making .6 words-per-week growth. It is the beginning of January and the goal will be set for the end of the year in May, which is 20 weeks from now. The calculation would be:

Baseline + # of weeks (growth rate) = goal
80 + 20(.6) = 92 words per minute

(continued)

FIGURE 6.5. Setting goals.

Intraindividual Framework

Finn is a first-grade student and the team has monitored him on oral reading fluency for the last 8 weeks. His baseline data points are 15, 17, 18, 18, 19, 19, 20, and 20. The difference between the highest and lowest score is 5: 5/8 weeks is .625, and when multiplied by 1.5 the result is .9375. This represents the student's growth rate per week: .9375 × 12 weeks of the intervention is 11.25 words total. The team adds that to Finn's baseline (19) and the result is 30.25 words. This will be the goal for the end of the intervention, which is 12 weeks later.

Taveon is a fifth-grade student and the team has monitored him on oral reading fluency for the last 8 weeks. His baseline data points are 110, 110, 111, 111, 111, 112, 112, and 112. The difference between the highest and lowest score is 2: 2/8 weeks is .25, and when multiplied by 1.5 the result is .375. This represents the student's growth rate per week: .375 × 16 weeks of the intervention is 6 words total. The team adds that to Finn's baseline (111) and the result is 117 words. This will be the goal for the end of the intervention, which is 16 weeks later.

FIGURE 6.5. *(continued)*

data on the graph actually means something. Without fidelity, the data is lacking in meaning, and data-based decision-making rules cannot be used. As mentioned in Chapter 5, supporting fidelity systemically is essential for the adoption of new programs. If the team finds that an intervention was not implemented with fidelity, those issues should be addressed first. Once full implementation occurs, data can be reviewed using data-based decision-making rules to determine effectiveness.

When teams evaluate data on a regular basis, it is because they are competent with three core components: (1) graphing conventions, (2) goal setting (as was discussed earlier), and (3) data-based decision-making rules. The basic conventions of graphing are reviewed and the utility and application of data-based decision-making rules are described. With these core skills, teams will be able to create, analyze, and use progress monitoring graphs to make instructionally relevant and beneficial decisions for students.

Graphing Conventions

For teams using a commercially available benchmarking system, the graphs are built for you and are often easily understood. There are a number of features built into the graphs that help teams analyze data. For teams collecting data but not entering it into a commercially available system, graphing conventions can be more difficult, only because you are creating the graph yourself. For these teams, it is important to understand the necessary components of graphs so that data can be effectively graphed.

In Figure 6.6, graphing conventions are presented. See *A* and *B* for the *x*- and *y*-axes. On the *y* axis, the dimension that is being measured will be listed. For example, if the measure is problems correct per minute, that is what would be written next to the *y*-axis. On the *x*-axis, time is represented by dates. The team then starts by collecting baseline data, represented by *C*. Once three baseline data points have been collected, a vertical line can be drawn after the baseline data points to represent the start of the intervention. The words *Baseline* and *Intervention* should be listed above the graph, as shown in *D*. To draw the goal line, the team should select a goal for the student and mark it on the graph. Then, the median of the baseline data points should

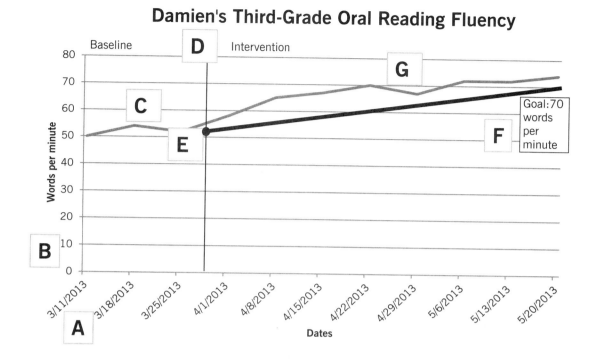

FIGURE 6.6. Graphing conventions.

be determined and it should be marked on the vertical line that separates the baseline and intervention, as in *E*. From the median baseline data point on the vertical line, the diagonal goal line can be drawn to the goal. This is represented by *F*. Now the team can begin collecting intervention data points, as shown in *G*. The next step would then be to use a data-based decision-making rule to evaluate the effectiveness of the intervention. There are a number of ways teams can evaluate student progress. How the data are evaluated depends on what data collection system you are using and what decision-making rule you choose to use. We will discuss the two most common approaches for decision making: which are the four-point rule and trendline analysis.

The Four-Point Decision-Making Rule

The four-point rule for decision making points our attention to the last four data points in the intervention phase. To use this rule, there should be at least six data points in the intervention phase and the intervention should have been occurring for at least 3 weeks. We discuss ascending goal lines first. If the last four data points are above the goal line, the decision is that the intervention is successful. The goal should be increased or the student should be phased out of the intervention. In this case, we have a positive outcome and can make one of two decisions. If the student has met the goal and is now performing similar to peers, this is a great opportunity to phase out the intervention and provide instruction solely in the general education setting. This is the best-case scenario, one that should be celebrated. In the second outcome related to positive growth, the student may have the last four data points above the line and the team decides to increase the goal and continue to provide the intervention. This is also something to celebrate, but here the team feels the student needs more intervention time before being phased completely out of the intervention. It's possible the student is not yet performing similar to peers or that the team feels the student needs more support before removing the intervention completely. To raise the goal, the steps are simple. Take the last three intervention data points and find the median, or the middle score. These last three data points are acting as your new baseline, to provide a starting point for selecting a new goal. Find the median and write a new goal that will continue to encourage ambitious growth. The team can create a new graph with a new goal and then continue to collect data and monitor progress (see Figure 6.7).

If the last four data points are below the goal line, the decision is that the intervention is not working and instructional modifications need to be made. In this case, the student is not responding to the intervention and his or her data indicates that inadequate progress has been made toward the goal. This is a critical moment where the team decides either to change the intervention or intensify the current intervention. This is a decision that should be made based on the student's needs, his or her problem analysis data, and the rate of progress. When a change is made, we indicate that by inserting a vertical phase-change line into the graph. After the phase change, we can indicate the name of the new intervention and continue to collect data with the revisions in place (see Figure 6.8).

The third option when using this rule is that the last four data points are both above and below the goal line. While the data may look like the intervention is working, because it is following the line, there are some data points that are still below the line. Because of this, the decision would be to continue the intervention and collect more data before a decision is made. By

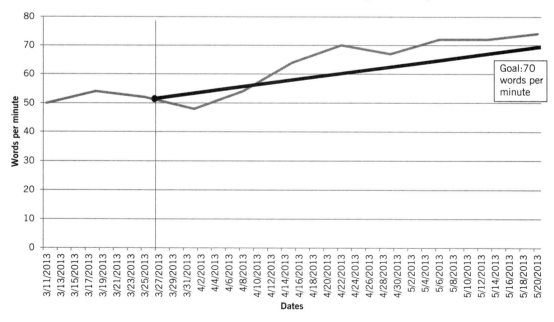

FIGURE 6.7. Four data points above with an ascending goal line.

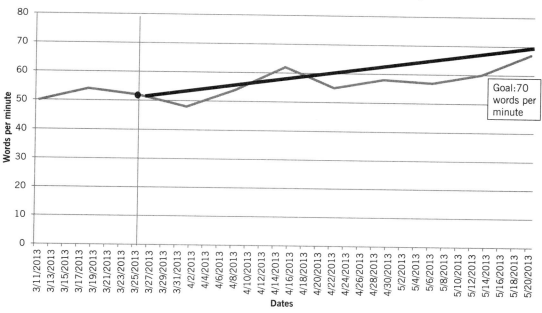

FIGURE 6.8. Four data points below with an ascending goal line.

collecting more data, teams can have more confidence in their decision to either keep or change the intervention (see Figure 6.9).

With descending goal lines, the rule is reversed to reflect the fact that we are monitoring behaviors that we want to decrease. Graphs with descending goals are used to monitor behaviors that occur too frequently for the school setting. While these graphs are necessary and appropriate, we also recommend monitoring positive prosocial behaviors for students as well. When students need to work on decreasing negative behaviors, it is equally important to monitor their display of positive behaviors (see Figure 6.10). With descending goal lines, the rule is that if the last four points are below the line, the decision is that the intervention is working. The goal can either be decreased or if the student has achieved the goal and the team feels like there is no more work to do, the intervention can be ceased, because the student is now successful. If the last four data points are above the line, the intervention is not working and an instructional change should be made. If the last four data points are both above and below the line, more data should be collected before a decision is made (see Figures 6.11–6.13).

Trendline Analysis

Trendline analysis is another way teams can choose to evaluate data. When using this method, teams evaluate the student's trendline compared to the goal line that was set. There are three possible decisions that can be made from evaluating the trendline in relation to the goal line. First, the trendline may be approaching the goal line, which would indicate a positive outcome. In this scenario, the student is making so much growth that his or her trendline is on target

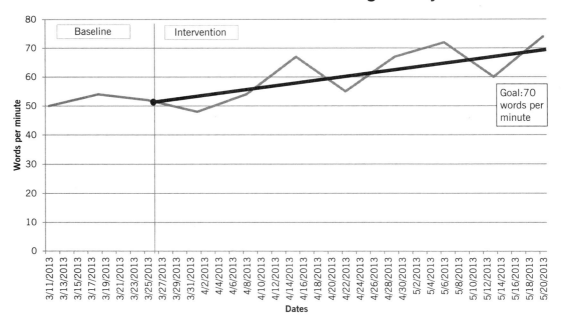

FIGURE 6.9. Four data points above and below with an ascending goal line.

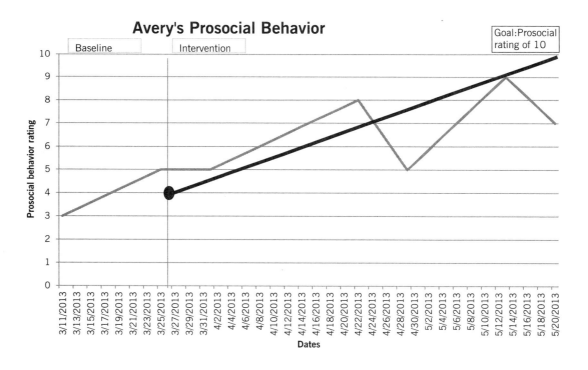

FIGURE 6.10. Prosocial behavior monitoring.

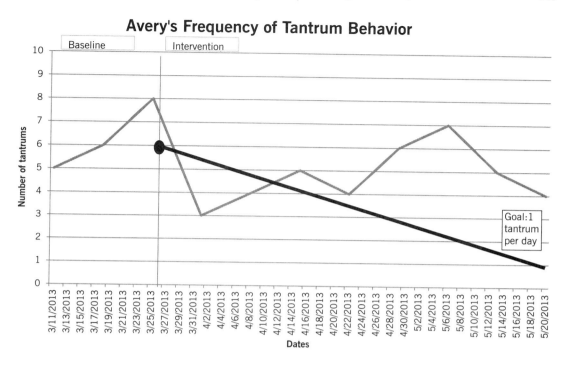

FIGURE 6.11. Four data points above with a descending goal line.

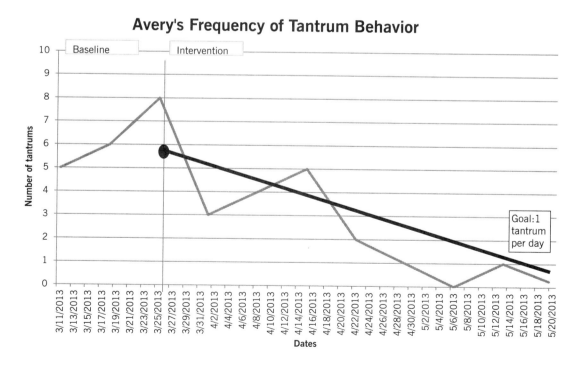

FIGURE 6.12. Four data points below with a descending goal line.

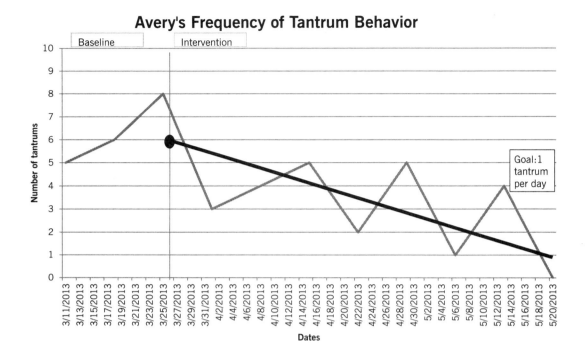

FIGURE 6.13. Four data points above and below with an ascending goal line.

for meeting the goal line. This is a successful outcome and the decision will be made to either increase the goal or fade out the intervention (see Figure 6.14). Second, the trendline may be increasing and it is following the goal line's path, but it does not appear that the trendline will ever meet the goal line. In this case, the outcome would be questionable. It's questionable because the trend is positive and the student is making progress, but not enough to meet the established goal. The team should be cautiously optimistic that the student is on the right path, but the intervention needs to be intensified. An instructional change needs to be made to ensure that the student will reach the specified goal (see Figure 6.15). Third, the outcome may be poor, because the student's trendline is not approaching the goal line, and in fact, the gap between the two lines may be getting larger. In this case, the intervention is clearly not working and a significant instructional change needs to be made immediately. The student is clearly not benefiting from the intervention and the team should take this information and make changes in an efficient manner. At this point, weeks have passed, the intervention has not worked, and so time has been underutilized. An intense, evidence-based, instructionally matched intervention should be selected next so that the student has an opportunity now to make growth (see Figure 6.16).

MODIFYING INTERVENTIONS FOR INDIVIDUAL STUDENTS

When students are not making progress with an intervention, the assumption is that the intervention is not matched to their needs and it should be changed. This may be the case if the intervention is not matched to their needs. If a student needs to improve his or her early phonics

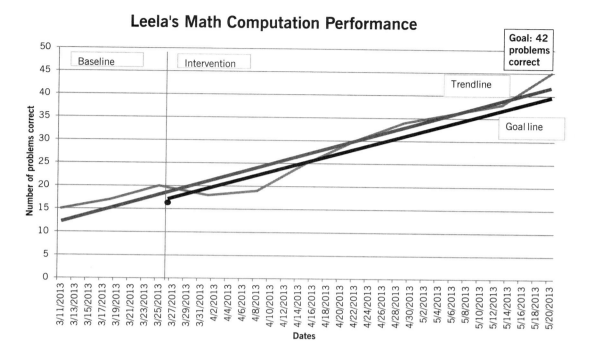

FIGURE 6.14. Positive RTI.

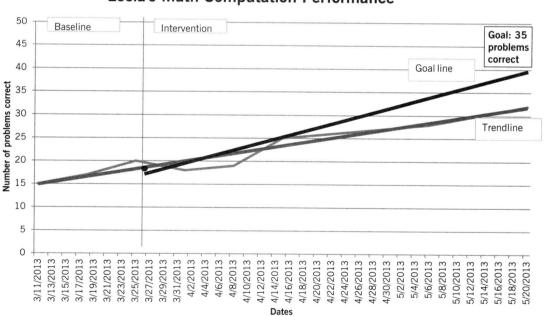

FIGURE 6.15. Questionable RTI.

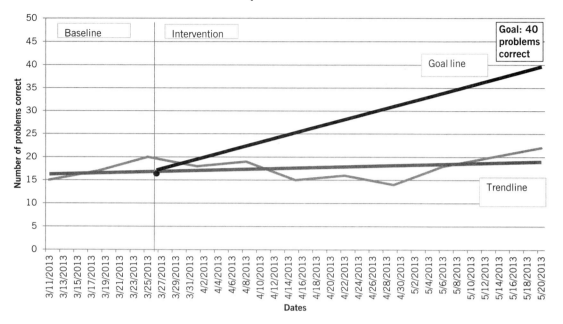

FIGURE 6.16. Poor RTI.

skills and the intervention targets advanced phonics skills, the match is off and the student will not improve the skills he or she needs to. If a student needs to improve his or her phonemic awareness skills and he or she is placed in a reading fluency intervention, the student will also not likely benefit from a program that is too difficult for him or her. In these cases, yes, the intervention program needs to be changed. If a student is appropriately matched to an intervention though, but is not making adequate progress, then it is likely the intervention needs to be intensified. To intensify instruction without changing the program, teams can modify the alterable variables. Alterable variables refer to the aspects of instruction that can be changed (see Figure 6.17). By changing the alterable variables, teams can intensify instruction for students without placing them into completely different intervention groups.

The first alterable variable is time. A student may be receiving an intervention for 45 minutes three times per week. Increasing the frequency of the intervention to 5 days per week and increasing the time to an additional 60 minutes would be an example of how time can be

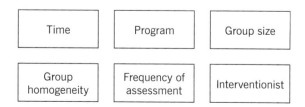

FIGURE 6.17. Alterable variables.

increased. Increasing the time is a decision the team must make based on student needs and availability in the schedule. While additional time may be hard to find, it can be a powerful factor in influencing student performance. Another alterable variable is grouping. The intervention group can be changed by size and constitution. First, group size can be reduced to provide more individualized attention to students. Second, who comprises the group can be changed so there is more homogeneity among the group. If all students have to work on the same skill, the instruction in the group can be targeted toward their areas of need. The students then have an opportunity to learn from the instructor and learn from each other as they respond to the same prompts.

The frequency of assessment can also be changed. With students placed in intervention groups, their progress should be monitored more frequently so it can be determined whether the intervention is successful. As mentioned earlier, students in Tier 2 can be progress monitored one to two times per month, and students in Tier 3 can be progress monitored one time per week. With these data, decisions can be made promptly about intervention effectiveness.

Another alterable variable that can be modified is who provides the intervention. The instructional delivery can be changed by (1) keeping the same interventionist and providing coaching as necessary, (2) keeping the same interventionist and providing more structured professional development, and (3) changing the interventionist if there continue to be issues with intervention implementation and fidelity. It is helpful to conduct regular fidelity checks using available checklists and observations so that this alterable variable can be addressed as need be. With regular checks, the team will have information about how the intervention is being presented, what is working, and what may need to be changed. If multiple aspects of intervention delivery need to be changed, the team then has to decide if coaching or professional development are provided, or the interventionist is changed completely.

Sample student files are provided in Figures 6.18–6.21 to demonstrate how alterable variables can be modified to increase the level of instructional support. In Emerson's original instructional planning form (IPF), she was receiving Corrective Reading twice per week for 45 minutes in a semilarge group (12 students) and was being progress monitored on seventh- and fifth-grade measures twice per month. Her teacher collected data over the next few months and the RTI team reconvened to review the data in February. They noticed that she made more progress at her instructional level (fifth grade) and made some progress at her current grade level (seventh grade) but did not meet her goals for either measure by February. After talking to the teacher, the team agreed that the Corrective Reading program was instructionally matched to Emerson's skills, so they decided to increase the intensity a bit. In the revised IPF, she received the program three times a week for an hour and 15 minutes. This increased intensity by modifying the alterable variables assisted her in making more progress by the end of the school year. (See Figure 6.18.)

In Smith's original IPF, he was receiving the Connecting Math Concepts program for three times per week for 40 minutes. After reviewing his progress weeks later, the team decided that it appeared that Smith was not making progress on the fifth-grade measures, which represent his current grade level. Knowing that Smith's instructional level was third grade, they decided to measure his progress using third-grade math computation and math concepts and applications probes as well. In the revised IPF, Smith is now being monitored using two different measures at two different grade levels (fifth and third). (See Figure 6.19.)

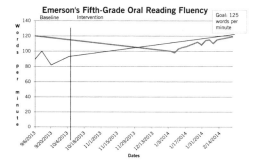

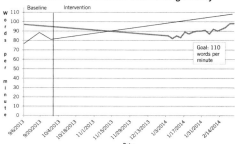

ORIGINAL INSTRUCTIONAL PLANNING FORM

Intervention Planning

Student: Emerson   Grade: Seventh grade   Intervention: Tier 2
Teacher: Mr. Dahl

Date	Target skills	Instructional strategies	Materials	Logistics (include who will teach, when, where, and how often)	Assessment (progress monitoring tools)	Follow-up date
October 5, 2013	Fluency and advanced decoding (multisyllabic words, irregular words, r-controlled vowels)	Corrective Reading	Corrective Reading materials	Who: Mrs. Barney When: Mondays and Wednesdays from 1:00 to 1:45 P.M. Where: Mrs. Barney's room How often: Twice per week for 45 minutes Group: Tier 2 students in study hall (12 students total in group)	AIMSweb oral reading fluency seventh- and fifth-grade measures twice per month	February 5, 2014

Goal: In 16 weeks, Emerson will read 110 words per minute when given a seventh-grade oral reading fluency probe for 1 minute. (seventh-grade goal for current grade level).

In 16 weeks, Emerson will read 125 words per minute when given a fifth-grade oral reading fluency probe for 1 minute. (fifth-grade goal for instructional reading level).

Parent signature: _____   Interventionist signature (if different from teacher): _____

Teacher signature: _____   RTI team facilitator signature: _____

REVISED INSTRUCTIONAL PLANNING FORM

Intervention Planning

Student: Emerson   Grade: Seventh grade   Intervention: Tier 2
Teacher: Mr. Dahl

Date	Target skills	Instructional strategies	Materials	Logistics (include who will teach, when, where, and how often)	Assessment (progress monitoring tools)	Follow-up date
February 5, 2014	Fluency and advanced decoding (multisyllabic words, irregular words, r-controlled vowels)	Corrective Reading	Corrective Reading materials	Who: Mrs. Barney When: Mondays, Wednesdays, and Fridays from 1:00 to 2:15 P.M. Where: Mrs. Barney's room How often: Three times per week for 1 hour and 15 minutes Group: Tier 2 students in study hall (12 students total in group)	AIMSweb oral reading fluency seventh- and fifth-grade measures twice per month	June 5, 2014

Goal: In 16 weeks, Emerson will read 110 words per minute when given a seventh-grade oral reading fluency probe for 1 minute (seventh-grade goal for current grade level).

In 16 weeks, Emerson will read 125 words per minute when given a fifth-grade oral reading fluency probe for 1 minute (fifth-grade goal for instructional reading level).

Parent signature: _____   Interventionist signature (if different from teacher): _____

Teacher signature: _____   RTI team facilitator signature: _____

FIGURE 6.18. Sample student file for Emerson.

Intervention Planning

Student: Smith   Grade: Fifth grade   Intervention: Tier 2
Teacher: Mr. Channen

Date	Target skills	Instructional strategies	Materials	Logistics (include who will teach, when, where, and how often)	Assessment (Progress monitoring tools)	Follow-up date
October 5, 2012	Math computation skills: single-digit by double-digit multiplication, double-digit by double-digit multiplication, geometry Math application (word problems) skills: comparisons, action word problems, money, time	Connecting Math Concepts	Connecting Math Concepts materials	Who: Mrs. Zander When: Tuesdays, Thursdays and Fridays from 3:00 to 3:40 P.M. Where: Mrs. Zander's room How often: Three times per week for 40 minutes Group: Tier 2 students (six students total in group)	AIMSweb math computation and math concepts and applications fifth measures twice per month	January 5, 2013

Goal: In 12 weeks, Smith will complete 10 math computation problems when given a fifth-grade math computation probe for 8 minutes.

In 12 weeks, Smith will complete eight math concepts and applications problems when given a fifth-grade math concepts and applications probe for 8 minutes.

Parent signature: _____   Interventionist signature (if different from teacher): _____

Teacher signature: _____   RTI team facilitator signature: _____

REVISED INSTRUCTIONAL PLANNING FORM

Intervention Planning

Student: Smith   Grade: Fifth grade   Intervention: Tier 2
Teacher: Mr. Channen

Date	Target skills	Instructional strategies	Materials	Logistics (include who will teach, when, where, and how often)	Assessment (progress monitoring tools)	Follow-up date
January 5, 2013	Math computation skills: single-digit by double-digit multiplication, double-digit by double-digit multiplication, geometry Math application (word problems) skills: comparisons, action word problems, money, time	Connecting Math Concepts	Connecting Math Concepts materials	Who: Mrs. Zander When: Tuesdays, Thursdays, and Fridays from 3:00 to 3:40 P.M. Where: Mrs. Zander's room How often: Three times per week for 40 minutes Group: Tier 2 students (six students total in group)	AIMSweb math computation and math concepts and applications fifth-grade measures twice per month AIMSweb math computation and math concepts and applications third-grade measures twice per month	June 5, 2013

Goal: In 12 weeks, Smith will complete 10 math computation problems when given a fifth-grade math computation probe for 8 minutes.

In 12 weeks, Smith will complete eight math concepts and applications problems when given a fifth-grade math concepts and applications probe for 8 minutes.

In 12 weeks, Smith will complete 18 math computation problems when given a third-grade math computation probe for 8 minutes.

In 12 weeks, Smith will complete 14 math concepts and applications problems when given a third-grade math concepts and applications probe for 8 minutes.

Parent signature: _____   Interventionist signature (if different from teacher): _____
Teacher signature: _____   RTI team facilitator signature: _____

FIGURE 6.19. Sample student file for Smith.

Intervention Planning

Student: Dahlia   Grade: Eighth grade   Intervention: Tier 3
Teacher: Mr. Shotten

Date	Target skills	Instructional strategies	Materials	Logistics (include who will teach, when, where, and how often)	Assessment (progress monitoring tools)	Follow-up date
October 5, 2012	Language arts and writing skills: capitalization, punctuation, spelling, writing complete sentences, paragraph structure	Expressive Writing	Expressive Writing materials	Who: Mrs. Gill When: Mondays, Tuesdays, Wednesdays, and Thursdays Where: Mrs. Gill's room How often: Four times per week for 50 minutes Group: Tier 3 students (nine students total in group)	Written expression story starters twice per month	February 5, 2013

Goal: In 16 weeks, Dahlia will write 40 total words when given a story starter with 1 minute to think and 3 minutes to write.

In 16 weeks, Dahlia will write 35 correct writing sequences when given a story starter with 1 minute to think and 3 minutes to write.

Parent signature: _____   Interventionist signature (if different from teacher): _____

Teacher signature: _____   RTI team facilitator signature: _____

REVISED INSTRUCTIONAL PLANNING FORM

Intervention Planning

Student: Dahlia   Grade: Eighth grade   Intervention: Tier 3
Teacher: Mr. Shotten

Date	Target skills	Instructional strategies	Materials	Logistics (include who will teach, when, where, and how often)	Assessment (progress monitoring tools)	Follow-up date
February 5, 2013	Language arts and writing skills: capitalization, punctuation, spelling, writing complete sentences, paragraph structure	Expressive Writing	Expressive Writing materials	Who: Mrs. Gill When: Mondays, Tuesdays, Wednesdays, and Thursdays Where: Mrs. Gill's room How often: Four times per week for 50 minutes Group: Tier 3 students (four students total in group)	Written expression story starters once per week	June 5, 2013

Goal: In 16 weeks, Dahlia will write 40 total words when given a story starter with 1 minute to think and 3 minutes to write.

In 16 weeks, Dahlia will write 35 correct writing sequences when given a story starter with 1 minute to think and 3 minutes to write.

Parent signature: _____   Interventionist signature (if different from teacher): _____

Teacher signature: _____   RTI team facilitator signature: _____

FIGURE 6.20. Sample student file for Dahlia.

ORIGINAL BEHAVIORAL SUPPORT PLAN

Name: Grant   Grade: Fourth grade   Teacher: Mrs. Franklin   Date: October 5, 2012

Problem Behavior: Following directions, waiting his turn, whining behaviors.
Hypothesized Function: To gain individual attention from the teacher and his peers.
Replacement Behavior: To raise his hand to obtain the same individual attention and follow directions to receive positive reinforcement.

Proactive/Preventative Strategies: *What antecedent and setting-event strategies will be used to decrease the problem behavior and/or increase the replacement behavior?*

Procedures/Strategies	Materials	Schedule (when/how often)	Where	Person(s) Responsible
Preferential seating close to the teacher.		Throughout day	General education setting	General education teacher and special education teacher
Precorrections and reminders when Grant comes in from recess to remember to (1) raise his hand, and (2) work quietly at his desk.		Every day after recess	General education setting	General education teacher and special education teacher

Alternative Strategies to Be Taught: *How will the coping skills be taught?*

Procedures/Strategies	Materials	Schedule (when/how often)	Where	Person(s) Responsible
Guided reflection times using Hassle Log to review problem behaviors and determine changes for next time.	Hassle log	Whenever Grant engages in a serious defiant behavior	General education classroom	Special education teacher

Reinforcement Strategies: *How will the behavior be reinforced?*

Procedures/Strategies	Materials	Schedule (when/how often)	Where	Person(s) Responsible
Positive reinforcement (earns points) for raising his hand during whole-class instruction. Earning a total number of points will result in a daily prize. Giving reinforcement will be paired with verbal praise specific to the behavior that earned it.	Classroom points Reinforcers like computer time, staying in for recess, and looking at the fish tank in the office or library	High rate of frequency throughout day	General education classroom	General education teacher

Consequence Strategies: *What consequence strategies will be used to decrease the problem behavior?*

Procedures/Strategies	Materials	Schedule (when/how often)	Where	Person(s) Responsible
When Grant engages in serious defiant behavior, he will complete a "Hassle Log," where he debriefs the situation with the general education teacher.	Designated Hassle Log sheet	Whenever Grant engages in defiant behavior	At his desk or in a quiet spot in the room with the teacher	Special education teacher

Decision-Making Plan: *What are the procedures in place to determine whether the plan is working and/or if changes are needed?*

How will the data be summarized? Data will be charted and graphed weekly.

How many data points/length of time is needed before decision making? Typically four data points.

What is the decision-making rule to be used to make decisions about the data? Four-point decision-making rule. If behavior increases, plan will be revised to address concerns. If Grant is successful, task demands will gradually increase and/or decrease in reinforcement schedule.

FIGURE 6.21. Sample student file for Grant. Form based on Heartland Area Education Agency, Iowa.

REVISED BEHAVIORAL SUPPORT PLAN

Name: Grant   Grade: Fourth grade   Teacher: Mrs. Franklin   Date: February 5, 2013

Problem Behavior: Following directions, waiting his turn, whining behaviors.
Hypothesized Function: To gain individual attention from the teacher and his peers.
Replacement Behavior: To raise his hand to obtain the same individual attention and follow directions to receive positive reinforcement.

Proactive/Preventative Strategies: *What antecedent and setting-event strategies will be used to decrease the problem behavior and/or increase the replacement behavior?*

Procedures/Strategies	Materials	Schedule (when/how often)	Where	Person(s) Responsible
Preferential seating close to the teacher.		Throughout day	General education setting	General education teacher and special education teacher
Precorrections and reminders when Grant comes in from recess to remember to (1) raise his hand, and (2) work quietly at his desk.		Every day after recess	General education setting	General education teacher and special education teacher
Verbally remind Grant and provide encouragement each morning about how to earn points on the reinforcement card.		Every day each morning	General education setting	General education teacher
Visual reminder on desk of hand raising	Picture cue	Throughout day	General education setting	General education teacher

Alternative Strategies to Be Taught: *How will the coping skills be taught?*

Procedures/Strategies	Materials	Schedule (when/how often)	Where	Person(s) Responsible
Ongoing instruction on how to wait his turn and follow directions in each setting in the school. "Grant, remember, you need to _____ when you're at lunch."		Daily basis	All school settings	General education teacher

Verbal prompts to listen quietly. "Grant, you need to be quiet while others are talking."		Throughout the day	All school settings	General education teacher
Guided reflection times using Hassle Log to review problem behaviors and determine changes for next time.	Hassle log	Whenever Grant engages in a serious defiant behavior	General education classroom	Special education teacher

Reinforcement Strategies: *How will the behavior be reinforced?*

Procedures/Strategies	Materials	Schedule (when/how often)	Where	Person(s) Responsible
Positive reinforcement (earns points) for raising his hand during whole-class instruction. Earning a total number of points will result in a daily prize. Giving reinforcement will be paired with verbal praise specific to the behavior that earned it.	Classroom points Reinforcers like computer time, staying in for recess, and looking at the fish tank in the office or library	High rate of frequency throughout day	General education classroom	General education teacher

FIGURE 6.21. *(continued)*

Consequence Strategies: *What consequence strategies will be used to decrease the problem behavior?*

Procedures/Strategies	Materials	Schedule (when/how often)	Where	Person(s) Responsible
When Grant engages in serious defiant behavior, he will complete a "Hassle Log," where he debriefs the situation with the general education teacher.	Designated Hassle Log sheet	Whenever Grant engages in defiant behavior	At his desk or in a quiet spot in the room with the teacher.	Special education teacher

Decision-Making Plan: *What are the procedures in place to determine whether the plan is working and/or if changes are needed?*

How will the data be summarized? Data will be charted and graphed weekly.

How many data points/length of time is needed before decision making? Typically four data points.

What is the decision-making rule to be used to make decisions about the data? Four-point decision-making rule. If behavior increases, plan will be revised to address concerns. If Grant is successful, task demands will gradually increase and/or decrease in reinforcement schedule.

FIGURE 6.21. *(continued)*

In Dahlia's original IPF, she was receiving Expressive Writing four times per week. The team collected progress monitoring data on her twice-per-month using story starters. After meeting to review her data weeks later, they noticed she had not made as much progress as they would have liked. To increase the intensity of the intervention, they broke the Tier 3 intervention group into two so now there were only four students total in Dahlia's group. They also began to monitor her progress more frequently because she is considered as part of the Tier 3 group. Her progress used to be monitored twice per month and now they are monitoring her once per week. (See Figure 6.20.)

In Grant's original behavioral support plan, a number of strategies were put in place to support Grant in seeking appropriate teacher and peer attention. After a few months, the team met again to review Grant's data. He was not making as much progress as the team would have liked. In talking to Grant's teacher, the team noted that Grant still needed support in raising his hand, a reminder about the reinforcement card, and ongoing precorrections and reminders to follow directions. The team added these components to his behavioral support plan, which made it more complete. The alterable variables that were changed include the number of teacher prompts and reminders and the visual cues that were added to Grant's desk. (See Figure 6.21.)

MEETING FACILITATION

In Chapter 4, we discussed the importance of establishing ground rules and assigning roles. In Chapter 5, we discussed the importance of including an action plan in the meeting. In this chapter, we review the importance of facilitation. Facilitation does not just occur simply because someone has been designated that role. Facilitation means many things: listening, summarizing, keeping everyone on track, focusing the conversation, managing disagreements, and moving the process forward (see Figure 6.22). As we have discussed, using an agenda and keeping the meeting going are important tasks that can improve the meeting's outcomes. But how do you keep people on track so that they are focused on the relevant content? It can be common

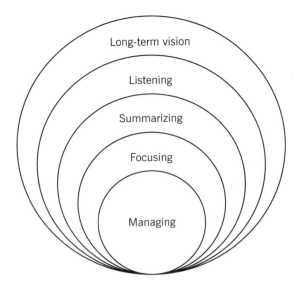

FIGURE 6.22. Facilitation.

for teams to get stuck on the "unalterable variables" when they are discussing students who are struggling. For example, it is easy to get off track and talk about a student's parents, home life, and other issues that may be at play. Although these are issues that are important, this is a different conversation that should be held at a different time with the necessary support staff. In a data day meeting, the focus should be on the data, the intervention, the student progress, and what is going to be done next.

The facilitator has this job: keeping people on track, talking about the data, discussing interventions, and reviewing the progress. To accomplish this, we suggest making it clear that the discussion will be timely, useful, and relevant. The goal of the meeting can be written on a whiteboard or large piece of paper to remind participants why they're there. For example, for a screening data review meeting, the goal could be: "Place all students into appropriate tiers of support," and for a progress monitoring data review meeting: "Evaluate student progress and make changes to interventions." Most participants will know what the goal of the meeting is ahead of time, but it helps to remind everyone why they are there and it serves as a gentle reminder to stay on track.

Second, it is important to respect everyone's time. The meeting should be focused and targeted to the relevant issues. If participants have been asked to do some work ahead of time with regarding to data analysis, intervention planning, or anything else, and they have not done so, the meeting should be stopped and rescheduled. Unless everyone is ready and willing to be on the same page, the meeting will not move forward productively. If some people have done their homework and some have not, and the meeting continues anyway, the facilitator has taught the people who did their work that it is not really valued, and for those who did not do their homework, they have just learned that it's OK not to. To be respectful of everyone's time and to take control, all participants should be held accountable. It also sends a message that preparation is not optional. Being prepared means being dedicated to the task at hand. That should be the goal for all participants involved.

Unconventional Meeting Ideas

In previous chapters, the importance of having and using an agenda, establishing roles, creating action plans, and facilitation were discussed. And we know what you're thinking. "I have sat in meetings with those components and they still did not go well," or "None of those things matter. It really just depends on the personalities in the group any way," or our favorite, "I have yet to see a meeting run well with our facilitator. The meetings always run better when he is not there." And these statements have some element of truth. Simply having an agenda or establishing roles does not necessarily mean the meeting is going to run well. The personalities in the group do matter. The group dynamics are always influenced by who is there and who is participating. And yes, an ineffective facilitator can inhibit meeting progress. All of those situations are potential outcomes.

In light of this reality, it is worth trying some unconventional ideas. See Table 6.1 for a sample. These may offer quick solutions to persistent problems.

TABLE 6.1. Unconventional Meeting Ideas

Issue	Unconventional idea
You have a team member who is consistently late to meetings.	Find the person in his or her room and escort him or her to the meeting.
Issues are presented and people start chiming in immediately.	Use silence. Present an issue, and have participants spend 2 minutes in silence thinking about it. Have everyone share out after.
Certain participants always tend to sit together.	Change the seating arrangement. This can help people focus more on the meeting if they are less distracted by a friend sitting next to them.
The meetings have a negative tone.	Start the meeting with positives. State what has been successful in recent weeks, what has worked, and who deserves acknowledgement for his or her actions. Celebrate the successes first.
Participants seem unhappy or do not participate.	Pass out cards at the end of the meeting and have participants rate the meeting on a scale of 1 to 10. For those who did not give a 10, ask them to provide one way the meeting could be improved. Use the feedback to make changes.
Participants feel overwhelmed and busy with the amount of work that needs to get done.	Surprise participants by covering content at the beginning and then allowing for the rest of the meeting to be planned work time. Or inform participants that for the rest of the year, planned work time will be incorporated into each meeting.
The meeting is comprised of updates and little decision making is needed.	Ask yourself if you really need to hold a meeting. If the answer is no, then don't have it. Provide updates in another way and respect others' time by only holding meetings when absolutely necessary.

PREVENTING AND CONFRONTING COMMON ROADBLOCKS DURING PROGRESS MONITORING MEETINGS

There are a number of roadblocks that can occur during meetings. The following is a list of actions that can be taken to address common roadblocks:

- **Roadblock 1:** Participants do not collect progress monitoring data.
  - *Cause 1:* There may not be enough time to collect the data.
  - *Solution 1:* Determine why data is not being collected and provide the necessary support. Find others to collect the progress monitoring data or provide additional time to do so. Help the teacher prioritize data collection and remove a different activity from his or her plate to provide for more time.
  - *Cause 2:* There may be confusion on how to administer or score the measures.
  - *Solution 2:* Determine what is confusing about administration or scoring. Provide the needed training.

- **Roadblock 2:** Participants do not bring their progress monitoring graphs to the meeting.
  - *Cause 1:* The purpose of the meeting may be unclear or there may be little accountability in the meetings.
  - *Solution 1:* Clarify the purpose of the meeting. Require participants to bring their graphs each time. Cancel the meeting unless everyone is prepared. If certain participants continue to be unprepared, determine the reasons why. Assess if it's because of lack of knowledge, training, or agreement regarding collecting ongoing data.

- **Roadblock 3:** There is disagreement regarding student progress and what to do next with the intervention support.
  - *Cause 1:* There is confusion regarding how to use decision-making rules.
  - *Solution 1:* Clarify what decision-making rule is being used, how to use it, and review the student data as a team.
  - *Cause 2:* The decision-making rules (four-point and trendline analysis) yield two different results. Team members disagree about next steps.
  - *Solution 2:* Decide on one decision-making rule beforehand. Or decide that a group consensus process will be used during times when there is confusion about next steps. In this situation, those most familiar with the student and those skilled with intervention design and progress monitoring should be involved in decision making.

- **Roadblock 4:** After using data-based decision making, the team realizes that multiple students are not responding to intervention.
  - *Cause 1:* The intervention is not being implemented with fidelity.
  - *Solution 1:* Conduct fidelity checks, provide support to those implementing the intervention. Change the interventionist if need be.
  - *Cause 2:* The intervention is not matched to the students' needs.
  - *Solution 2:* Gather additional problem analysis data to determine why the students are struggling and what skills they need to specifically improve. Find an intervention that matches those skills.

- *Cause 3:* The intervention is not being delivered with intensity.
- *Solution 3:* Make intervention delivery a priority. Secure the time in the schedule for the intervention to occur frequently. Find and train additional interventionists so that the group size can be reduced.

- **Roadblock 5:** There are too many students to discuss at each meeting and too many graphs to review.
  - *Cause 1:* There are too many students who are in Tier 2 and Tier 3.
  - *Solution 1:* Add to the core curriculum. Have general education teachers bump up the core curriculum to address more students' needs.
  - *Cause 2:* The meetings comprise too many teachers.
  - *Solution 2:* Reduce the meetings to grade-level teams and necessary support staff. Allow enough time for each teacher to review the progress monitoring graphs.

SUMMARY

In this chapter, we've examined steps your team can take to set the stage for efficient progress monitoring. Because progress monitoring can get lost in the mix, a number of planning tools and considerations are provided. We've considered how to select progress monitoring measures, collect and analyze the data, and use it to make decisions about student growth. In providing multiple graphs, teams will have a deeper understanding of graphing conventions and use of the data-based decision-making rules. The importance of alterable variables and how to modify these to increase the intensity of interventions was also discussed. During the meeting, we encourage teams to try unconventional meeting ideas as needed to see how they improve the meeting structure.

In the next chapter, we shift our focus to planning the roadmap for the RTI process. We provide multiple planning tools that teams can use to facilitate their work.

PART III

AFTER THE TEAM MEETING

CHAPTER 7

The Roadmap
Planning for Data-Based Decision Making

It is Year 3 of RTI implementation. The RTI team has engaged in multiple planning sessions, reviewed data, and organized interventions for students. The teachers are comfortable with the process. The principal is pleased with the changes and believes more students are receiving necessary support. As things are moving along, the RTI process continues to be in full swing, but there are a few missteps here and there that might indicate an "implementation dip," or a faltering of implementation. We might say the team became complacent, believing that everything would just continue to run smoothly. We might say the principal began to focus on other school priorities and RTI took a back seat to the new initiatives. We might say that the teachers began to skip intervention sessions here and there, because they were being asked to do other things that took up their time. Regardless of the reason, what we do know is that implementation is slowing a bit, and a reflective stance needs to be taken. With a step back, a full view, and a critical eye, the principal and RTI team can begin to see what is still working well and what needs to be improved.

The "implementation dip" is described by Michael Fullan (2011), an author on systems change, as the inevitable bumpiness that comes along with people being asked to engage in new behaviors and adopt new skills (see Figure 7.1). This dip in performance can occur early on as people are being asked to engage in new tasks, or later as time passes on and fidelity of implementation falters over time. When the dip occurs early on, it is often related to adults' anxiety and fear regarding their ability to adopt these new behaviors. People may feel overwhelmed or cautious because they are unclear about what is being asked of them and question their ability to perform the new behaviors. When the dip occurs later (as in Years 3 and 4 of implementation), it can be related to a dulled sense of vigilance. In a school where data day meetings initially occurred monthly or intervention checks were routinely conducted, they now occur every so often. The school may have reoriented their focus to another initiative and it makes RTI seem like less of a priority.

Whether the "implementation dip" occurs in your school early on in the adoption process or a bit later, it is important to acknowledge it, respond, and move forward with new changes and modifications that can support ongoing implementation. Rather than dwell on it, we encour-

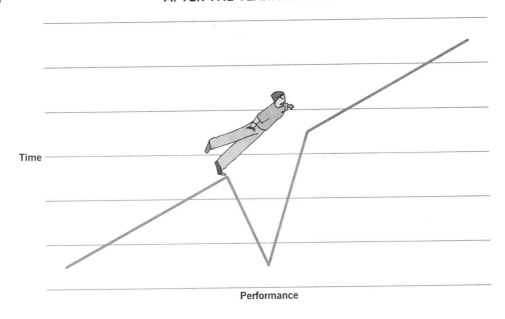

Time

Performance

FIGURE 7.1. The implementation dip.

age teams to identify what needs to be changed and create measurable action steps that prompt people to move forward. In this stage, we emphasize the importance of balance. This means

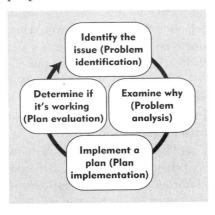

having enough self-awareness to know that an implementation dip has occurred but also not spending too much time focusing on the errors that have occurred. It is important to identify the dip, acknowledge it, determine the reasons for it, create measurable action steps that address the reasons, and then enforce the action with new teaching, reinforcement, or accountability.

In this chapter, we highlight a larger systems approach, providing tools that support long term planning and by providing assessments that can be used to identify strengths and areas of need. The focus will be on asking the question, "What question am I trying to answer?" so that teams can refocus as implementation occurs over time and continue to evaluate individual teacher needs while balancing whole-school systems needs. We discuss how to define your decisions and identify the necessary data for decision making. Finally, we provide tools and handouts that schools can use for planning and decision making.

TYPES OF DECISIONS
THAT NEED TO BE MADE WITHIN AN RTI FRAMEWORK

Let's take a step back and review the types of decisions that need to be made in an RTI framework. But first, let's review what RTI does not represent. RTI does not represent the new way to find students eligible for special education. It is not the "Let's put a student into a Tier 2 intervention first and a Tier 3 intervention next, both for 6 to 12 weeks, so we can complete the formality and then staff him or her anyway" or "The student really needs Reading Mastery but it is only available in special education so we better staff him or her." RTI also does not represent an enhanced focus on data collection without data analysis. Often early on, teams get bogged down in the data collection process itself and find themselves forgetting about data analysis. With so much effort devoted to collection, an equal amount of time should be devoted to analysis, so there is a purpose to the whole process. Finally, RTI does not stand for "really terrible idea," as one teacher liked to call it. Overwhelmed and fed up by the requirement for new work and lack of sufficient training, this teacher believed that RTI was not worth it. Instead, with a clear rationale and ongoing support, RTI can change from a "really terrible idea" into a "really terrific idea."

The types of decisions that need to be made in an RTI framework center around the four purposes of assessment: screening, progress monitoring, outcomes, and problem analysis. RTI addresses each of these purposes by focusing on individual and systemic decision making about students (see Figure 7.2). Screening measures answer the questions "How well is everyone doing?" "Is our core curriculum effective?" and "Which students need additional support?" By engaging in a screening process that includes all students three times per year, teams have enough information to determine whether the core curriculum is effective for these students and which students need additional support. Progress monitoring decisions center around if the intervention is working for the students, if students are making adequate progress, and how instructional changes impact student performance. By collecting these data on a monthly or weekly basis, teams have enough information to assess how students are performing over time. Diagnostic decisions refer to what specifically needs to be done to help a student. With diagnostic information, teams can determine patterns of strengths and weaknesses that can be used to select interventions that are targeted toward those needs. Outcomes decisions are made based on an evaluation of the effectiveness of instruction and indicate student year-end aca-

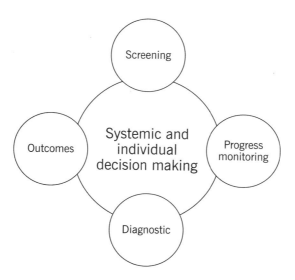

FIGURE 7.2. Types of decision making.

demic achievement when compared to grade-level performance standards. These assessments are administered to all students at the end of a grading period and/or school year.

DEFINING YOUR DECISIONS:
WHICH DECISIONS WILL BE MADE, AND WHEN?

As indicated above, the timing of decision making depends on what assessments students are administered. Knowing this makes the planning process fairly straightforward. Screening three times per year. Check. Progress monitoring monthly or weekly depending on student need. Check. Diagnostic is ongoing for students who need it. Check. And outcomes are assessed at the end of the school year. Check. It is one thing to acknowledge this timeline, and another to implement it and make it happen. Figures 7.3 and 7.4 are examples of master schedules of districts, buildings, and grade-level team meetings to promote opportunities for collaboration and data-based decision making. The types of meetings are highlighted and are reflected in regular intervals throughout the year. Using a schedule such as this allows for all types of necessary decisions to be made and allows teams time to plan for what is required during the meetings.

Once the meetings are built into the schedule, the team should spend time planning for space for the meetings, how many substitutes will be needed to cover the general education teachers, and start planning a basic agenda for each type of meeting. By taking care of these action items up front, teams reduce their work load later on as other activities fill up the year.

IDENTIFYING THE NECESSARY DATA
FOR DECISION MAKING:
WHICH DATA WILL YOU NEED, AND WHEN?

Data collection is an ongoing process that guides regular decision making among educators. When strategically planned at the outset of the school year, data collection is manageable and predictable. It becomes a constant that all staff are familiar with. When data collection is planned haphazardly, it becomes a more cumbersome process that takes additional time and resources to implement. These are the instances where *assessment* becomes the "dirty word" in education. It feels like there is too much assessment and too little teaching. Instead, the goal is to facilitate efficient assessment processes that are used to modify instruction. To accomplish this, we encourage teams to spend the time up front creating a feasible grade-level plan for data collection and management. This section addresses the main considerations and provide tools for planning all types of data collection.

Screening will be addressed first. Because this is a process that takes place three times per year, it needs to be run like a well-oiled machine. Assessors should be trained, logistics determined, and students organized so that all students can be assessed quickly and return to class. Some schools prefer to assess all students in a few days and others take a couple of weeks. Regardless, it is worth taking the time up front to plan for an efficient and smooth process.

MIDDLE SCHOOL EXAMPLE
2011–2012 SCHOOL YEAR CALENDAR

FIGURE 7.3. Schoolwide calendar.

SCHOOL DISTRICT

2011–2012 CALENDAR

AUGUST

S	M	T	W	Th	F	S
	1	2	3	4	5	6
7	8	9	10	11	12	13
14	15	16	17	18	19	20
21	22	23	24	25	26	27
28	29	30	31			

SEPTEMBER

S	M	T	W	Th	F	S
				1	2	3
4	5	6	7	8	9	10
11	12	13	14	15	16	17
18	19	20	21	22	23	24
25	26	27	28	29	30	

OCTOBER

S	M	T	W	Th	F	S
						1
2	3	4	5	6	7	8
9	10	11	12	13	14	15
16	17	18	19	20	21	22
23	24	25	26	27	28	29
30	31					

NOVEMBER

S	M	T	W	Th	F	S
		1	2	3	4	5
6	7	8	9	10	11	12
13	14	15	16	17	18	19
20	21	22	23	24	25	26
27	28	29	30			

DECEMBER

S	M	T	W	Th	F	S
				1	2	3
4	5	6	7	8	9	10
11	12	13	14	15	16	17
18	19	20	21	22	23	24
25	26	27	28	29	30	31

JANUARY

S	M	T	W	Th	F	S
1	2	3	4	5	6	7
8	9	10	11	12	13	14
15	16	17	18	19	20	21
22	23	24	25	26	27	28
29	30	31				

FEBRUARY

S	M	T	W	Th	F	S
			1	2	3	4
5	6	7	8	9	10	11
12	13	14	15	16	17	18
19	20	21	22	23	24	25
26	27	28	29			

MARCH

S	M	T	W	Th	F	S
				1	2	3
4	5	6	7	8	9	10
11	12	13	14	15	16	17
18	19	20	21	22	23	24
25	26	27	28	29	30	31

APRIL

S	M	T	W	Th	F	S
1	2	3	4	5	6	7
8	9	10	11	12	13	14
15	16	17	18	19	20	21
22	23	24	25	26	27	28
29	30					

MAY

S	M	T	W	Th	F	S
		1	2	3	4	5
6	7	8	9	10	11	12
13	14	15	16	17	18	19
20	21	22	23	24	25	26
27	28	29	30	31		

JUNE

S	M	T	W	Th	F	S
					1	2
3	4	5	6	7	8	9
10	11	12	13	14	15	16
17	18	19	20	21	22	23
24	25	26	27	28	29	30

JULY

S	M	T	W	Th	F	S
1	2	3	4	5	6	7
8	9	10	11	12	13	14
15	16	17	18	19	20	21
22	23	24	25	26	27	28
29	30					

School year may be extended due to inclement weather. Calendar subject to change.

IMPORTANT DATES

Sep 5	Labor Day	Dec 19–30	Winter break	Jun 5	Last day of school
Sep 6	First day of school	Jan 1	New Year's Day	Jun 12	Grades due
Sep 27	Benchmark meeting	Jan 16	M. L. King Jr. Day		
Oct 3–5	Conferences	Jan 31	RTI meeting (B)		
Oct 10	Columbus Day	Feb 20	Presidents' Day		
Oct 25	RTI meeting (B)	Feb 28	RTI meeting (PM)		
Nov 11	Veteran's Day	Mar 27	RTI meeting (PM)		
Nov 24–25	Thanksgiving	Apr 24	RTI meeting (B)		
Nov 29	RTI meeting (PM)	May 28	Memorial Day		

KEY

⟋ Check Important Dates section			
■ No school	▨ Half day	□ First/ last day	

FIGURE 7.4. Districtwide calendar.

Form 7.1 at the end of this chapter is a planning sheet for the screening process. As part of the planning sheet, we've included a section on data analysis dates, so the team can start planning for when data will be analyzed at each grade level. Because the analysis of the data is the purpose of collection, we encourage teams to have staff members sign a data analysis commitment letter at the beginning of the year. This is a letter that everyone will sign, including the staff, RTI team, and administrators. It acts as a commitment to the analysis process, so that the data is used as it was intended, and that instructional changes are made accordingly. To further encourage this process, we've included commitment letters for teachers and the RTI team in Forms 7.2 and 7.3 at the end of this chapter. Commitment letters act as a more formal agreement about our responsibilities as educators and our acknowledgment of the benefits of the RTI process. RTI teams are encouraged to use these at the beginning of the school year and keep them on file as data collection and analysis takes place throughout the year.

Progress monitoring and problem analysis are the next types of data collection that should be planned. Because these are ongoing processes that require consistency and commitment, it is necessary to plan who will collect the progress monitoring data and when meetings will occur to review it. Additionally, problem analysis data should be collected on students who are not making progress in Tier 2 or Tier 3 interventions. This is a data collection process that will be instituted as needed, when students are not making progress with their current interventions. The important part about collecting these types of data is that the data are then used to make decisions. Thus, scheduling regular data review meetings can support analysis and implementation of instructional changes as necessary. (See Form 7.4 at the end of this chapter for a planning sheet for the progress monitoring and problem analysis processes.)

Finally, outcome assessment data should be reviewed at the end of the year. This is summative data that the RTI team can analyze with the administrators and make some decisions regarding the effectiveness of the support process. Outcome data can include criterion-referenced tests, state tests, and other standardized measures of achievement that are administered to all students. (See Form 7.5 at the end of this chapter for a planning sheet to evaluate outcome data.)

DEFINING THE CONTINUUM OF INSTRUCTIONAL SUPPORTS FOR YOUR GRADE LEVEL

Once a plan is created for data collection and analysis, the next component to address is what interventions will be provided for students in each tier in each grade level. Creating a map of interventions that will be implemented to meet the needs of students at each grade level is an important first step. It helps the team conceptualize what interventions are currently in place and which ones are needed. It also provides teachers a clear method of understanding what is available to their students in need. Teams can use the intervention planning map (see Form 5.1 at the end of Chapter 5) to complete this step.

After a clear outline of the interventions available is provided, teams can move to completing IPFs with teachers. There are many IPFs available online and teams can decide to select the template that works best for them. We suggest starting with the problem analysis data first (which highlights areas of need) and then completing the IPF based on that information. (See Form 7.6 at the end of this chapter for a problem analysis planning form.) The reason for this is twofold. First, what often happens in schools is that we place students in tiers of support based on their screening results, without getting a sense of what specific skills they need to work on.

Identify early on in the planning process who will implement the Tier 2 and Tier 3 interventions. This will help ensure that once students are identified, they receive immediate support. If general education teachers are selected, something else should be removed from their list of responsibilities. If support staff are selected, ensure that they are part of all planning meetings, so everyone is on the same page.

By filling out the problem analysis form first, teams are directed to thinking about patterns, to ensure a better intervention match. Second, it encourages teams to review all sources of information and create a complete picture, rather than just using one data source to make tier decisions. By listing all the data sources, creating a summary, and writing a recommendation based on the summary, teams can ensure that students are placed in the appropriate intervention. School psychologists can play a role in this process, by helping to analyze the data and make instructional recommendations. Using these forms and a team approach increases the chances that students are getting the support they need.

It is also important to take a step back and consider all of the steps that go into working on a student case. For students who are struggling in academics or behavior, there are a lot of resources that go into assisting the student and there are a lot of steps that comprise the process. From start to finish, there are many sources of information collected and many decisions along the way that determine how and by how much a student is supported. Figure 7.5 is a sample problem-solving work sheet for an individual student. (Form 7.7 at the end of this chapter is a blank worksheet.). School psychologists can use these steps to walk through cases, and determine what interventions are appropriate and how goals should be established and monitored.

Throughout the book, we have talked a lot about defining team members' roles and responsibilities. The more planning that occurs up front, the less time will be needed later for organization and management. To continue this theme, a data collection planning form is provided in Form 7.8 at the end of this chapter to plan for administration of the measures. Finally, Form 7.9 at the end of this chapter is a template of a multiyear RTI action plan. We've also included a partially completed version from a school in Figure 7.6. The purpose of these forms is to support your current instructional framework and use them to enhance team functioning. With adequate planning and sustained commitment, teams can learn to function effectively, which will then better support student performance and achievement over time.

Bryan is a sixth-grade student who just moved into the district this year. He appears to be struggling in reading. His fall benchmark scores indicate he is performing below peers and requires additional support. He has been referred to the problem-solving team. The school psychologist begins to collect more data and works with the team to determine the best course of action.

Step 1: The school psychologist and teacher complete the RIOT and ICEL framework. They gather data on the instruction, curriculum, environment, and learner using record review, interview, observe, and test techniques. To complete the test portion, they put in Bryan's CBM scores. The results are summarized below.

	Review	Interview	Observe	Test
Instruction	Instruction is a combination of whole class and small group.	Teacher feels that combination of whole class and small group benefits some students, but not all. Bryan needs more individualized support.	Instruction is 45 minutes whole class and 30 minutes small group.	
Curriculum	Record review indicates it is a whole-language curriculum. Direct teaching is not emphasized. Student independence is the focus.	Teacher feels the curriculum is not addressing Bryan's needs.	Curriculum was a more independent learning approach.	
Environment	Classroom rules evident, regular letters home to parents found.	Teacher feels environment is calm. Students participate, complete their work, participate when asked.	Structured classroom rules, positive reinforcement delivered, class participation encouraged.	
Learner	Bryan has experienced difficulty with reading since last year. His grades started to drop last year and he did not perform well on the state test.	Teacher indicates that Bryan seems unengaged during reading. He does not complete his reading homework. He has been struggling since the beginning of the year.	Bryan did not participate in reading class. He stared at the floor or fumbled with materials in his desk. He was on task 40% of the time, whereas peers were on task an average of 92% of the time.	Bryan's median CBM reading performance was 90 words per minute and 10 errors. This places him in the intensive category.

Step 2: Verify discrepancy.

Local norms: The team reviews Bryan's fall CBM scores to determine how discrepant he is from peers. They ask the questions "How does the student compare to local norms?" and "If the student is not in the average range (25th–75th percentile), how low is the student?"

Local Norms (25th–75th percentile)

Grade	Fall	Winter	Spring
1	10–25	30–50	60–80
2	50–75	80–100	100–115
3	80–115	120–130	135–140
4	100–130	130–140	140–155
5	130–150	150–165	165–175
6	135–150	150–170	170–185

Bryan's oral reading fluency CBM score was 90 words per minute. The range for fall sixth-grade measures is 135–150 words per minute. The team verifies that Bryan is discrepant.

(continued)

FIGURE 7.5. Student example of problem solving in reading.

Step 3: The team now wants to determine at what instructional level Bryan is reading. The school psychologist offers to sample back using earlier grade-level passages to determine Bryan's instructional level. Bryan reads three passages at the fifth-, fourth-, and third-grade levels. The school psychologist takes the median of the words read correct (WRC) and errors (E) and uses the local norms above to determine where Bryan is performing.

Reading Assessment Passages	Passage 1 (WRC/E)	Passage 2 (WRC/E)	Passage 3 (WRC/E)	Median (WRC/E)	Fall Performance Level
6	90/10	85/12	92/7	90/10	Reading problem
5	100/6	95/8	101/7	101/7	Reading problem
4	95/7	98/10	100/5	98/10	Reading problem
3	110/5	108/7	105/5	105/5	Average

Problem Analysis

Step 4: The team found Bryan to be reading well at the third-grade level. Now, the team wants to know more about why Bryan is struggling. What specific skills in reading does he need to improve? The school psychologists administer some additional measures in reading to determine patterns of strengths and weaknesses. Bryan's results are summarized below.

Student Name: Bryan		Grade: 6		Date: October 1	
Problem Analysis Data					
Big Idea	Phonemic Awareness	Phonics	Fluency	Vocabulary	Comprehension
Measures	None	Problem analysis phonics measures	Oral reading fluency	None	Retell
Findings	Does not appear to be an issue.	Long vowels, consonant digraphs, vowel teams, trigraphs, variant vowels, and multisyllabic words.	Needs to improve fluency, but accuracy is more of an issue. Frequent errors indicate a phonics and decoding issue.	Does not appear to be an issue.	Does not appear to be an issue. Greater fluency over time will lead to increased comprehension.

Summary:
Bryan has proficient skills in phonemic awareness, vocabulary, and comprehension. His areas to work on include fluency and advanced phonics. His oral reading fluency scores place him in the "intensive" range and his instructional level was found to be third-grade passages. Problem analysis measures in phonics indicate that Bryan needs instruction in long vowels. Bryan was unable to differentiate when to say a long- or short-vowel sound. Digraphs should also be an area of focus, as Bryan was unable to pronounce words with the /ch/, /gh/, /ng/, /sc/, and /ph/ digraphs. Bryan also needs to work on vowel teams that include the /ea/, /ee/, /ai/, /ei/, and /ou/ teams. Trigraphs can be another area of focus. Bryan experienced difficulty with /sch/, /ing/, and /ion/. Variant vowels should also be targeted, specifically the /ar/, /or/, /ou/, and /oo/ sounds. Multisyllabic words including *teacher, computer, pencil, necklace, magnet, dollhouse, playground, basketball*, and *watermelon* should be targeted.

Recommendations:
Bryan should be placed in an intervention group that targets the above skills. A Tier 3 intervention provided at Willow Brook Middle School is Corrective Reading, a direct instruction program. It contains **decoding** and **comprehension** strands that can be used separately as a supplemental reading intervention or combined for use as a comprehensive reading intervention program. We recommend the decoding strand for Bryan because he does not read accurately and his oral reading is choppy. This program can target the phonics skills that he needs to improve.

Because Bryan requires extensive support, we recommend that he receive the Corrective Reading program for 5 days per week for 45 minutes each. This should occur in addition to his regular reading/language arts instruction. His progress will be monitored weekly and data-based decision-making rules will be used to determine progress.

(continued)

FIGURE 7.5. *(continued)*

Step 5: Confirm the intervention selection and complete the instructional planning form (IPF).

Student: Bryan

Teacher: Mr. Dahl

Grade: 6th grade

Intervention: Corrective Reading, Tier 3

Date	Target skills	Instructional strategies	Materials	Logistics (include who will teach, when, where, and how often)	Assessment (progress monitoring tools)	Follow-up date
October 25	Fluency and advanced decoding skills (long vowels, consonant digraphs, vowel teams, trigraphs, variant vowels, and multisyllabic words)	Corrective Reading program. Decoding strand. Cycle to be determined. Corrective Reading is a direct instruction program that targets specific decoding and comprehension skills.	Corrective Reading materials (placement test, teacher materials, student workbook, etc.)	Who: Mrs. Blith When: 1:45 P.M. daily Where: Mrs. Blith's room How often: 5 days per week, 45 minutes each session Group: Tier 3 students in study hall	AIMSweb oral reading fluency fifth- and third-grade measures twice per month	January 25

Parent signature: _____

Teacher signature: _____

Interventionist signature (if different from teacher): _____

RTI team facilitator signature: _____

(continued)

FIGURE 7.5. *(continued)*

177

Step 6: Now the team wants to select a goal for Bryan. There are multiple ways of doing this and the team has to consider how discrepant Bryan is, his current grade level, where he is performing on sixth-grade measures, where he is performing on third-grade measures, and where Bryan should be to catch up to peers.

Also, keep in mind that it is helpful to progress monitor using two different measures. For example, fifth and third grade (current grade level and instructional grade level) or first grade and DIBELS nonsense word fluency measures (current grade level and a phonics measure) or DIBELS nonsense word fluency measures and DIBELS phoneme segmentation measures (for a student who needs to work on both phonics and phonemic awareness).

Option 1: Select the end-of-the-year national norm benchmark goal for where the student should be. Bryan will be monitored on third- and sixth-grade measures. The team would check the national norms for oral reading fluency for third grade and sixth grade in the spring. They could find them to be 120 words per minute and 150 words per minute, respectively. Those would be the goals.

Option 2: Select the end-of-the-year local norm benchmark goal for where the student should be. Bryan will be monitored on third- and sixth-grade measures. The team would check the local norms for oral reading fluency for third grade and sixth grade in the spring. Based on the local norms above, this would be 135 words per minute and 165 words per minute, respectively. Those would be the goals.

Option 3: Use growth rates to determine what is appropriate growth between now and June. Bryan will be monitored on third- and sixth-grade measures. The growth rate for third grade could be 1 word per week and the growth rate for sixth grade could be .5 word per week. The team will use that to calculate Bryan's spring goals.

Third grade: 105 + 1(30) = 135 words per minute

Baseline + growth rate (weeks for intervention) = goal

Sixth grade: 90 + .5(30) = 105 words per minute

Baseline + growth rate (weeks for intervention) = goal

Option 4: Intraindividual framework. Bryan's first eight baseline data points on sixth-grade measures are 85, 90, 91, 92, 92, 93, 94, and 94. The difference between the highest and lowest score is 9; 9/8 weeks is 1.125 and when multiplied by 1.5 the result is 1.6875. This represents the student's growth rate per week; 1.6875 × 30 weeks of the intervention is 50.625 words total. The team adds that to Bryan's baseline (90 words per minute) and the result is 140.625 words. This will be the goal for the end of the intervention, which is 30 weeks later.

Bryan's Goals

The team decides to use the end-of-the-year local norms to establish goals for Bryan on third- and sixth-grade measures. They want to progress monitor him at his current grade level (to see if he is catching up to peers) and his instructional reading level (to see if he is making progress with the intervention).
In 12 weeks, Bryan will read 150 words per minute when given a sixth-grade oral reading fluency probe for 1 minute.
In 12 weeks, Bryan will read 120 words per minute when given a third-grade oral reading fluency probe for 1 minute.

178

FIGURE 7.5. (*continued*)

District: Southeast   School: Greenview Middle
RTI Leadership Team: Principal, asst. principal, school psychologist, special ed teacher, general ed teacher, social worker
Implementation Years: Five-year process
Data Sources: Interviews with administration, district guidelines for RTI, curriculum review, screening data review, state test scores, special ed rates

Planning Year

Objective 1: Clarify purpose and outcomes of RTI to teachers.

Purpose: To establish and maintain reasonable expectations regarding special education placement and the RTI process. To understand typical child development.

Action steps	Stakeholders responsible	Outcomes	By when	Resources/challenges
Provide ongoing professional development.	RTI leadership team	Clarity around the RTI process, Tiers 2 and 3, gen ed. versus spec ed., how to support students in the classroom, easy tips, and techniques		Professional development days Professional development provider
Secure time for weekly grade-level meetings.	Principal	Ongoing time to collaborate and discuss interventions. What is working? Weekly mini presentations by teachers to their grade-level teams		When? How much time?

Objective 2: Organize current data and plan for the upcoming school year.

Purpose: To evaluate needs, determine next steps, and modify this action plan as needed.

Action steps	Stakeholders responsible	Outcomes	By when	Resources/challenges
Summarize all academic and behavior data sources.	RTI leadership team	Determine strengths of current programs, areas of need, plan for next steps. What is our data telling us?		Data review day. Time for analysis and planning.
Use results to create a step-by-step action plan with built-in accountability, reinforcement, and timelines.	RTI leadership team	A clear, detailed plan for the upcoming school year. Time allocated toward grade-level team meetings, professional development, RTI leadership team meeting times, and an intervention block.		Use this action plan to start. Allocate time to review, modify, and use. Secure understanding and support among the team.

(continued)

FIGURE 7.6. RTI action plan example.

Implementation Year 1

Objective 1: Establish Tier 2 interventions in reading.

Purpose: To provide students evidence-based instruction in reading that occurs daily.
A balanced literacy approach is not enough for students struggling in reading.

Action steps	Stakeholders responsible	Outcomes	By when	Resources/challenges
Secure daily intervention block time.	Principal	Daily intervention period that is uninterrupted <u>protected</u> time. No assemblies, <u>special</u> events, or other activities occur during this time. Interventions occur for the whole time.		Half hour? 45 minutes? Does this fit into the schedule?
Select evidence-based Direct Instruction reading strategies.	RTI leadership team	Evidence-based reading instruction based on the five big ideas. Students are exposed to phonemic awareness, phonics, fluency, vocabulary, and comprehension instruction on a regular basis. Phonics is especially emphasized.		www.FCRR.org www.Interventioncentral.org 100 Easy Lessons to Teach your Child to Read SRA Reading Mastery
Train teachers in evidence-based strategies.	RTI leadership team; professional development provider	Teacher accuracy and fluency with selected strategies or programs. Teachers take assessment at the end of the training to demonstrate competence. Teachers are rewarded for their efforts. Modeling and demonstration are used throughout.		Professional development days

Objective 2: Evaluate Tier 2 interventions in reading.

Purpose: Determine what is effective and what can be improved.
How can interventions be incorporated into Tier 1? How can we "beef up" the core?

Action steps	Stakeholders responsible	Outcomes	By when	Resources/challenges
Data review day	RTI leadership team	What data do we have? What data do we need? What does our current data indicate about reading performance? Are the reading interventions working? Do they need to be changed completely or just intensified?		A full day to meet with all grade-level teams. Review data. Make decisions.

(continued)

FIGURE 7.6. (continued)

Make data-based decisions	RTI leadership team	Based on the data review day, what needs to be kept? What needs to be changed? Review all student progress reports on a group and individual level. How does this impact the curriculum and interventions currently in use?		Select new programs as needed. Modify current interventions.

Implementation Year 2

Objective 1: Establish a reading progress monitoring system related to skills (five big ideas in beginning reading).

Purpose: To monitor Tier 2 students monthly, Tier 3 students weekly, and use graphs to make decisions about reading instruction.

Action steps	Stakeholders responsible	Outcomes	By when	Resources/challenges
Select EasyCBM, DIBELS, or AIMSweb	RTI leadership team; Principal	A progress monitoring system focused on the big ideas		Pricing, finances available
Train teachers on progress monitoring system.	Professional development provider or RTI leadership team	Teachers who are accurate and fluent in administration and scoring of the measures.		Professional development days
Train the RTI leadership team on data analysis.	Professional development provider	A train-the-trainers model where the RTI leadership team then trains the teachers in data analysis.		Training time
"Data days"	RTI leadership team	The RTI leadership team meets with grade-level teams monthly to review progress monitoring data. Decisions are made based on data.		Built into the schedule monthly

Objective 2: Select evidence-based math interventions that can be used as Tier 2 or in Tier 1.

Purpose: To support struggling students in math using evidence-based strategies.

Select evidence-based Direct Instruction math strategies.	RTI leadership team	Evidence-based math instruction provided in the form of interventions or strategies. Students are exposed to math facts, math computation, and math application (word problems) instruction on a regular basis. A direct instruction approach is emphasized.		Corrective Math Connecting Math Concepts DISTAR arithmetic Intervention central
Train teachers in evidence-based strategies.	RTI leadership team; professional development provider	Teacher accuracy and fluency with selected strategies or programs. Teachers take assessment at the end of the training to demonstrate competence. Teachers are rewarded for their efforts. Modeling and demonstration are used throughout.		Professional development days

FIGURE 7.6. (*continued*)

SUMMARY

In this chapter, we've provided a roadmap for planning an efficient and effective RTI approach. Sample calendars are provided to encourage teams to get the benchmark, intervention, and progress monitoring meetings on the books early. Sample RTI commitment letters are provided to show teams how all members of a school can show their dedication to the process by indicating their agreement at the beginning of the year. Planning forms for the types of decisions are included to show teams how data can be utilized in different ways. A problem analysis individual student case is provided to show teams how to walk through each step of the process in the area of reading. Finally, an action plan template and example are provided to demonstrate how to set long-term goals to facilitate systems change. In the final chapter, we discuss considerations for capacity building to sustain the practices that constitute an RTI approach.

Schoolwide Screening Planning

Administration Days

When will the measures be administered?	Start date	End date	Make-up days	Notes
Fall				
Winter				
Spring				

Assessor Commitment

Who will be the assessors?	Names	Names	Names
Fall			
Winter			
Spring			

Data Entry

Who will enter the data?*	Start date	End date	Notes
Fall			
Winter			
Spring			

*If using paper-based scoring

Data Analysis Commitment Dates

Data analysis dates	K	1	2	3	4	5	6	7	8	Notes
Fall										
Winter										
Spring										

Data Analysis Commitment Letter for Staff

Date

Name of School

Dear *Name of School*,

This letter is to indicate that I, _____, will commit to analyzing the data collected by the schoolwide benchmark screening process. At the three designated times during the year (fall, winter, and spring), I will attend the scheduled data day meeting(s). I will review the data before the meeting by reviewing patterns and determining who is in need. During the meeting I agree to discuss the data, ask questions as needed, and assist others with their data. I am committing to this because I understand this process will support all students.

I also agree to complete the action steps determined by the team during the meeting. I understand that the action steps may include but not be limited to: implementing additional Tier 1 instructional strategies with all of my students, implementing a Tier 2 or Tier 3 intervention with a small group, collecting progress monitoring data, meeting with parents to discuss the data, and continuing to meet with my team to review the data.

I agree to all of the above steps because I understand that they alone or in combination are necessary for an effective RTI process and ultimately support enhanced student achievement.

_____   _____

Signature   Date

_____

Print Name

Data Analysis Commitment Letter for RTI Team Member

Date

Name of School

Dear *Name of School*,

This letter is to indicate that I, _____, will commit to analyzing the data collected by the schoolwide benchmark screening process. At the three designated times during the year (fall, winter, and spring), I will attend the scheduled data day meeting(s). I will review the data before the meeting by reviewing patterns and determining who is in need. During the meeting I agree to discuss the data, ask questions as needed, and assist others with their data. I agree to facilitate the meeting as needed. I am committing to this because I understand that this process will support all students.

I also agree to complete the action steps determined by the team during the meeting. I understand that the action steps may include but not be limited to: supporting teachers with progress monitoring data collection, supporting teachers with data analysis, providing professional development on designated topics as needed, meeting with the administrator to review the core curriculum, implementing a Tier 2 or Tier 3 intervention with a small group, collecting progress monitoring data, meeting with parents to discuss the data, and continuing to meet with the RTI team to review the data.

I agree to all of the above steps because I understand that they alone or in combination are necessary for an effective RTI process and ultimately support enhanced student achievement.

_____   _____

Signature   Date

_____

Print Name

Schoolwide Program Monitoring and Problem Analysis Planning

Schoolwide Progress Monitoring Planning

Administration Days

Which students will be progress monitored?	Tier 2	Assessor names	Person responsible for data entry	Data analysis meeting dates	Tier 3	Assessor names	Person responsible for data entry	Data analysis meeting dates
Kindergarten								
First								
Second								
Third								
Fourth								
Fifth								
Sixth								
Seventh								
Eighth								

(continued)

Schoolwide Problem Analysis Planning

Which students require problem analysis?	Tier 2	Assessor names	Data analysis meeting dates	Tier 3	Assessor names	Data analysis meeting dates
Kindergarten						
First						
Second						
Third						
Fourth						
Fifth						
Sixth						
Seventh						
Eighth						

Schoolwide Outcome Data Analysis Planning

Grade	Assessment	Grade-Level Results	Individual Students in Need		Intervention Planning	Notes
			Previously identified by screening measures?	Not previously identified by screening measures?		
Kindergarten						
First						
Second						
Third						
Fourth						
Fifth						
Sixth						
Seventh						
Eighth						

Individual Student Problem Analysis Planning by Subject

Individual Student Reading Problem Analysis Planning

Student Name: _____ Grade: _____ Date: _____

Big Idea	Problem Analysis Data			
	Phonemic Awareness	Phonics	Fluency	Vocabulary	Comprehension
Measures					
Findings					

Summary:

Recommendations:

(continued)

Individual Student Problem Analysis Planning by Subject *(page 2 of 4)*

Individual Student <u>Math</u> Problem Analysis Planning

Student Name: _____   Grade: _____   Date: _____

Big Idea	Early Numeracy	Math Facts	Computation	Application/Word Problems	Algebra
			Problem Analysis Data		
Measures					
Findings					

Summary:

Recommendations:

(continued)

Individual Student Problem Analysis Planning by Subject *(page 3 of 4)*

Individual Student Written Language Problem Analysis Planning

Student Name: _____   Grade: _____   Date: _____

Big Idea		Problem Analysis Data			
	Spelling	Punctuation	Capitalization	Grammar	Story Composition
Measures					
Findings					

Summary:

Recommendations:

(continued)

Individual Student Problem Analysis Planning by Subject *(page 4 of 4)*

Individual Student Behavior Problem Analysis Planning

Student Name: Grade: Date:

Problem Analysis Data

Function (circle one)	Negative Reinforcement (student escapes demands or situations by engaging in problem behavior)	Positive Reinforcement (student gains something by engaging in problem behavior)	Multiple Functions (student both escapes and gains something by engaging in problem behavior)	Automatic (student escapes or gains something biologically by engaging in problem behavior, e.g., flicking the lights off and on, pressing a button that makes noise repeatedly, rubbing arm repeatedly)

Data Sources That Confirm Function
(circle one and write notes below)

Teacher Interview	ABC Observations	Student Interview	Paired Choice Assessment	Functional Analysis

Behavior Intervention Plan Brainstorming

Antecedent strategies (strategies to prevent the behavior from occurring):

Instructional strategies (strategies to teach new skills):

Positive reinforcement strategies (strategies to reward positive behaviors):

Consequence strategies (strategies to discourage negative behaviors):

192

From Start to Finish: Problem Solving for an Individual Student

Directions: Complete the steps below. Fill in the information as it is collected. Use these forms to guide team discussions and create action plans for students.

Step 1: Complete the RIOT and ICEL framework. Gather data on the instruction, curriculum, environment, and learner using record review, interview, observe, and test techniques. Summarize the results below.

	Review	Interview	Observe	Test
Instruction				
Curriculum				
Environment				
Learner				

(continued)

Step 2: Verify discrepancy.

Local norms: Use local norms to answer the questions "How does the student compare to local norms?" and "If the student is not in the average range (25th–75th percentile), how low is the student?"

National norms: Or the team can use national norms to answer the questions "How does the student compare to local norms?" and "If the student is not in the average range (25th–75th percentile), how low is the student?"

Step 3: Sample back. Sample back using earlier grade-level measures to determine where the student's instructional level is.

Grade level	Measure 1	Measure 2	Measure 3	Median	Performance level

(continued)

Problem Analysis

Step 4: Find out more about why the student is struggling. Administer problem analysis measures to determine patterns of strengths and weaknesses. Summarize the results below.

Student Name:		Grade:	Date:	
Problem Analysis Data				
Big Idea				
Measures				
Findings				

Summary:

Recommendations:

(continued)

From Start to Finish: Problem Solving for an Individual Student *(page 4 of 5)*

Step 5: Confirm the intervention selection and complete the instructional planning form (IPF).

Student: Grade: Intervention:

Teacher:

Date	Target skills	Instructional strategies	Materials	**Logistics** (include who will teach, when, where, and how often)	**Assessment** (progress monitoring tools)	**Follow-up date**
				Who: When: Where: How often: Group:		

Parent signature: _____   Interventionist signature (if different from teacher): _____

Teacher signature: _____   RTI team facilitator signature: _____

(continued)

Step 6: Select a goal for the student. Consider selecting two goals and monitoring progress on two different measures. For example, fifth and third grade (current grade level and instructional grade level) or first grade and DIBELS nonsense word fluency measures (current grade level and a phonics measure) or DIBELS nonsense word fluency measures and DIBELS phoneme segmentation measures (for a student who needs to work on both phonics and phonemic awareness).

Option 1: Select the end-of-the-year national norm benchmark goal for where the student should be.

Option 2: Select the end-of-the-year local norm benchmark goal for where the student should be.

Option 3: Use growth rates to determine what is appropriate growth between now and June.

Option 4: Intraindividual framework. Determine the growth the student has been making and use that to set a goal.

Student Goals

Current grade level:

Instructional level:

Measures used to progress monitor:

Fill in the blanks below:

GOAL 1

By _____ , _____ will _____ _____ when given _____
   (Time)   (Student)   (Behavior)   (Criterion)   (Conditions)

GOAL 2

By _____ , _____ will _____ _____ when given _____
   (Time)   (Student)   (Behavior)   (Criterion)   (Conditions)

197

FORM 7.8

Data Collection Plan

Reading screening

Grade Level	Number of Students	Minutes per Student	Number of Days for Assessing	Number of Assessors Needed	Measures

Math screening

Grade Level	Number of Students	Minutes per Student	Number of Days for Assessing	Number of Assessors Needed	Measures

(continued)

Writing screening

Grade Level	Number of Students	Minutes per Student	Number of Days for Assessing	Number of Assessors Needed	Measures

Behavior screening

Grade Level	Number of Students	Minutes per Student	Number of Days for Assessing	Number of Assessors Needed	Measures

RTI Action Plan

District:

Implementation Years:

Data Sources:

School:

Date:

RTI Leadership Team:

Planning Year

Objective 1			
Purpose:			
Action steps	Stakeholders responsible	Outcomes	By when	Resources/challenges
Objective 2			
Purpose:			
Action steps	Stakeholders responsible	Outcomes	By when	Resources/challenges
Objective 3			
Purpose:			
Action steps	Stakeholders responsible	Outcomes	By when	Resources/challenges

(continued)

RTI Action Plan *(page 2 of 6)*

Implementation Year 1

Objective 1

Purpose:

Action steps	Stakeholders responsible	Outcomes	By when	Resources/challenges

Objective 2

Purpose:

Action steps	Stakeholders responsible	Outcomes	By when	Resources/challenges

Objective 3

Purpose:

Action steps	Stakeholders responsible	Outcomes	By when	Resources/challenges

(continued)

RTI Action Plan *(page 3 of 6)*

Implementation Year 2

Objective 1			
Purpose:			
Action steps	Stakeholders responsible	Outcomes	By when	Resources/challenges

Objective 2			
Purpose:			
Action steps	Stakeholders responsible	Outcomes	By when	Resources/challenges

Objective 3			
Purpose:			
Action steps	Stakeholders responsible	Outcomes	By when	Resources/challenges

(continued)

RTI Action Plan *(page 4 of 6)*

Implementation Year 3

Objective 1			
Purpose:			
Action steps	Stakeholders responsible	Outcomes	By when	Resources/challenges

Objective 2			
Purpose:			
Action steps	Stakeholders responsible	Outcomes	By when	Resources/challenges

Objective 3			
Purpose:			
Action steps	Stakeholders responsible	Outcomes	By when	Resources/challenges

(continued)

RTI Action Plan *(page 5 of 6)*

Implementation Year 4

Objective 1

Purpose:

Action steps	Stakeholders responsible	Outcomes	By when	Resources/challenges

Objective 2

Purpose:

Action steps	Stakeholders responsible	Outcomes	By when	Resources/challenges

Objective 3

Purpose:

Action steps	Stakeholders responsible	Outcomes	By when	Resources/challenges

(continued)

204

RTI Action Plan *(page 6 of 6)*

Implementation Year 5

Objective 1

Purpose:

Action steps	Stakeholders responsible	Outcomes	By when	Resources/challenges

Objective 2

Purpose:

Action steps	Stakeholders responsible	Outcomes	By when	Resources/challenges

Objective 3

Purpose:

Action steps	Stakeholders responsible	Outcomes	By when	Resources/challenges

CHAPTER 8

Making It Happen
Implementing and Sustaining Data-Based Decision Making in Collaborative RTI Teams

In this final chapter, the importance of capacity building for sustaining RTI data-team practices within the context of schoolwide RTI implementation is discussed. There are four types of teams needed within the organizational structure of school systems implementing RTI: district RTI leadership teams, school RTI leadership teams, grade-level RTI data teams, and problem-solving teams. When implementing collaboration and data-based decision making within this team structure, it is important to keep in mind that although these teams can take steps to develop and implement evidence-based practices, the success of these practices will be impacted by the success of broader RTI model implementation throughout the school and district. To promote long-term sustainability of RTI team practices, we must first focus on the school system as a "host environment" and build a sustainable schoolwide RTI system at that level (Kame'enui & Simmons, 1998).

Sustainability is the "durable, long-term implementation of a practice at a level of fidelity that continues to produce valued outcomes" (McIntosh, Horner, & Sugai, 2009, p. 328). It is said to occur if and when school personnel continue to implement enough critical features of the practice that valued outcomes are produced, but not when the practice is implemented with low fidelity (McIntosh, Filter, Bennett, Ryan, & Sugai, 2009). Taking a systems perspective, and based on their experience with large-scale systems change efforts, Sugai and Horner (2006) describe an approach to promoting accurate and sustained implementation of positive behavioral interventions and supports (PBIS), a systemwide prevention and intervention model with many parallels to RTI models focused on academic achievement. The approach requires districts to make a formal and long-term commitment to evidence-based PBIS practices, investments in coordination, leadership, an organizational structure that promotes capacity building, outcome-driven decision making, and contingencies that promote high fidelity of implementation. Over time, sustainable practices are promoted by a district-level leadership team consisting of district-level leaders with policy and programmatic decision-making responsibilities, with representation from key stakeholders (e.g., general and special education, administration, mental health, families). The leadership team leads and coordinates capacity-building efforts in the following areas (Sugai & Horner, 2006):

- *Funding*: securing stable and recurring funding for a PBIS coordinator and annual activities.
- *Visibility*: ensuring stakeholders remain aware of PBIS activities and accomplishments, promoting communication, accountability, and acknowledgement of successful implementation.
- *Political support*: maintaining PBIS as a high priority within the district through the supportive actions of policymakers and decision makers.
- *Training*: establishing the capacity to provide effective and ongoing training, with decreased reliance on outside expertise.
- *Coaching*: making an overt link between training experience and actual implementation of PBIS systems and practices through the use of coaching; making this link durable by integrating coaching functions into job descriptions of existing personnel.
- *Evaluation*: using outcome data to inform decision making; evaluating learner outcomes and fidelity of implementation.
- *Local school teams and demonstrations*: initially implementing PBIS in a small number of schools to demonstrate success and make contextual adaptations; systematically expanding implementation based on capacity and success.

School districts should take a systematic approach, such as the one outlined by Sugai and Horner (2006), to building capacity for long-term sustainability of the multicomponent RTI model.

RTI TEAMS AND THE CHANGE PROCESS

As a critical component of schoolwide RTI models, RTI teams should be afforded careful consideration regarding the change process required to attain full implementation status, and then sustained practice. It is difficult to establish initial implementation of team practices, as illustrated by the findings of a recent survey that only about one in four school districts report full implementation of RTI leadership teams in all school buildings, or regularly held collaborative data-team meetings focused on evaluating student outcomes at the grade or individual student levels (Spectrum K12 School Solutions, 2011). Further, the literature indicates similar difficulty with sustained implementation of other problem-solving team models in which teachers receive support with data-based decision making in their work with struggling students. For example, despite years of training, support, and adaptation to promote contextual fit, the mainstream assistance team model failed to achieve sustained implementation when external supports were removed from the school system (D. Fuchs, L. Fuchs, Harris, & Roberts, 1996). Kovaleski, Gickling, Morrow, and Swank (1999) found that teachers' use of instructional support teams (ISTs) resulted in improved outcomes for students (compared to controls), but only in schools with high overall implementation of the IST model. As Kovaleski et al. stated, "What is striking about these results is the implication that half-hearted efforts at IST implementation are no better for at-risk students than what is traditionally practiced in non-IST schools" (1999, p. 180).

Achieving initial and sustained implementation of RTI leadership and data teams within a school building is a large task requiring systemwide change, given that *all* educators (including administrators, teachers, specialists, and related service providers) will become active participants on one or more teams. Adelman and Taylor (1997) outlined a framework for scaling up promising practice innovations in which there are four overlapping phases of change:

1. Creating readiness: enhancing the climate for change.
2. Initial implementation.
3. Institutionalizing new approaches.
4. Ongoing evolution and renewal.

Table 8.1 provides a summary of each phase, along with implications for RTI teams. Although this model clearly has broad implications for promoting large-scale implementation of RTI across a school, district, state, or beyond, we also find it a useful framework from which to consider the process of "scaling up" implementation of the many RTI teams within a school building. A brief description of the four phases of the Adelman and Taylor (1997) model follows, along with a discussion of implications for the adoption and implementation of school-level RTI teams.

Phase I: Creating Readiness

When initially implementing an RTI model, meaningful teaming is not likely to occur if it is simply mandated as one of the required RTI practices. It begins with a vision of the new practice and an understanding of how to facilitate the desired changes. Initial commitment, ownership, and ongoing support of policymakers is critical to substantive and lasting change (Adelman & Taylor, 1997). During this phase, developing a vision, involving *all* stakeholders, allocating time, and establishing leadership and policy commitment are recommended (Ervin & Schaughency, 2008).

> **Creating readiness requires efforts by leaders to create interest in the new practice among those who will be asked to change.**

In this phase, school RTI leaders (e.g., RTI leadership team members, RTI coaches, principals, school psychologists) describe RTI-team collaboration and data-based decision-making practices, the benefits and costs of implementation, and the steps that will be required for implementation to stakeholders who will be expected to implement RTI teams (i.e., *all* educators within the school). Part I of this book describes many strategies for creating readiness for RTI-team implementation at the school level. RTI team members are led through the process of developing a vision and goals (i.e., mission statement), and building team member commitment to both a shared purpose and individual roles and responsibilities. School principals work with RTI teams to redesign aspects of the school infrastructure (e.g., adjust teaching schedules to create shared planning time, develop annual calendar of RTI team meetings) to create time for team development, planning, and decision-making activities.

TABLE 8.1. Adelman and Taylor's (1997) Phases of Systems Change

Phase	Guidelines/activities for scale-up
Creating readiness	Leading the way • Dissemination of new ideas to create interest • Evaluating indications of interest Policy direction, support, and protection for restructuring • In-depth interactive presentations to build consensus • Negotiating a policy framework and conditions for engagement • Ratification and sponsorship by stakeholders Redesigning organizational and programmatic mechanisms • Modification of regular mechanisms • Clarifying the need for temporary mechanisms • Restructuring time • Stakeholder foundation building
Initial implementation	Steering the prototype and phasing in change • Temporary mechanisms to facilitate the diffusion process • Adapting and phasing in the prototype Guidance and support for change • Stakeholder development • Facilitating day-to-day stakeholder performance and prototype implementation Establishing formative evaluation procedures
Institutionalization	Ownership, guidance, and support Ongoing leadership Maintenance of planning, implementation, and coordination mechanisms Continuing education
Ongoing evolution	Formative and summative evaluation Pursuing outcome efficacy

Phase II: Initial Implementation

Temporary mechanisms are added to facilitate the change process, with an emphasis on building capacity for implementation, and new practices are adapted to fit specific contexts. Examples of temporary mechanisms that may facilitate initial implementation of new innovations include steering teams, coaches, and change agents. Support is provided to stakeholders to develop attitudes, knowledge, and skill needed for implementation. Finally, formative evaluation procedures are established for ongoing improvement of processes and outcomes (Adelman & Taylor, 1997).

> The initial implementation phase involves the phasing in of new practices, with guidance and support.

Just as RTI models must be adapted to fit the context of each district and school building, RTI teams must also be adapted to fit the school context in which they operate. This book describes ways in which team organization, structure, and membership may vary depending on features of the local context. Each RTI team should identify the strengths of team members and resources available, and draw upon these to define individual roles and responsibilities and establish routines for data-based decision making to accomplish their identified goals. Specific data-based decision-making practices need to be defined for screening, instructional planning, progress monitoring, and outcomes-evaluation decisions. As RTI teams begin to implement team meetings using data for decision making, they may benefit from the support of an RTI coach or mentor. For school-level RTI leadership teams, this may be an external mentor, or change agent, with experience guiding the RTI adoption and implementation process at a district or school level. For grade-level data teams, coaching may be provided by a member of the school leadership team, or schools may invest in hiring RTI coaches on a temporary or permanent basis to support implementation of RTI teams (and other RTI practices).

During this phase, RTI teams should invest heavily in initial professional development. Teachers and other educators often have little training in team-based collaboration or data-based decision making, so knowledge and skill in these areas will need to be developed to build the capacity for independent team functioning. A commitment to ongoing team development and improvement should be established during this phase. Teams should identify strategies to collect data for formative evaluation of team process and outcomes. In this book, several strategies have been described for gathering formative evaluation data from sources both internal (e.g., debriefing, self-assessment) and external (e.g., outside observer of team meetings, feedback on decisions documented in minutes/action plans) to the team. RTI teams also have access to student achievement data at the systems level, which can be used to formatively and summatively evaluate the success of data teams in improving student outcomes at the classroom or grade levels.

Phase III: Institutionalizing New Approaches

Initial implementation does not necessarily indicate that a new practice will be sustained over time. To promote sustained implementation, the practice should be officially integrated into the infrastructure of an organization through institutionalization. Plans for ongoing adherence to underlying values of the practice, leadership, coordination, and continuing education are critical to this phase. Steps should also be taken to detect and address forces that may erode ongoing implementation (Adelman & Taylor, 1997).

> Institutionalization involves maintaining and enhancing new practices by ensuring that an organization assumes long-term ownership of the practices.

Schools can take steps to formalize an initiative as part of the school infrastructure by ensuring enough team members to keep the workload manageable, providing adequate resources, and mechanisms for ongoing capacity building (Ervin & Schaughency, 2008). External supports such as team coaching should be gradually reduced as teams develop increasing independence. However, it will be important for schools to enact structures to sustain team-based collaboration and decision making over time. Examples of such structures include:

- Allocation of time allocated for collaborative planning and team meetings in teacher contracts and schedules.
- Financial commitment to support RTI implementation (e.g., staff positions such as RTI coaches, contracts with data management systems).
- Documentation of policies and procedures related to team practices, such as data-based decision making for screening, instructional planning, progress monitoring, and outcomes evaluation.
- Incorporation of data-based decision-making resources (e.g., intervention maps for multi-tiered systems of support, worksheets for screening and instructional planning) into RTI procedural manuals.
- Access to technical assistance.
- Ongoing professional development, for new and returning team members.
- Incentives for effective teaming practices or meeting team goals (e.g., improving student outcomes).

Using activities described in this book, or similar strategies, RTI teams should periodically reassess members' commitment to the mission statement, including the underlying values, purpose, and goals of the team. This is particularly important after changes in team membership, but should be considered at least every few years. Formative evaluation data collected through periodic team-debriefing activities should also be used to identify roadblocks to implementation of effective teaming and data-based decision making, and address areas of team process or outcomes needing improvement. Teams should plan ahead for predictable threats to sustained implementation of practices, such as the hiring of new teachers and/or retirement of key team members (e.g., facilitators, coaches). Systems should be established to proactively introduce new team members to the underlying values and mission of the team, assign specific roles and responsibilities for participation, and provide professional development regarding team practices.

Phase IV: Ongoing Evolution and Renewal

Ongoing evolution "is the product of efforts to account for accomplishments, deal with changing times and conditions, generate renewal, and incorporate new knowledge" (Adelman & Taylor, 1997, p. 222). Renewal is an important aspect of this phase, in which organizations respond to waning motivation for implementation over time. Adelman and Taylor emphasize that although evaluating outcomes is an important aspect of this phase, evaluation should be done in a supportive manner that celebrates accomplishments and focuses on using data for quality improvement.

Ongoing evolution is fostered by continuing education, exposure to new ideas, and ongoing formative and summative evaluation.

In the context of implementing a comprehensive RTI model, RTI teams will likely face accountability pressures because an overarching goal of RTI is the prevention of academic problems and the improvement of student achievement. Principals and RTI leaders should work to establish a school culture in which educators support one another, and data are used to drive decisions in the best interests of children. Although it can be anxiety provoking for teachers to examine student outcome data in a public forum, these anxieties can be minimized when school administrators establish that student performance data are not used to evaluate or punish teachers; although, it may be used to identify the need to allocate additional resources (e.g., coaching, instructional assistants, materials) to teachers. Team facilitators and school leaders should publicly celebrate the accomplishments of each RTI team, and offer other incentives for success to maintain buy-in and motivation of team members over time.

As schools implement the full range of practices involved in RTI (e.g., evidence-based instruction and intervention, screening and progress monitoring, data-based decision making) over time, the complex school system itself will evolve. RTI teams, as a part of the school's organizational structure, will need to evolve simultaneously. This process will be unique to each school and team, and will be impacted by team members' development of new attitudes, knowledge, and skill.

CONCLUSION

This book is designed to promote effective collaboration and data-based decision-making practices within the context of RTI teams. Specific practices that promote team development and effective functioning before, during, and after team meetings have been described, with a focus on the needs of RTI data teams. We've provided ideas, strategies, and resources to assist teams throughout the process of creating readiness for teaming, initial implementation of collaboration and data-based decision making in the team setting, institutionalization, and ongoing evolution of RTI teams.

Finally, RTI teams are implemented within the context of a schoolwide RTI model. Teams can take steps to develop and implement evidence-based practices for team-based collaboration and data-based decision making, but the sustainability of these practices will be impacted by the extent to which sustainable RTI practices are developed throughout the school and district. Sufficient stakeholder buy-in, administrative support, and allocation of resources, infrastructure, and ongoing professional development are necessary to ensure that implementation and long-term institutionalization of RTI team practices will occur.

References

Adelman, H. S., & Taylor, L. (1997). Toward a scale-up model for replicating new approaches to schooling. *Journal of Educational and Psychological Consultation, 8(2)*, 197–230.

AIMSWEB data system (2012). What is AIMSWEB? Retrieved from *http://www.aimsweb.com.*

Behavioral and Emotional Screening System (BASC-2 BESS) (2012). Pearson assessments. Retrieved from *http://www.pearsonassessments.com/HAIWEB/Cultures/en-us/Productdetail.htm? Pid=PAaBASC2bess.*

Brown-Chidsey, R., & Steege, M. W. (2010). *Response to intervention: Principles and strategies for effective practice* (2nd ed.). New York: Guilford Press.

Burns, M. K., & Gibbons, K. (2012). *Implementing response-to-intervention in elementary and secondary schools: Procedures to assure scientific-based practices* (2nd ed.). New York: Routledge.

Burns, M. K., Riley-Tillman, T. C., & VenDerHeyden, A. (2012). *RTI applications, Volume 1: Academic and behavioral interventions.* New York: Guilford Press.

Bursuck, B., & Blanks, B. (2010), Evidence-based early reading practices within a response to intervention system. *Psychology in the Schools, 47*, 421–431.

Carnine, D. (1997). Bridging the research-to-practice gap. *Exceptional Children, 63(4)*, 513–521.

Compton, D. L., Fuchs, D., & Fuchs, L. S. (2010). Rethinking response to intervention at middle and high school. *School Psychology Review, 39(1)*, 22–28.

Delehant, A. M. (2007). *Making meetings work: How to get started, get going, and get it done.* Thousand Oaks, CA: Corwin Press.

Deno, S., Fuchs, L. S., Marston, D., & Shin, J. (2001). Using curriculum-based measurement to establish growth standards for students with learning disabilities. *School Psychology Review, 30(4)*, 507–524.

DIBELS Data System (2012). DIBELS data system. Retrieved from *https://dibels.uoregon.edu.*

DuFour, R., DuFour, R., Eaker, R., & Karhanek, G. (2004). *Whatever it takes.* Bloomington, IN: Solution Tree.

Ervin, R. A. & Schaughency, E. (2008). Best practices in accessing the systems change literature. In A. Thomas & J. Grimes (Eds.), *Best practices in school psychology–V*, (pp. 853–873), Washington, DC: National Association of School Psychologists.

Fixsen, D. L., Naoom, S. F., Blase, K. A., Friedman, R. M., & Wallace, F. (2005). *Implementation research: A synthesis of the literature* (FMHI Publication No. 231). Tampa, FL: University of South Florida, Louis de la Parte Florida Mental Health Institute, National Implementation Research Network.

Fletcher, J. M., Lyon, G. R., Fuchs, L. S., & Barnes, M. A. (2007). *Learning disabilities: From identification to intervention.* New York: Guilford Press.

Florida Center for Reading Research. (2012). Use of ongoing progress monitoring to improve reading instruction. Retrieved from *www.fcrr.org/forf_mazes/pdf/OPM_improve_reading_instruction.pdf.*

Fuchs, D., & Fuchs, L. S. (2006). Introduction to responsiveness-to-intervention: What, why, and how valid is it? *Reading Research Quarterly, 4,* 93–99.

Fuchs, D., Fuchs, L., Harris, A., & Roberts, P. (1996). Bridging the research-to-practice gap with mainstream assistance teams: A cautionary tale. *School Psychology Quarterly, 11*(3), 244–266.

Fuchs, L. S. (1986). Monitoring progress among mildly handicapped pupils: Review of current practice and research. *Remedial and Special Education, 7,* 5–12.

Fuchs, L. S., & Deno, S. L. (1991). Paradigmatic distinctions between instructionally relevant measurement models. *Exceptional Children, 57*(6), 488–500.

Fuchs, L. S., & Fuchs, D. (1999). Monitoring student progress toward the development of reading competence: A review of three forms of classroom-based assessment. *School Psychology Review, 28*(4), 659–671.

Fuchs, L. S., & Fuchs, D. (2004). *What is scientifically based research on progress monitoring?* Washington, DC: National Center on Progress Monitoring, American Institute for Research, Office of Special Education Programs.

Gersten, R., Vaughn, S., Deshler, D. D., & Schiller, E. (1997). What we know about using research findings: Implications for improving special education practice. *Journal of Learning Disabilities, 30*(5), 466–476.

Glasgow, R. E. (2002). Evaluation of theory-based interventions: The RE-AIM model. In K. Glanz, F. M. Lewis, & B. K. Rimer (Eds.), *Health behavior and health education: Theory, research, and practice* (3rd ed., pp. 531–534). San Francisco: Wiley.

Glasgow, R. E., Lichtenstein, E., & Marcus, A. (2003). Why don't we see more translation of health promotion research to practice?: Rethinking the efficacy to effectiveness transition. *American Journal of Public Health, 93*(8), 1261–1267.

Glover, T. A., & Diperna, J. C. (2007). Service delivery for response to intervention: Core components and directions for future research. *School Psychology Review, 36*(4), 526–540.

Greenwood, C. R., & Abbot, M. (2001). The research to practice gap in special education. *Teacher Education and Special Education, 24*(4), 276–289.

Gresham, F. M., MacMillan, D. L., Beebe-Frankenberger, M. E., & Bocian, K. M. (2000). Treatment integrity in learning disabilities intervention research: Do we really know how treatments are implemented? *Learning Disabilities Research and Practice, 15*(4), 198–205.

Haring, N. G., Lovitt, T. C., Eaton, M. D., & Hansen, C. L. (1978). *The fourth R: Research in the classroom.* Columbus, OH: Merrill.

Heartland Area Education Agency. (n.d.). Treatment integrity checklists. Retrieved from *www.aea11.k12.ia.us/idm/checkists.html.*

Individuals with Disabilities Education Improvement Act of 2004 (IDEIA). (2003). In GovTrack.us (database of federal legislation). Retrieved September 17, 2012, from *www.govtrack.us/congress/bills/108/hr1350.*

Kame'enui, E. J., & Simmons, D. C. (1998). Beyond effective practice to schools as host environments: Building and sustaining a school-wide intervention model in beginning reading for all children. *Australasian Journal of Special Education 23,* 100–122.

Kennedy, M. M. (1997). The connection between research and practice. *Educational Researcher, 26*(7), 4–12.

Kovaleski, J. F., Gickling, E. E., Morrow, H., & Swank, P. R. (1999). High versus low implementation of instructional support teams: A case for maintaining program fidelity. *Remedial and Special Education, 20*(3), 170–183.

Kovaleski, J. F., & Pedersen, J. (2008). Best practices in data analysis teaming. In A. Thomas & J. Grimes (Eds.), *Best practices in school psychology V* (pp. 115–130). Bethesda, MD: National Association of School Psychologists.

Lembke, E., McMaster, K., & Stecker, P. (2010). The prevention science of reading research within a response to-intervention model. *Psychology in the Schools, 47,* 22–35.

Marzano, R. J., Pickering, D. J., & Pollock, J. E. (2001). *Classroom instruction that works: Research-based strategies for increasing student achievement.* Upper Saddle River, NJ: Pearson.

McDougal, J. L., Graney, S. B., Wright, J. A., & Ardoin, S. P. (2009). *RTI in practice: A practical guide to implementing effective evidence-based interventions in your school.* New York: Wiley.

McIntosh, K., Filter, K. J., Bennett, J. L., Ryan, C., & Sugai, G. (2009). Principles of sustainable prevention: Designing scale-up of school-wide positive behavior support to promote durable systems. *Psychology in the Schools, 47(1),* 5–21.

McIntosh, K., Horner, R. H., & Sugai, G. (2009). Sustainability of systems-level evidence-based practices in schools: Current knowledge and future directions. In W. Sailor, G. Dunlap, G. Sugai, & R. H. Horner (Eds.), *Handbook of positive behavior support* (pp. 327–352). New York: Springer.

Merrell, K. W., & Buchanan, R. (2006). Intervention selection in school-based practice: Using public health models to enhance systems capacity of schools. *School Psychology Review, 35,* 167–180.

Merriam-Webster's online dictionary (11th ed.). (2012). [*Fidelity* definition.] Retrieved from *http://www.merriam-webster.com/dictionary/fidelity.*

National Association of State Directors of Special Education (NASDSE). (2005). *Response to intervention: Policy considerations and implementation.* Alexandria, VA: Author.

National Center on Response to Intervention (NCRTI). (2012). The essential components of RTI. Retrieved from *www.rti4success.org.*

National Council of Teachers of Mathematics. (2012). NCTM home page. Retrieved from *www.nctm.org.*

National Institute for Direct Instruction. 2012). Research and publications. Retrieved from *www.nifdi.org/15.*

National Staff Development Council. (2012). Standards for professional learning. Retrieved from *www.learningforward.org/index.cfm.*

National Research Center on Learning Disabilities. (2012). *Integrating research with improved policies and practice.* Retrieved from *www.nrcld.org.*

Oregon Response to Intervention. (n.d.). Fidelity checklists. Retrieved from *oregonrti.org/node/33.*

Parker, C., Fleischmann, J., Loughlin, J. E., & Ryan, A. (2010). Practice-based perspectives on implementing a three-tier reading model. In M. Shinn & H. Walker (Eds.), *Interventions for achievement and behavior problems in a three-tier model including RTI* (pp. 125–150). Bethesda, MD: National Association of School Psychologists.

Reschly, D., & Tilly, W. D. III (1999). Reform trends and system design alternatives. In D. Reschly, W. D. Tilly III, & J. Grimes (Eds.), *Special education in transition: Functional assessment and noncategorical programming* (pp. 19–48). Longmont, CO: Sopris West.

Reynolds, G. (2008). *Presentation zen: Simple ideas on presentation design and delivery.* Berkley, CA: New Riders.

Robinson, V. M. J. (1998). Methodology and the research-practice gap. *Educational Researcher, 27(1),* 17–26.

Schiola, S. A. (2011). *Making group work easy: The art of successful facilitation.* Lanham, MD: Rowman & Littlefield Education.

Scholtes, P. R., Joiner, B. L., & Streibel, B. J. (2003). *The team handbook* (3rd ed.). Madison, WI: Oriel.

Shinn, M. R. (2010). Building a scientifically based data system for progress monitoring and universal screening across three tiers including RTI using curriculum-based measurement. In M. R. Shinn & H. Walker (Eds.), *Interventions for achievement and behavior problems in a three-tier model, including RTI* (pp. 259–293). Bethesda, MD: National Association of School Psychologists.

Shinn, M. R., & Hubbard, D. (1992). Curriculum-based measurement and problem solving assessment: Basic procedures and outcomes. *Focus on Exceptional Children, 24*(5), 1–20.

Shinn, M. R., & Walker, H. (Eds.). (2010). *Interventions for achievement and behavior problems in a three-tier model, including RTI.* Bethesda, MD: National Association of School Psychologists.

Simmons, D. K., Kame'enui, E. J. & Good, R. H. (2002). Building, implementing, and sustaining a beginning reading improvement model: Lessons learned school by school. In M. Shinn, H. Walker, & G. Stoner (Eds.), *Interventions for academic and behavior problems II: Preventive and remedial approach* (pp. 537–570). Bethesda, MD: National Association of School Psychologists.

Spectrum K12 School Solutions (2011). *Response to intervention (RTI) adoption survey 2011.* Towson, MD: Author. Retrieved 1/17/12, from *http://www.spectrumk12.com/rti/the_rti_corner/rti_adoption_report.*

Sugai, G & Horner, R. (1999). Discipline and behavioral support: Preferred processes and practices. *Effective School Practices, 17*(4), 10–22.

Sugai, G., & Horner, R. H. (2006). A promising approach for expanding and sustaining school-wide positive behavior support. *School Psychology Review, 35*(2), 245–259.

School-Wide Information System (SWIS) (2012). *About SWIS.* Retrieved from *http://www.swis.org/.*

St. Croix River Education District. (n.d.). *Response to Intervention Center.* Retrieved from *www.scred.k12.mn.us.*

U.S. Department of Education, National Center on Response to Intervention. (2012). Essential components of RTI: A closer look at response to intervention. Retrieved from *www.rti4success.org/pdf/rtiessentialcomponents_042710.pdf.*

Vaughn Gross Center for Reading and Language Arts at the University of Texas at Austin. (2005). *Introduction to the 3-tier reading model: Reducing reading disabilities for kindergarten through third grade students* (4th ed.). Austin, TX. Author.

Willingham, D. T. (2009). *Why don't students like school: A cognitive scientist answers questions about how the mind works and what it means for the classroom.* San Francisco: Jossey-Bass.

Index

An *f* following a page number indicates a figure; a *t* following a page number indicates a table.